MINNESOTA

a photographic journey

featuring photography
by Max Foster

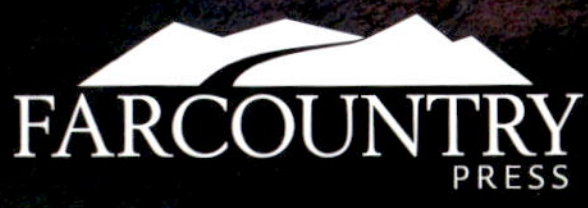

To Mom, for instilling confidence and determination in me;
to Amy, for unwavering love and support; and to Isla Ray, the light of my life.
— Max Foster

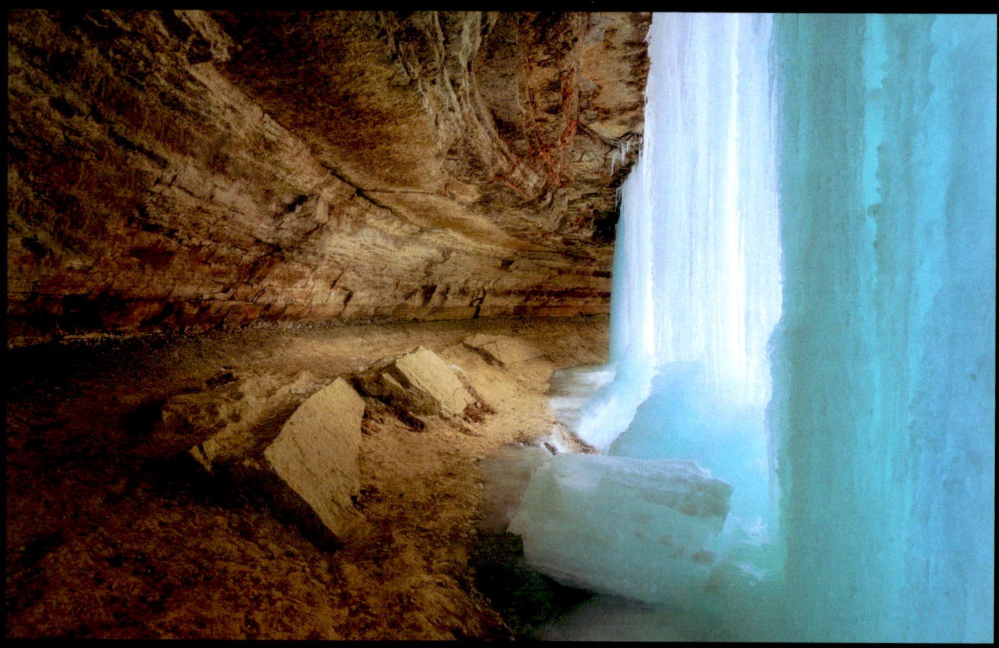

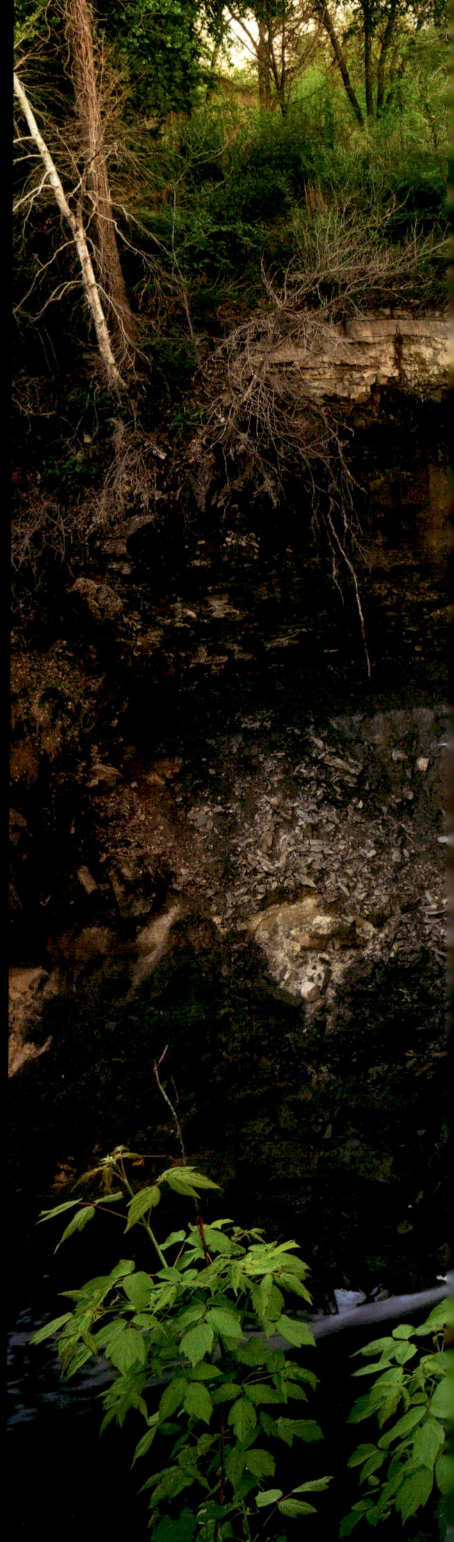

Above: From behind the frozen curtain of Minnehaha Falls, the hubbub of the Twin Cities feels miles away. MAX FOSTER

Right: Minnehaha Falls plunges 53 feet over a limestone rim at Minnehaha Regional Park in Minneapolis. MAX FOSTER

Title page: Sunrise spans Lake Superior's 31,700 square-mile surface. MAX FOSTER

Front cover: The Pigeon River plunges over Minnesota's highest waterfall in Grand Portage State Park. MAX FOSTER

Back cover: Split Rock Lighthouse is perhaps the most visited scenic spot on Lake Superior's North Shore. MAX FOSTER

ISBN: 978-1-56037-845-7

Design by Steph Lehmann

For more information about our books, write Farcountry Press, P.O. Box 5630, Helena, MT 59604; call (800) 821-3874; or visit www.farcountrypress.com.

Produced in the United States of America. Printed in China.

28 27 26 25 24 1 2 3 4 5

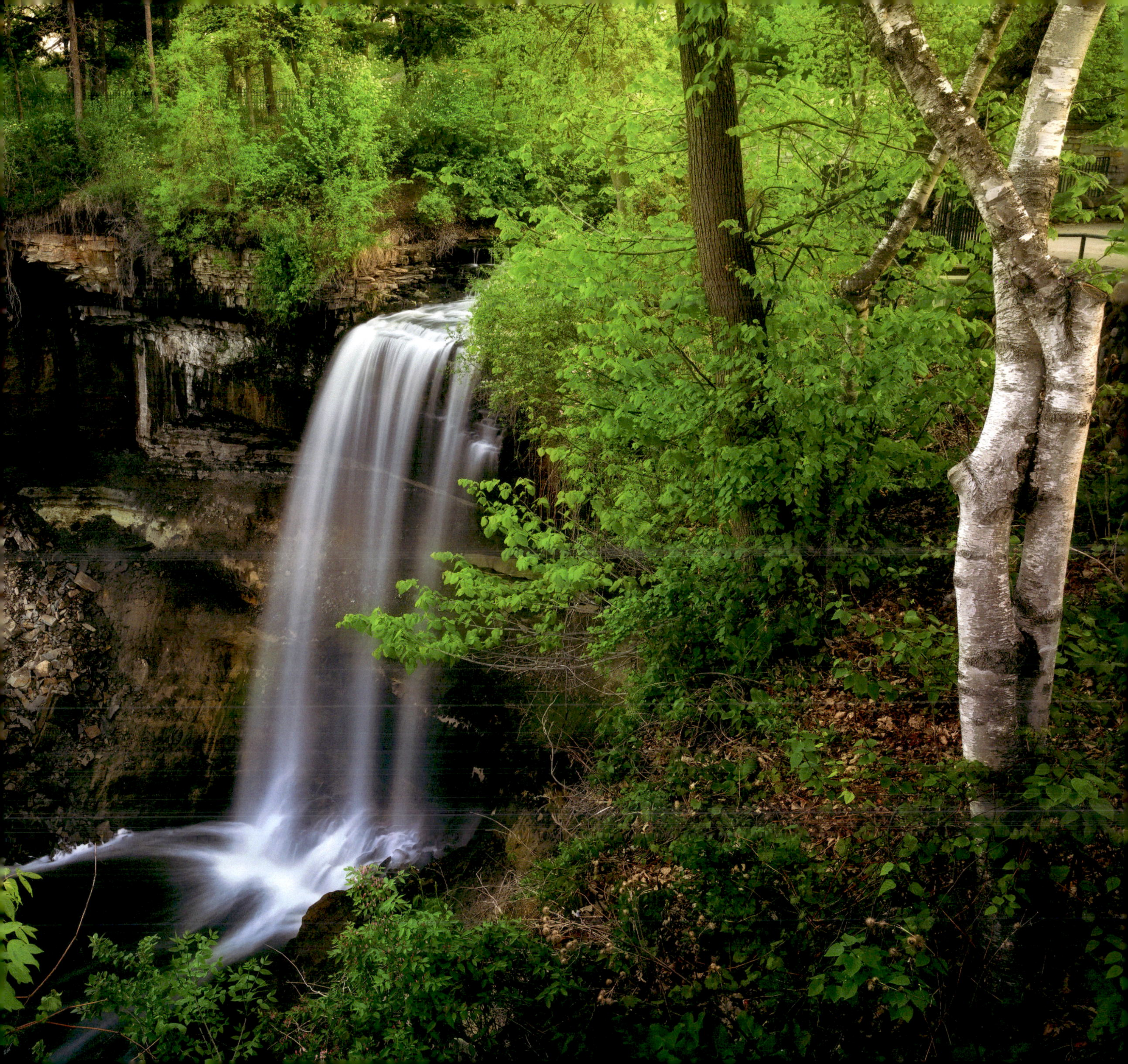

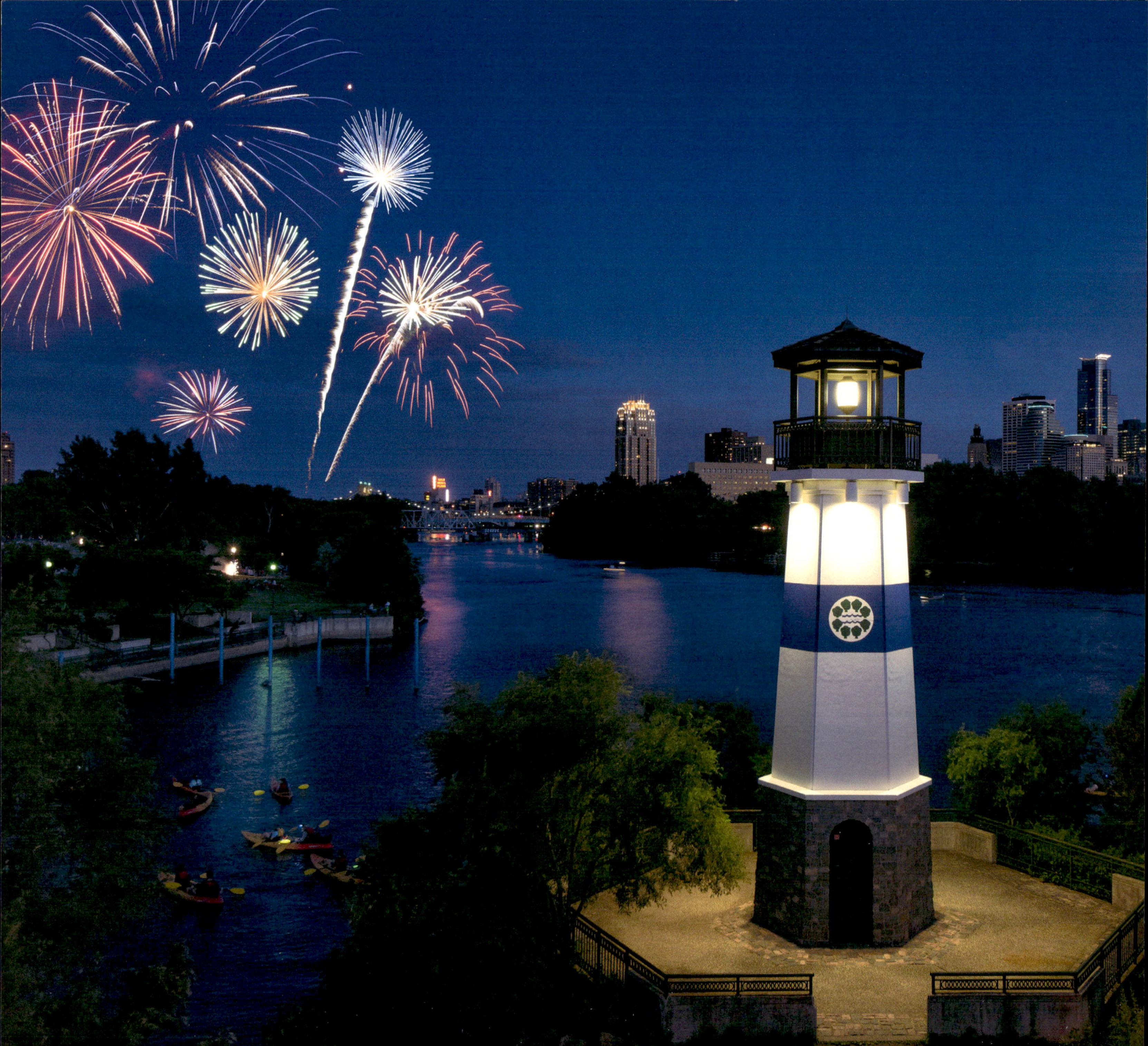

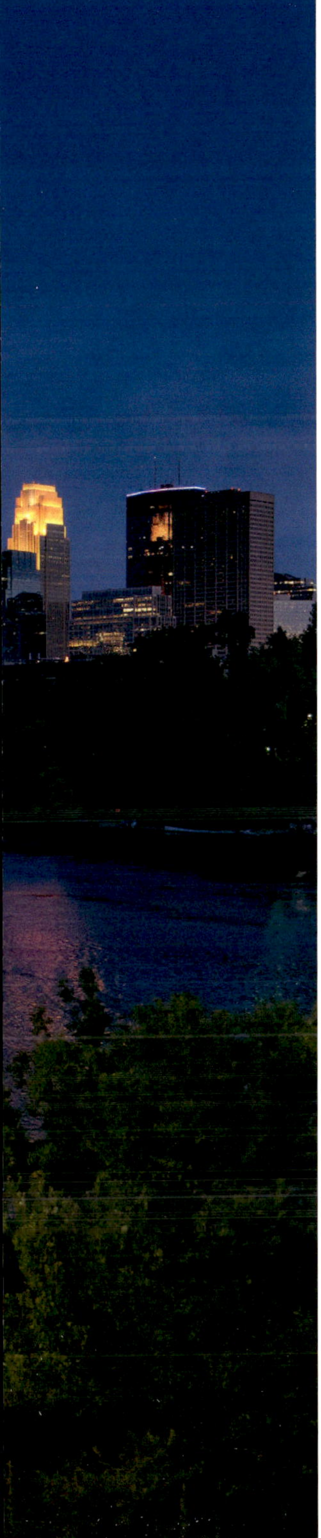

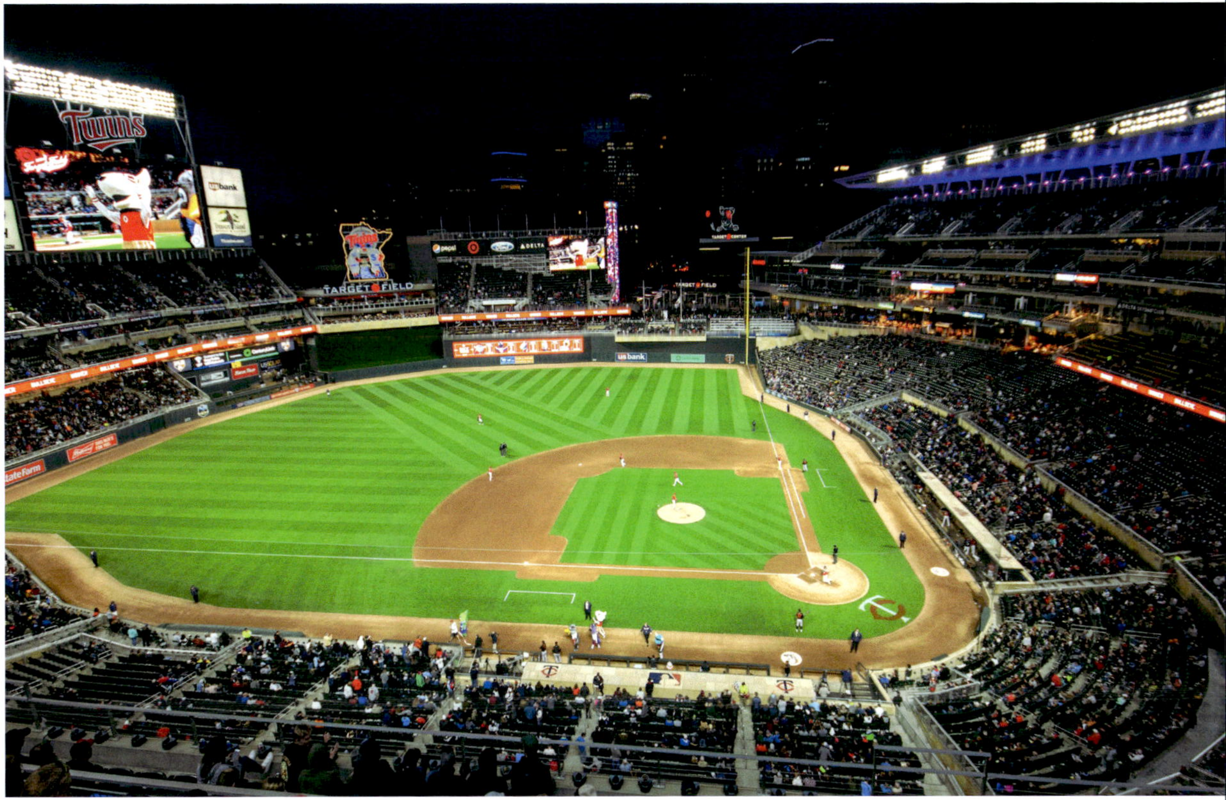

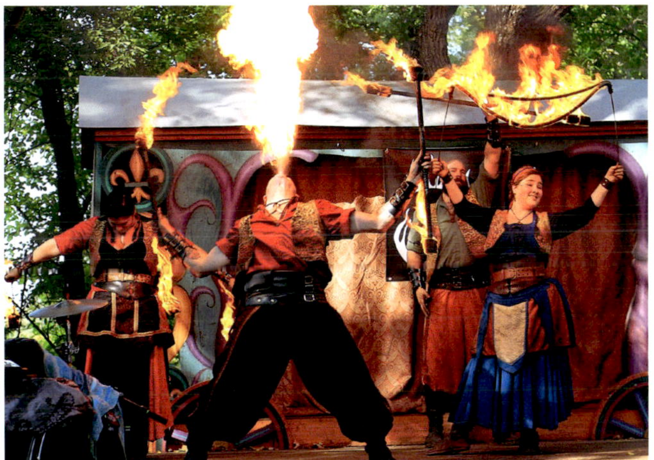

Above: Opening in 2010, Target Field is the home of Major League Baseball's Minnesota Twins. Seating more than 38,000 fans, the stadium also hosts music concerts and other sports events. KLEMENS KÖPFLE/UNSPLASH

Left: The annual Minnesota Renaissance Festival in Shakopee runs on weekends for six weeks in August and September, with games, rides, artisan wares, food, music, juggling school, jousting, and more. GRETCHEN GUNDA ENGER/SHUTTERSTOCK

Far left: The miniature Boom Island Lighthouse on the Mississippi River stands just across from Boom Island Park, which offers a boat docks, a picnic area, bicycle and pedestrian paths, and beautiful views of the Minneapolis skyline. MAX FOSTER

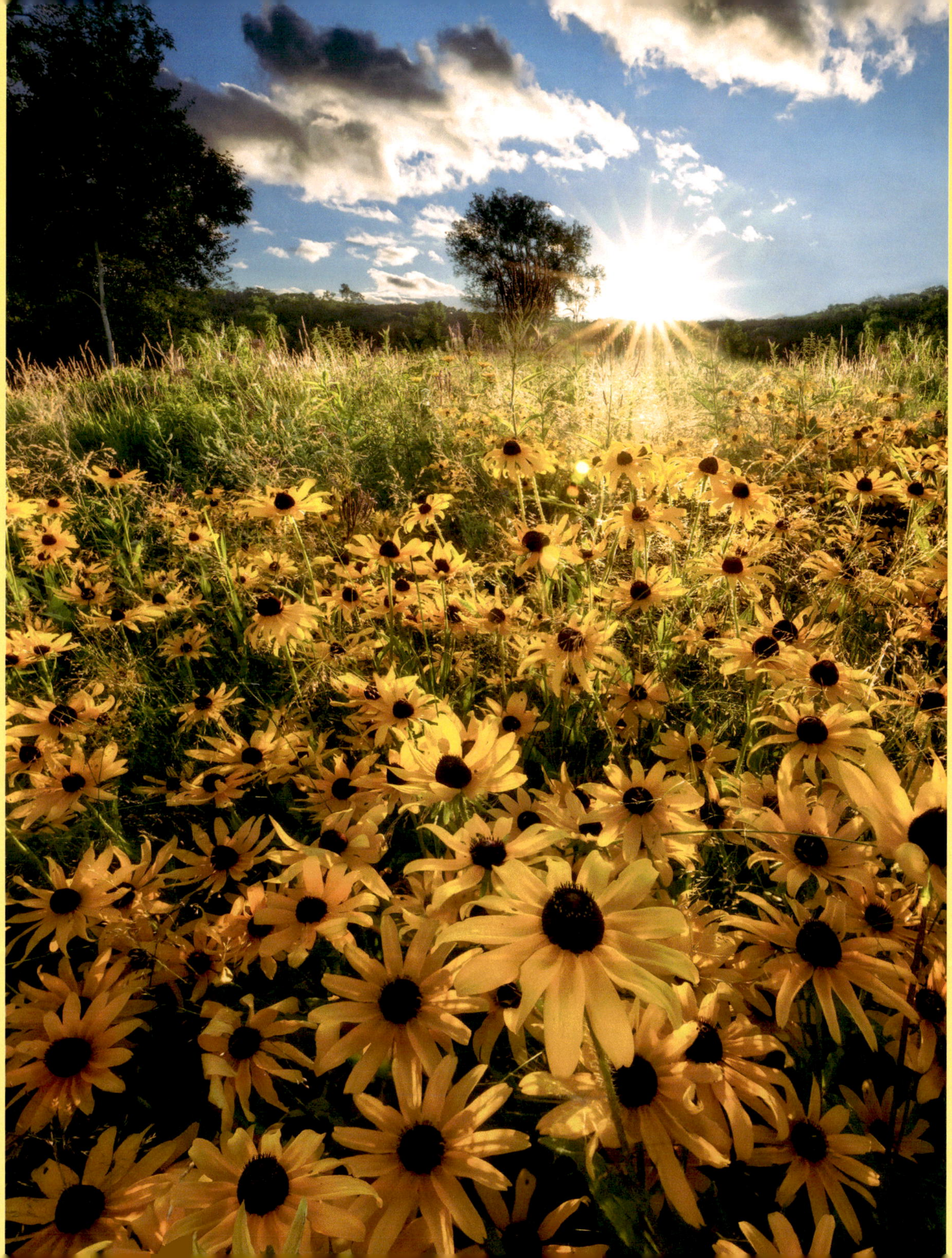

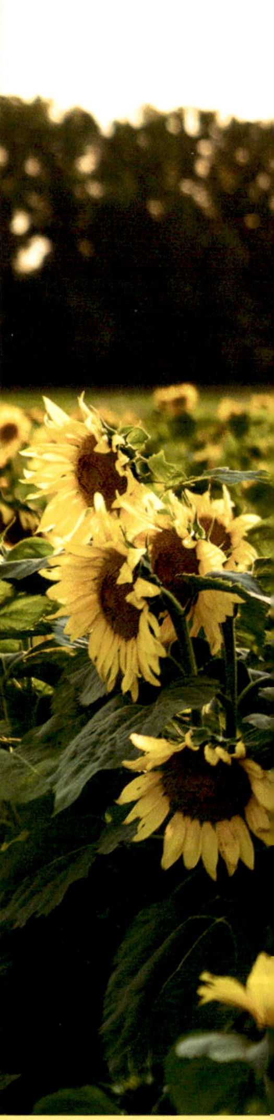

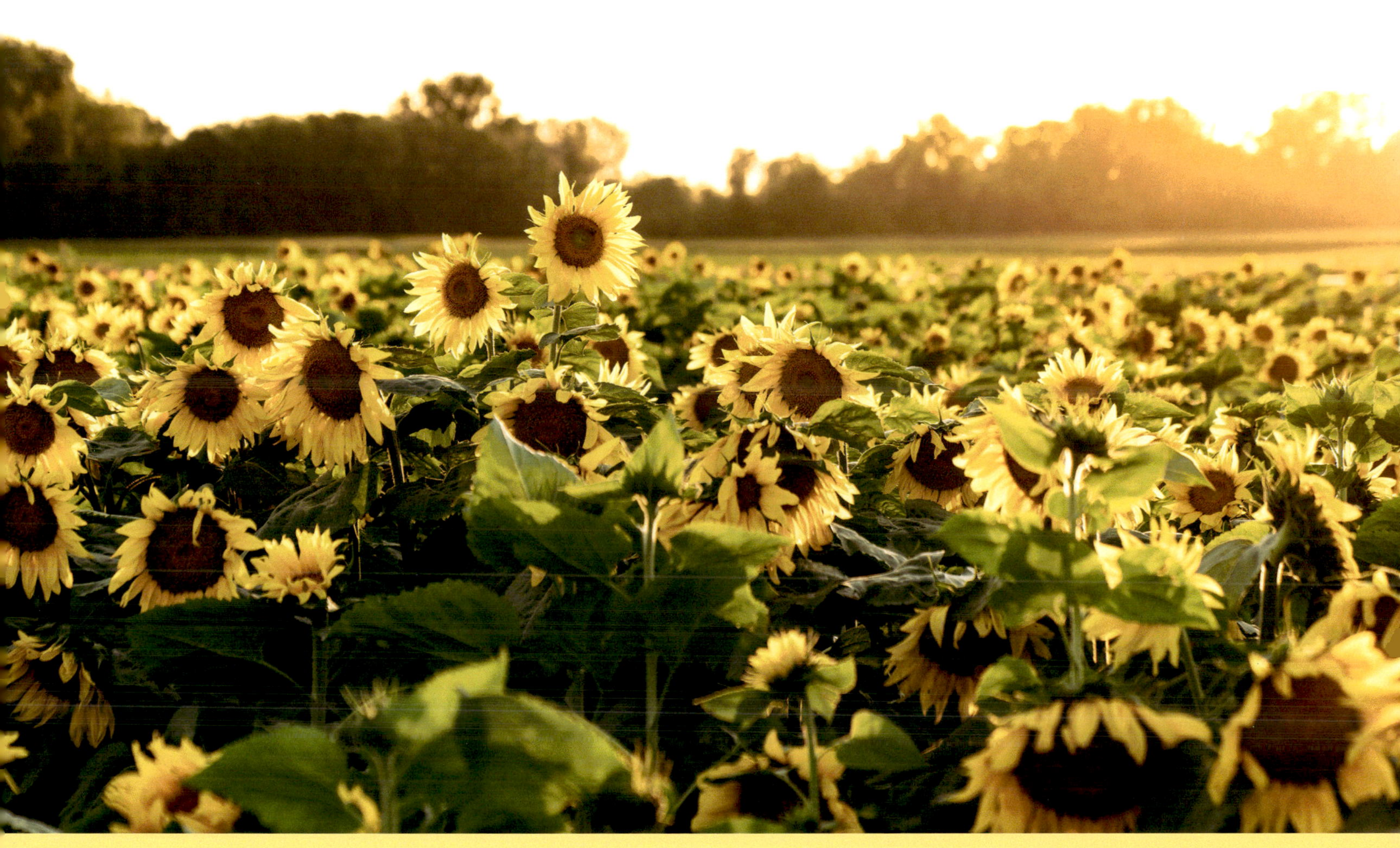

Above: Minnesota is the third largest producer of sunflowers in the United States. KRISTEN PERRINE/UNSPLASH

Facing page: Wildflowers in the sunflower family blanket a meadow in Plymouth, northwest of Minneapolis. MAX FOSTER

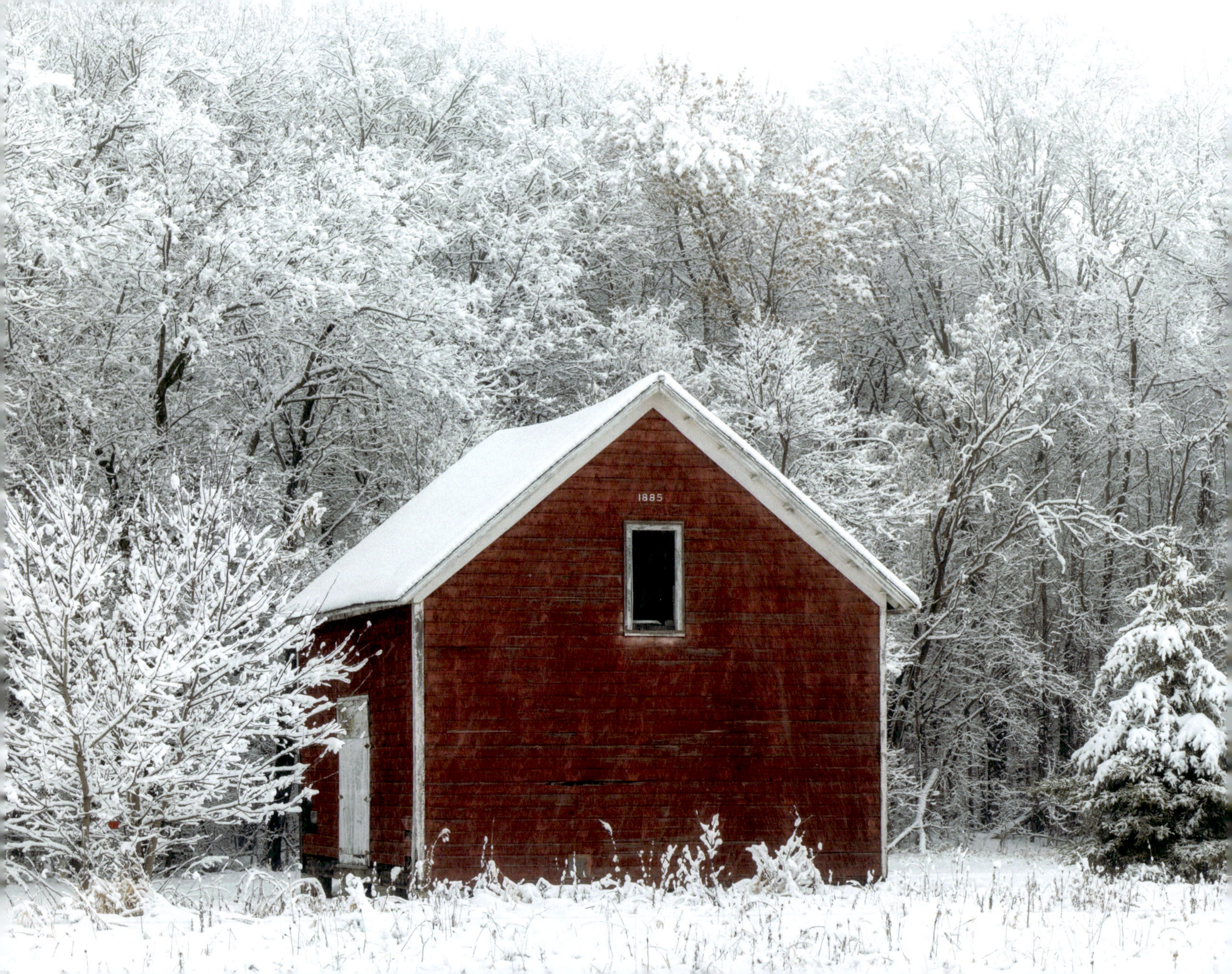
1885

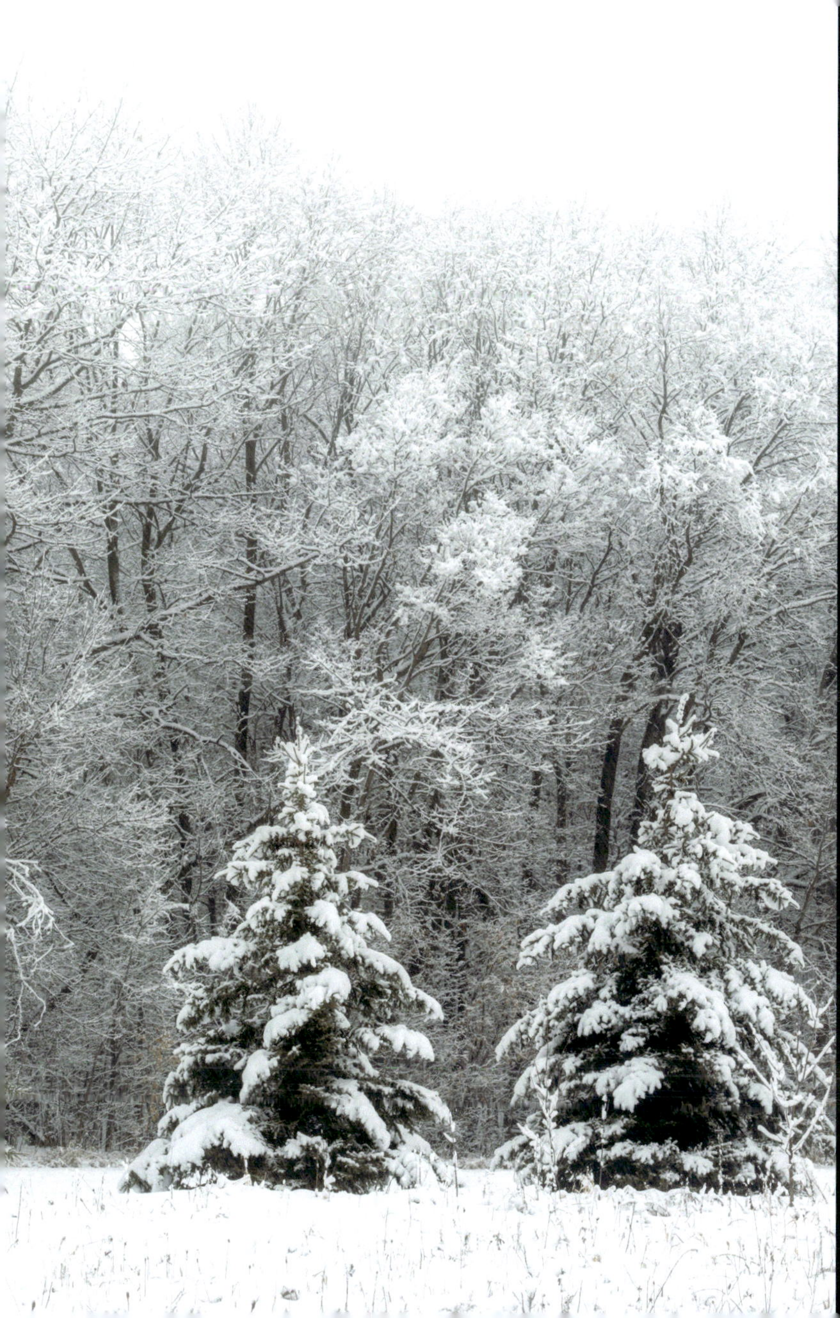

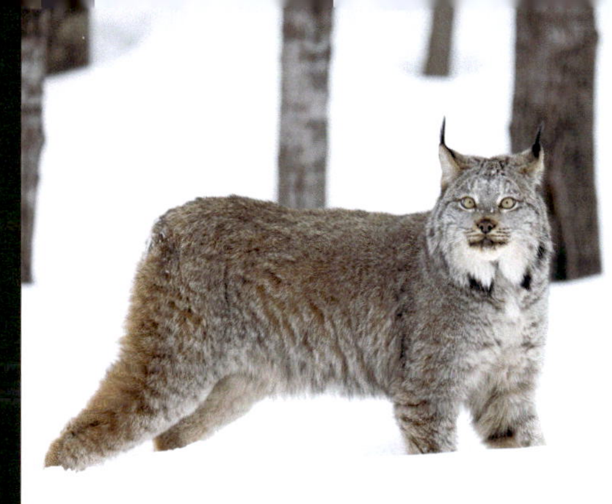

Above: Due to declining populations, Minnesota gave Canada lynx protected status in 1984, followed by federal protection in 2000. AGNIESZKA BACAL/SHUTTERSTOCK

Left: Henry's Woods Park near Roger is a 45-acre remnant of the hardwood forest that once spanned a swath of central Minnesota. Homesteading here, the Henry family built this sugar shack for making maple syrup. MAX FOSTER

Below: Minnesota's white-tailed deer are well adapted to many habitats, from wood lots and forests to swamps, prairies, and farm fields. ROBIN/UNSPLASH

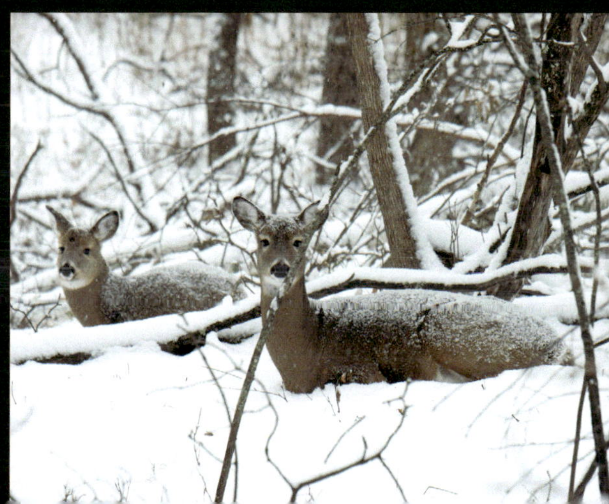

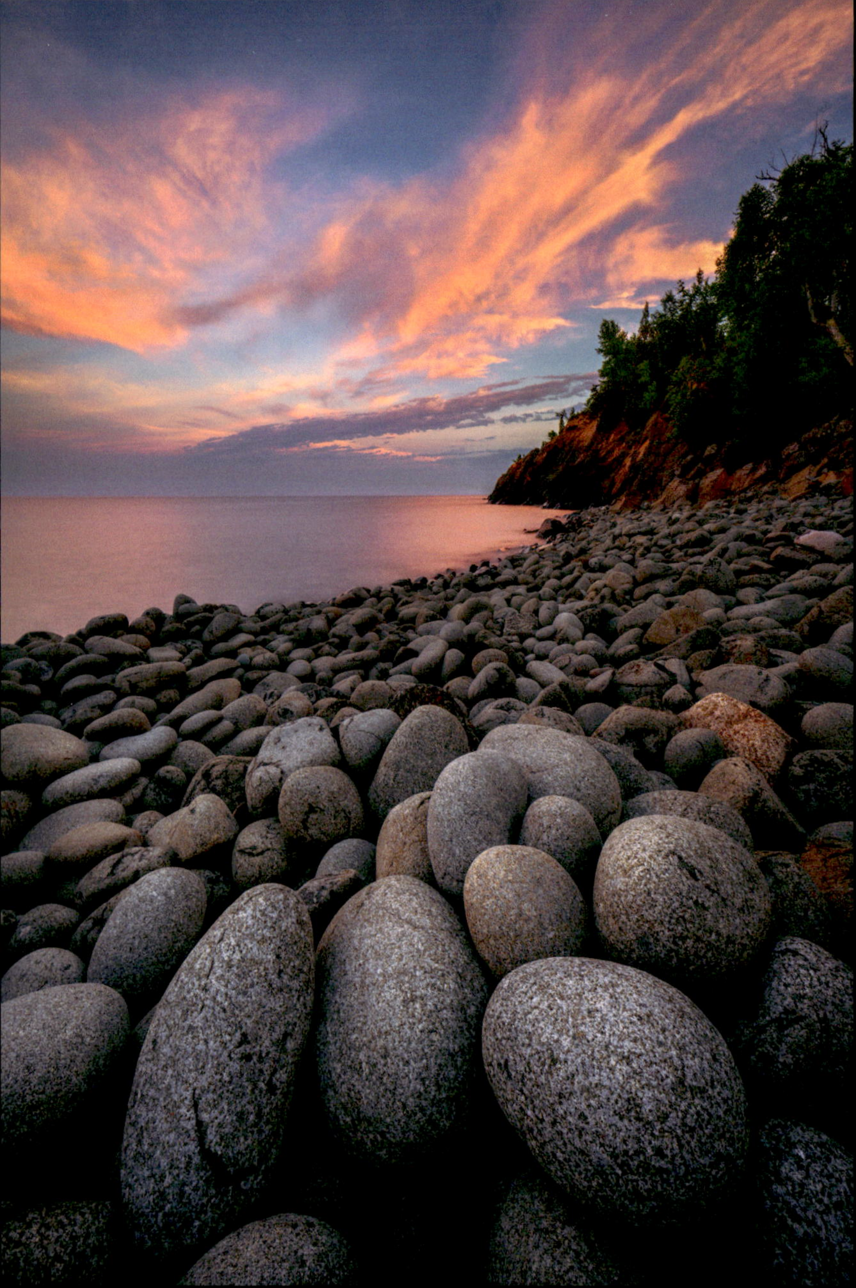

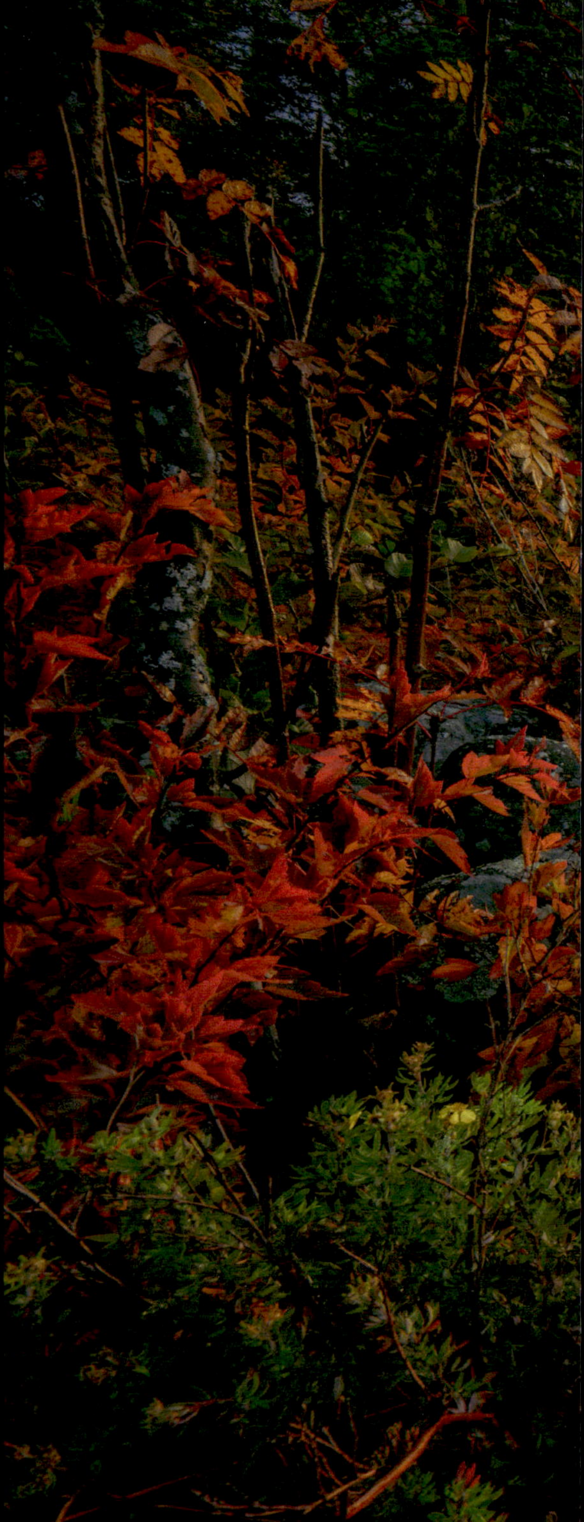

Above: Lake Superior's ceaseless waves reduce most beach cobble to small pebbles, but this "secret" beach is populated with smooth, rounded stones the size of bowling balls. MAX FOSTER

Right: Scarlet and golden leaves by slate-gray waters, with dark clouds on the horizon, portend winter's approach. MAX FOSTER

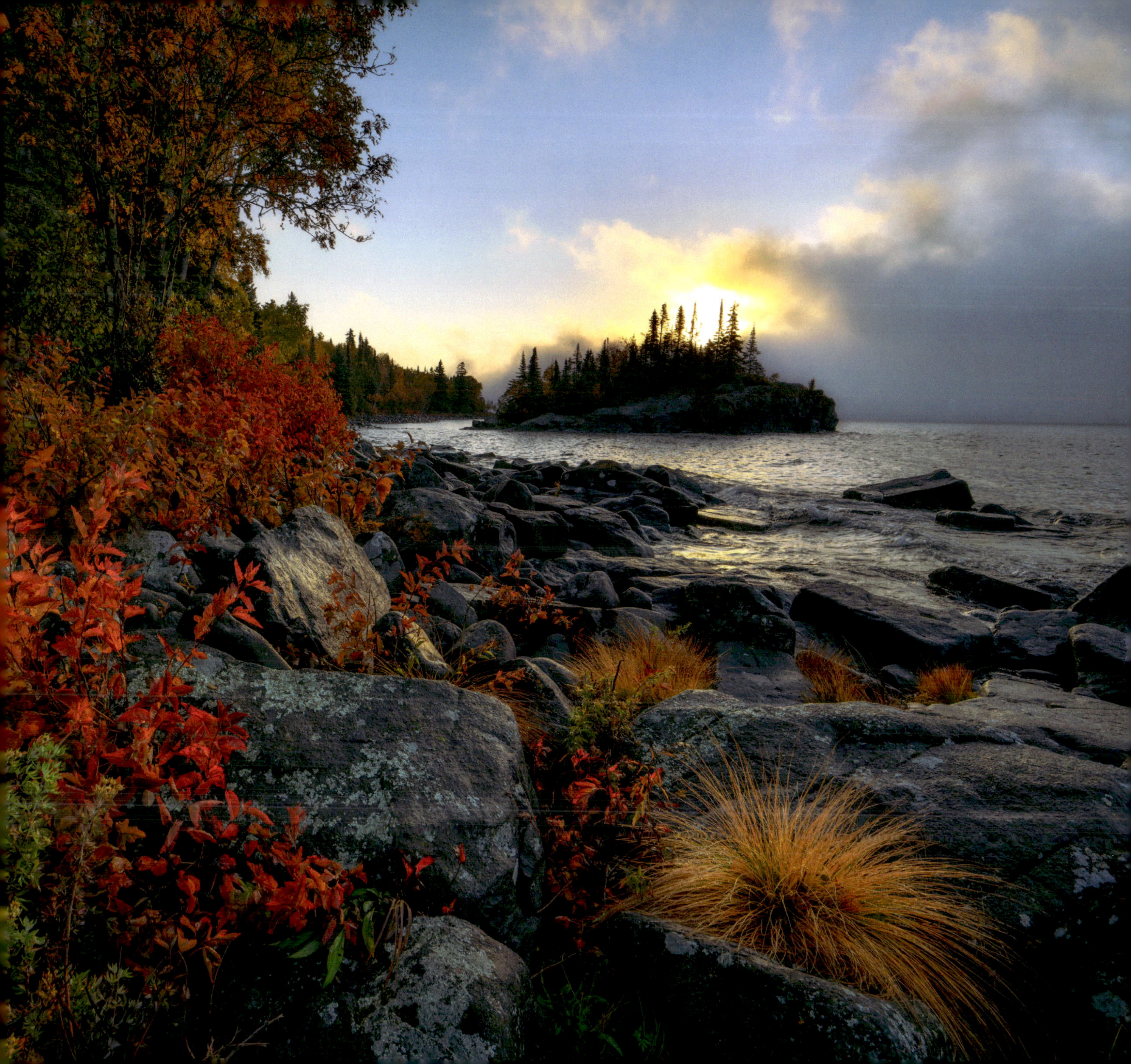

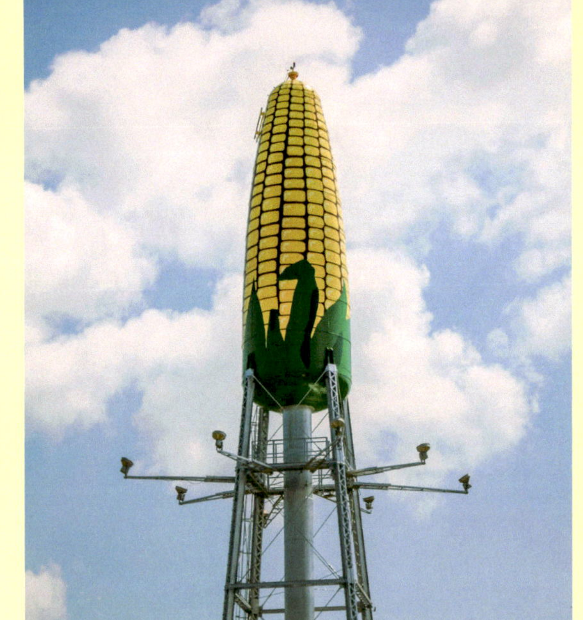

Right: Soaring to 151 feet, the Ear of Corn is a functioning 50,000-gallon water tower near Graham Park south of downtown Rochester. CODY OTTO/UNSPLASH

Far right: Cattle graze near an abandoned homestead near the town of Fountain in the state's southeastern corner. MAX FOSTER

Below: Southwest of Minneapolis-St. Paul, a classic red barn near Chanhassen serves as an emblem of the area's agricultural heritage. MAX FOSTER

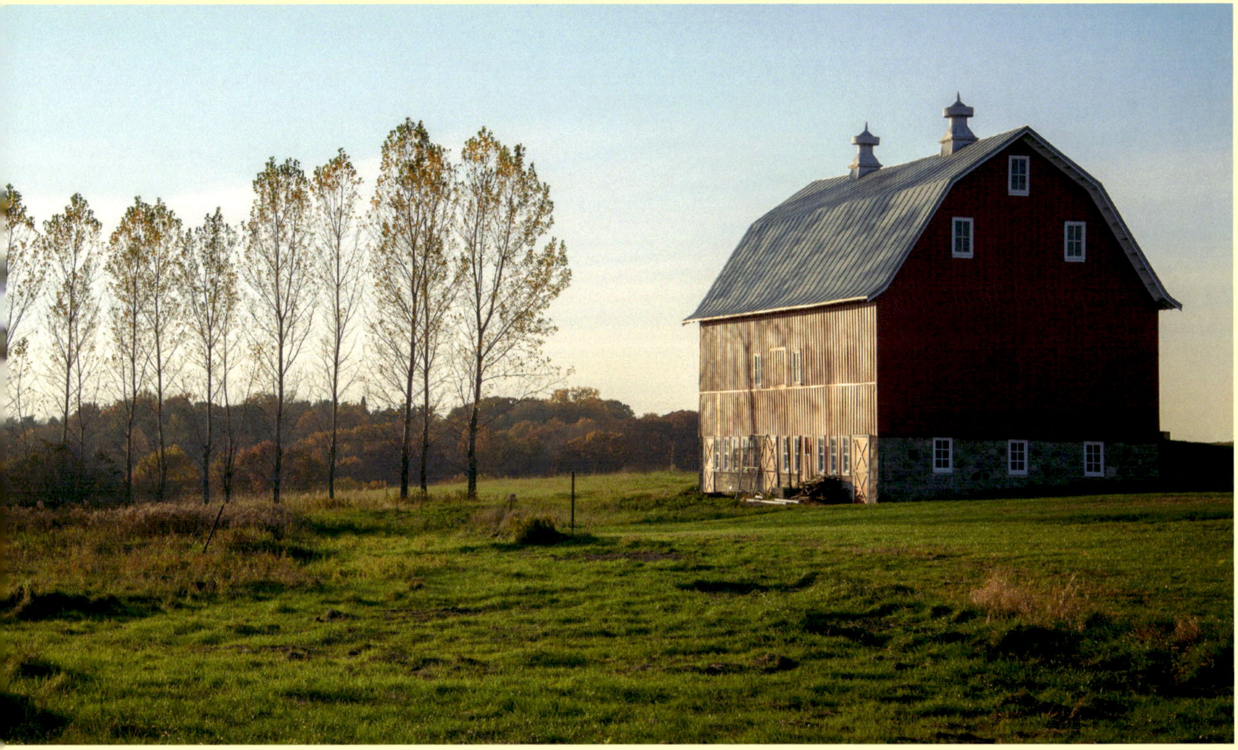

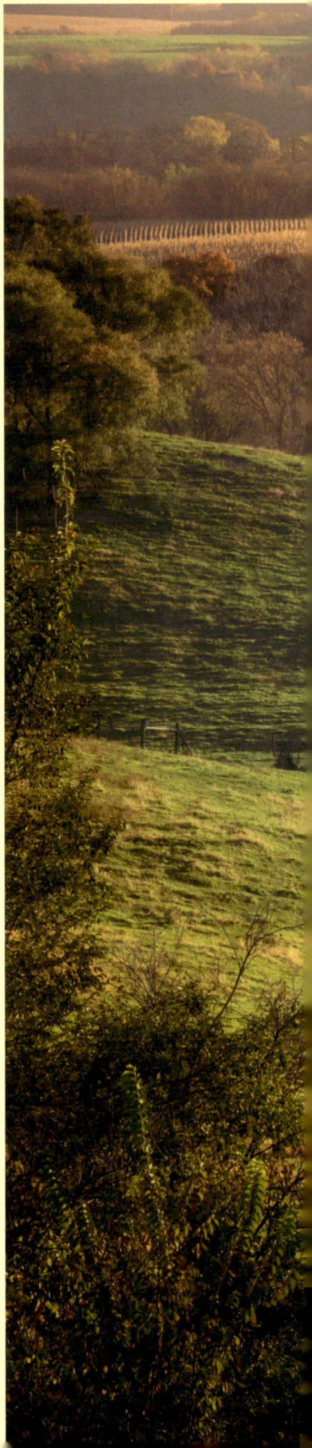

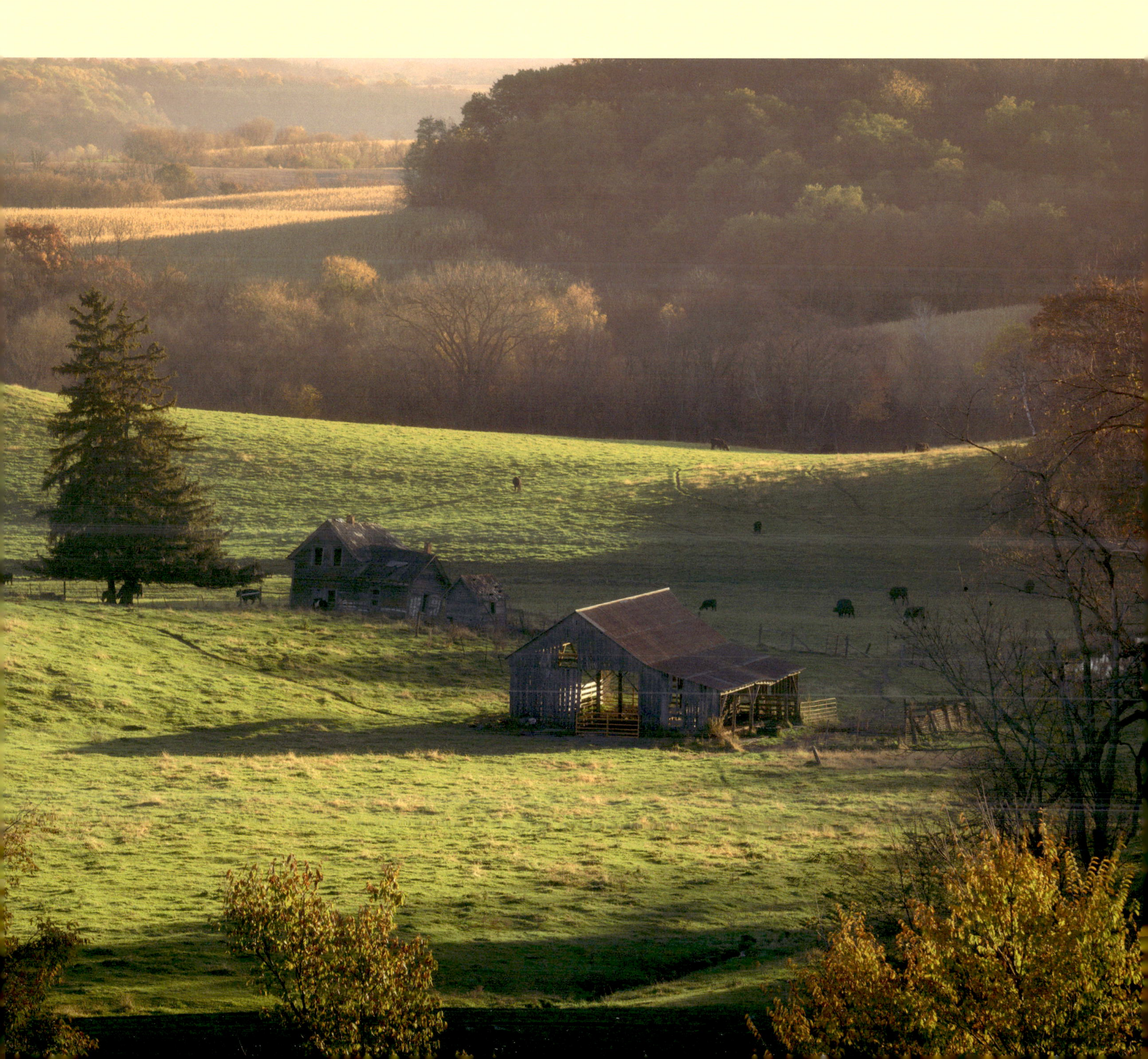

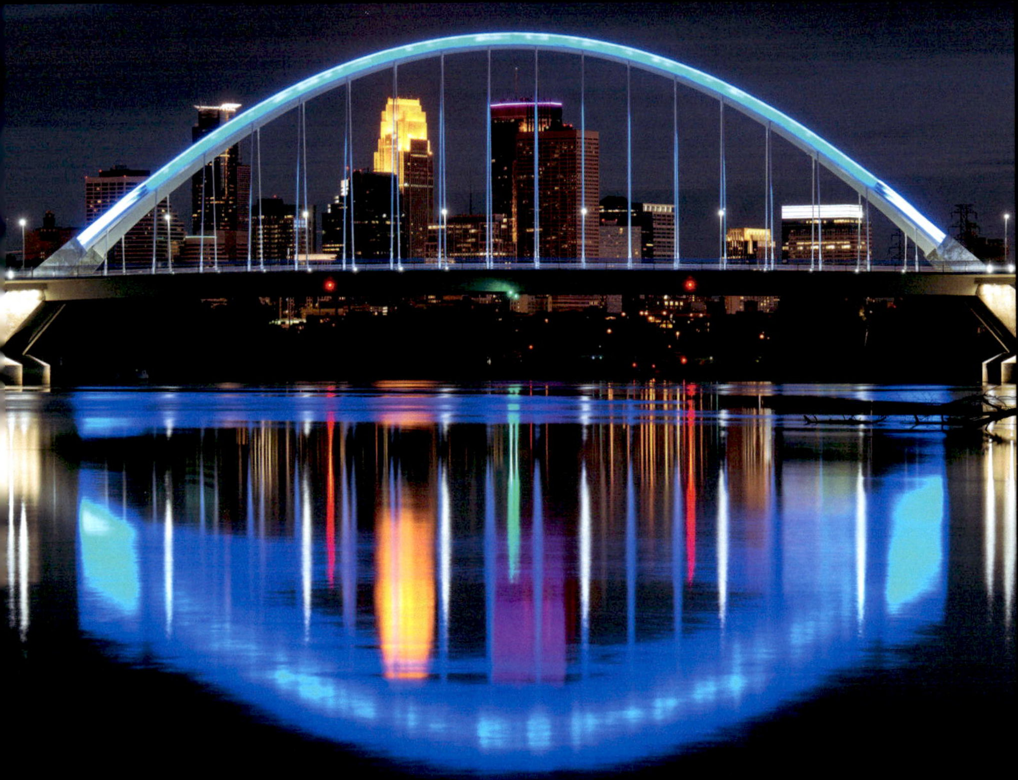

Above: The illuminated arches of the Lowry Avenue Bridge, completed in 2012, frame the equally colorful Minneapolis skyline. MAX FOSTER

Right: Downtown Minneapolis hosts a vibrant mix of four-star hotels, shopping, arts and culture centers, and eateries serving an array of world cuisines. JOSH HILD/UNSPLASH

Far right: Spanning the Mississippi River just below St. Anthony Falls, the Stone Arch Bridge was built in 1883 to carry the Great Northern Railroad. Today, the bridge carries pedestrians and cyclists. MAX FOSTER

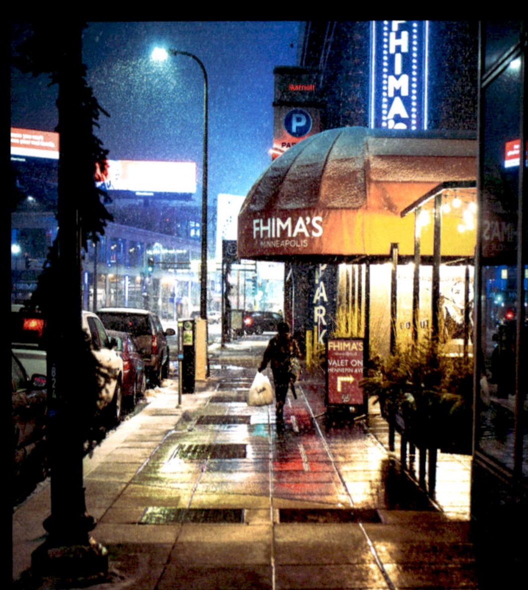

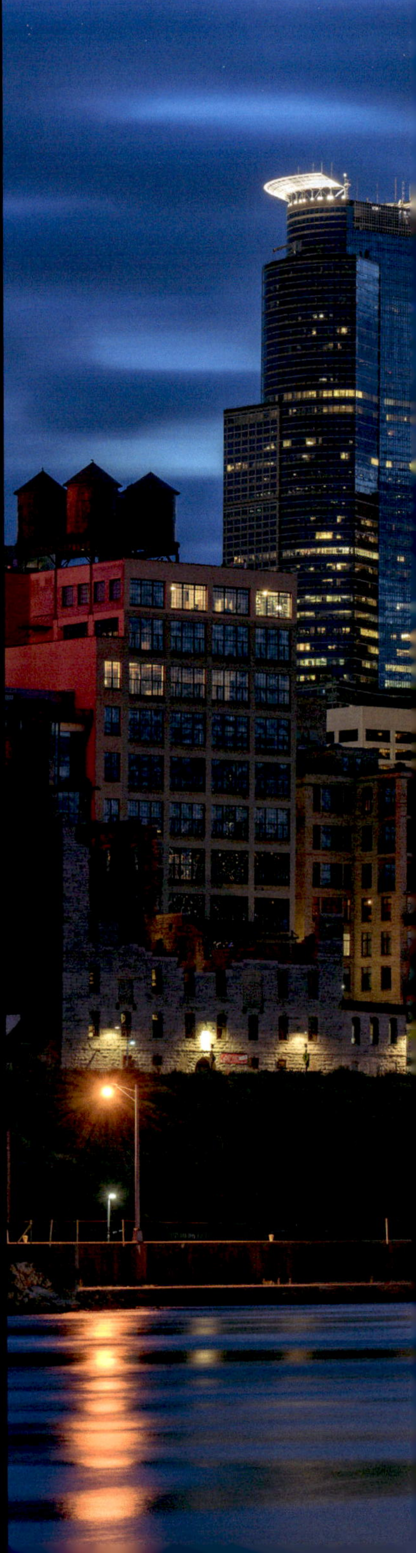

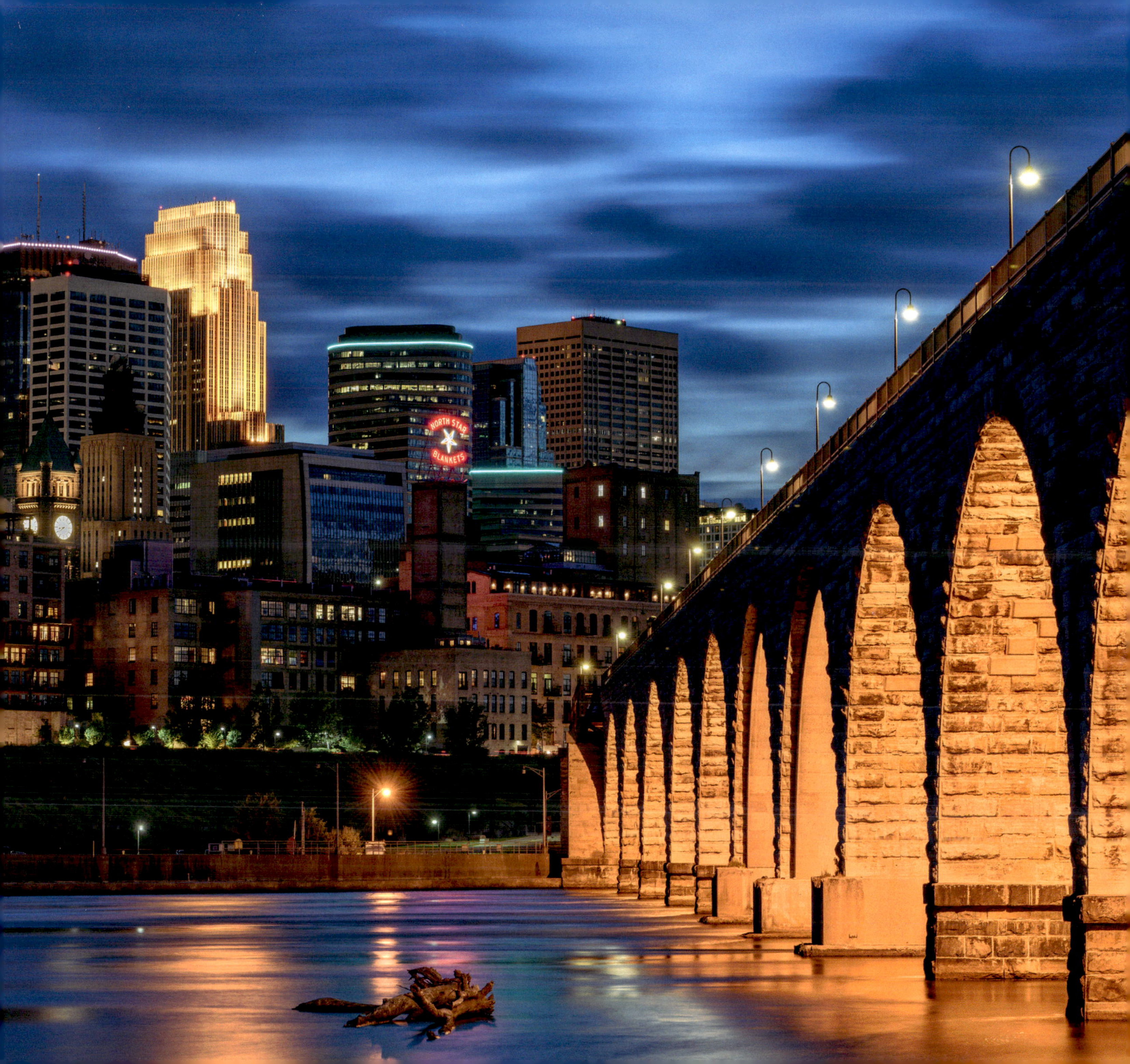
NORTH STAR
BLANKETS

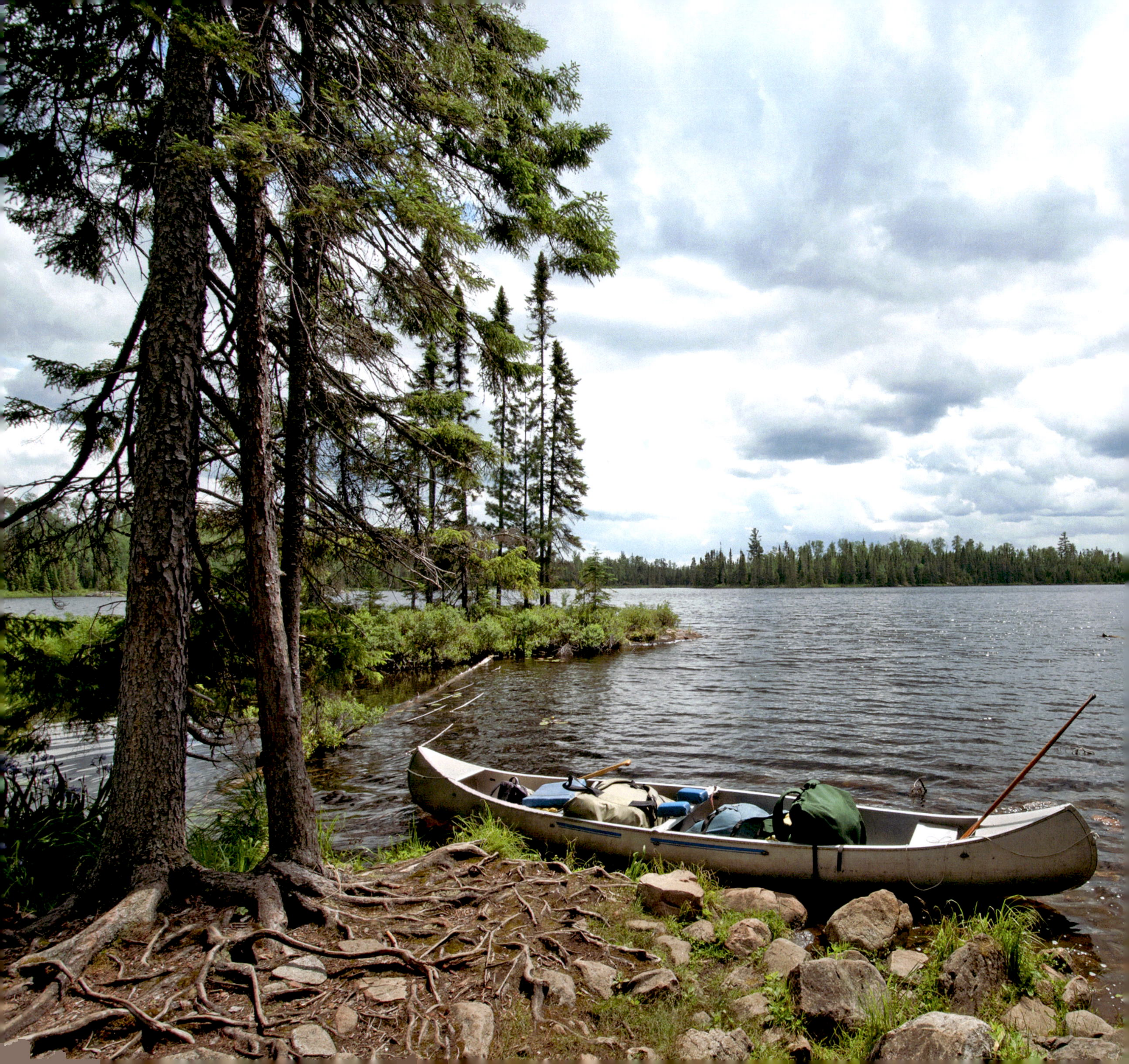

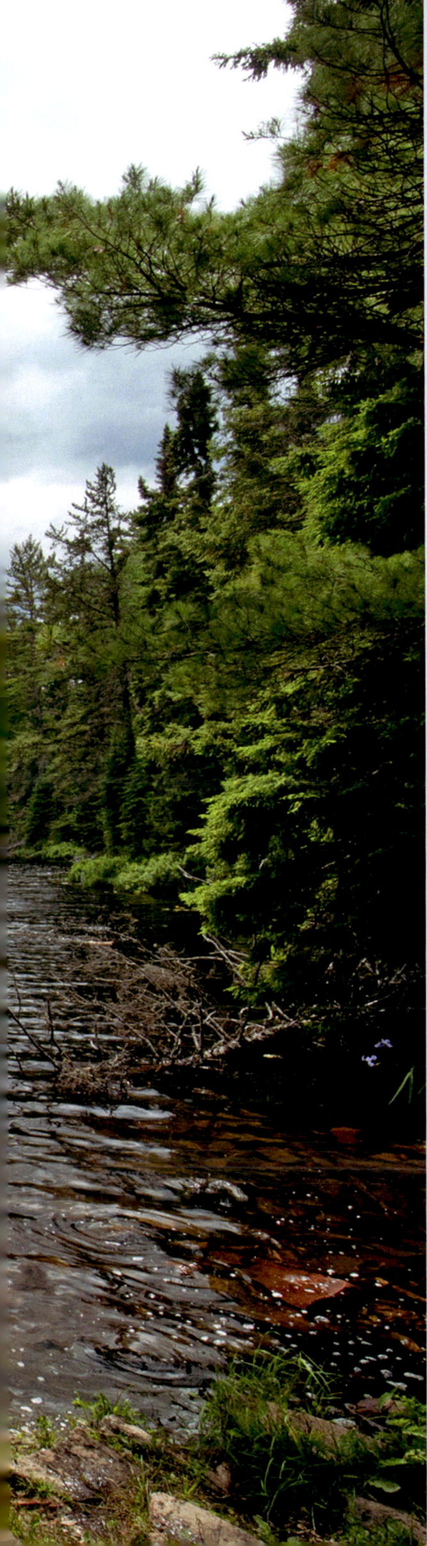

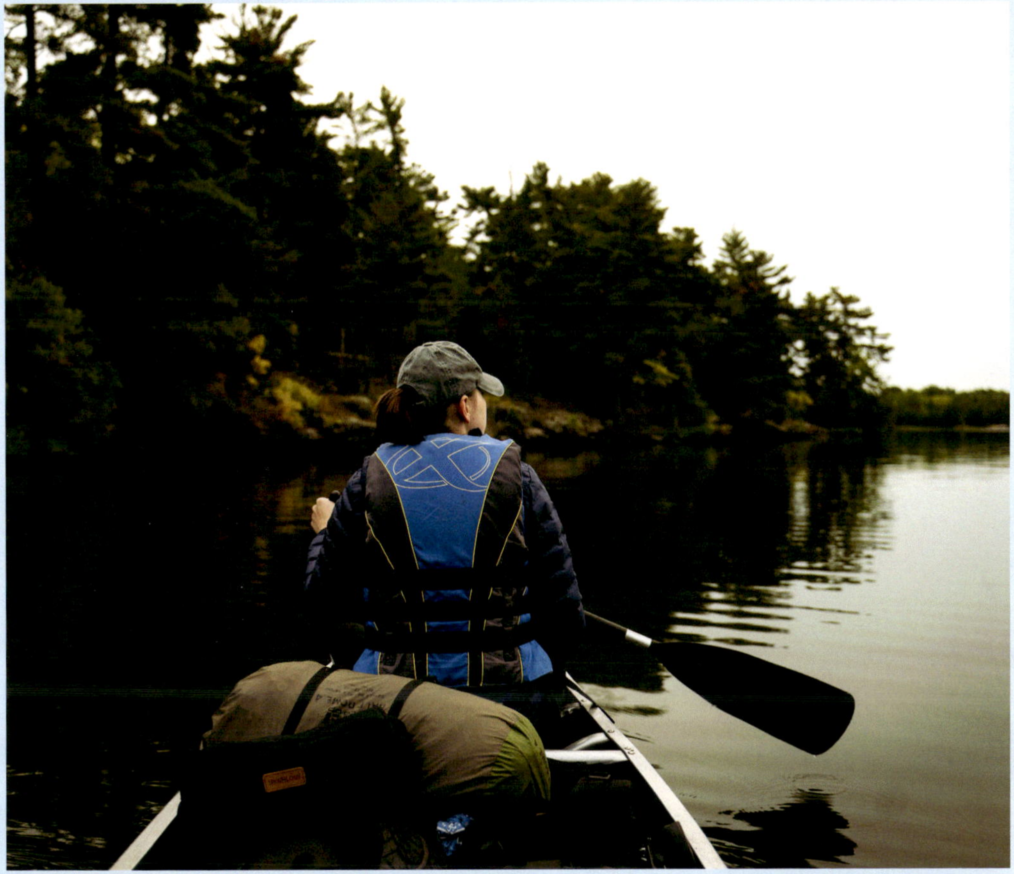

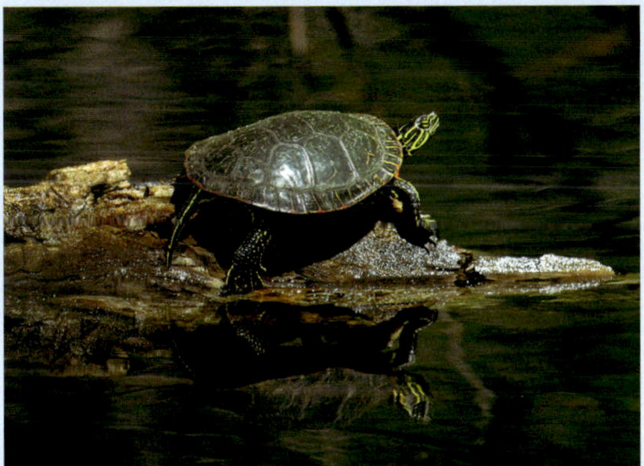

Above: Canoeists venture out on Kabetogama Lake in Voyageurs National Park near the Canadian border. TIM UMPHREYS/UNSPLASH

Left: The painted turtle is the most common of thirteen turtle species found across the northern Midwest. MATHEW BENOIT/UNSPLASH

Far left: The Boundary Waters Canoe Area Wilderness spans over 1 million acres, with more than 1,200 miles of canoe routes and 2,000 designated backcountry campsites. WILDNERDPIX/SHUTTERSTOCK

Right: Minnesota's highest waterfall (on the border with Ontario) is found in the far northeastern tip, where the High Falls of the Pigeon River plummet 120 feet into a narrow gorge in Grand Portage State Park. MAX FOSTER

Below: Autumn is a colorful time for exploring. JOSH HILD/SHUTTERSTOCK

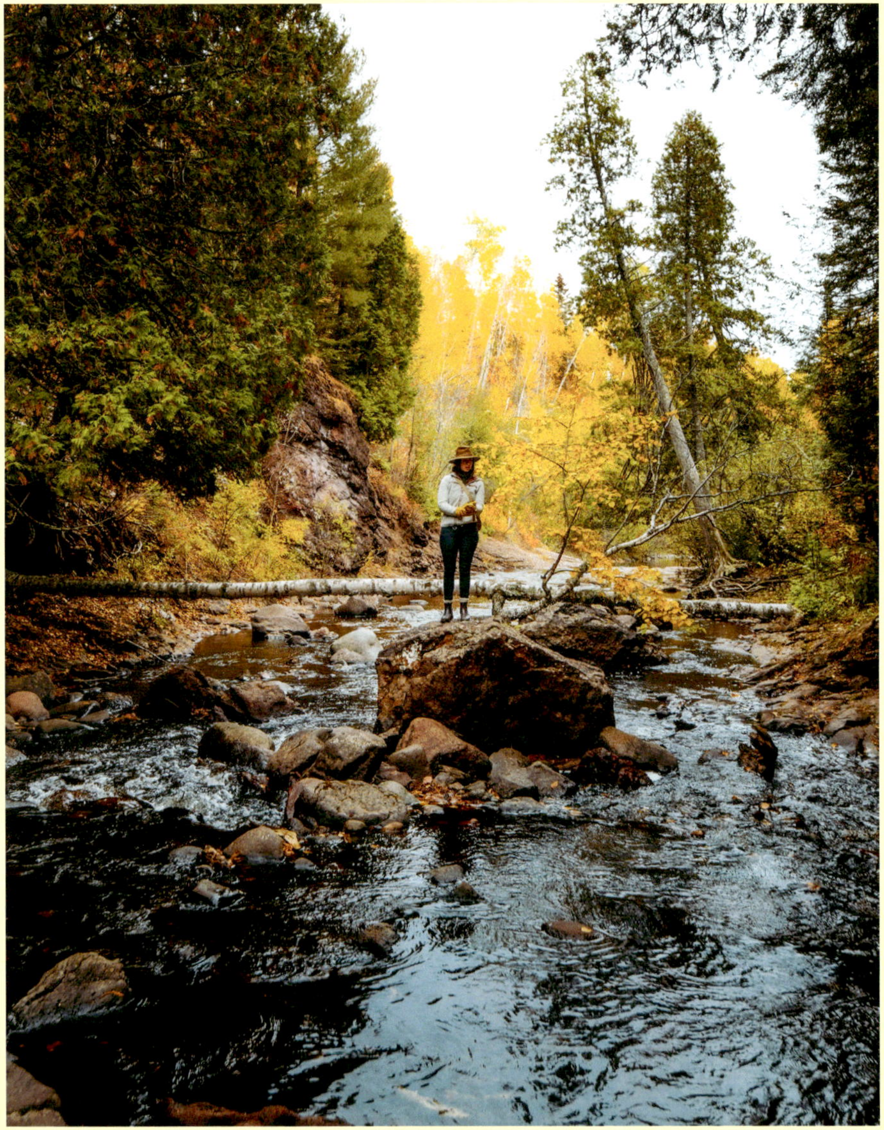

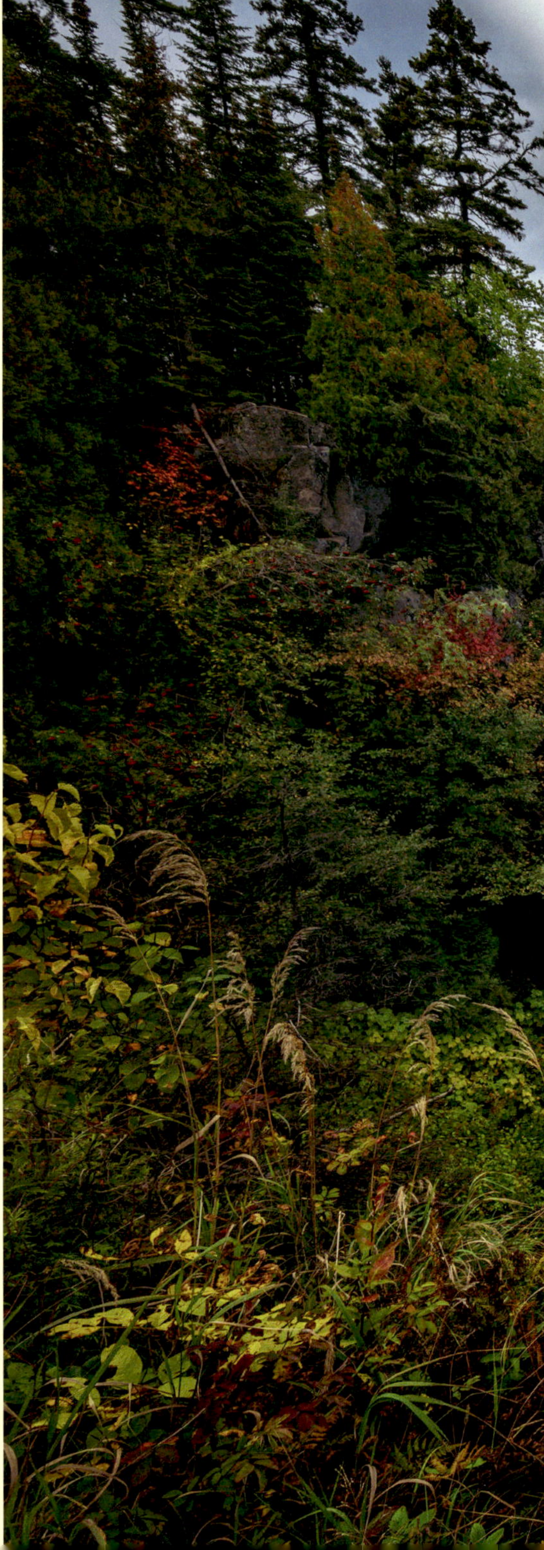

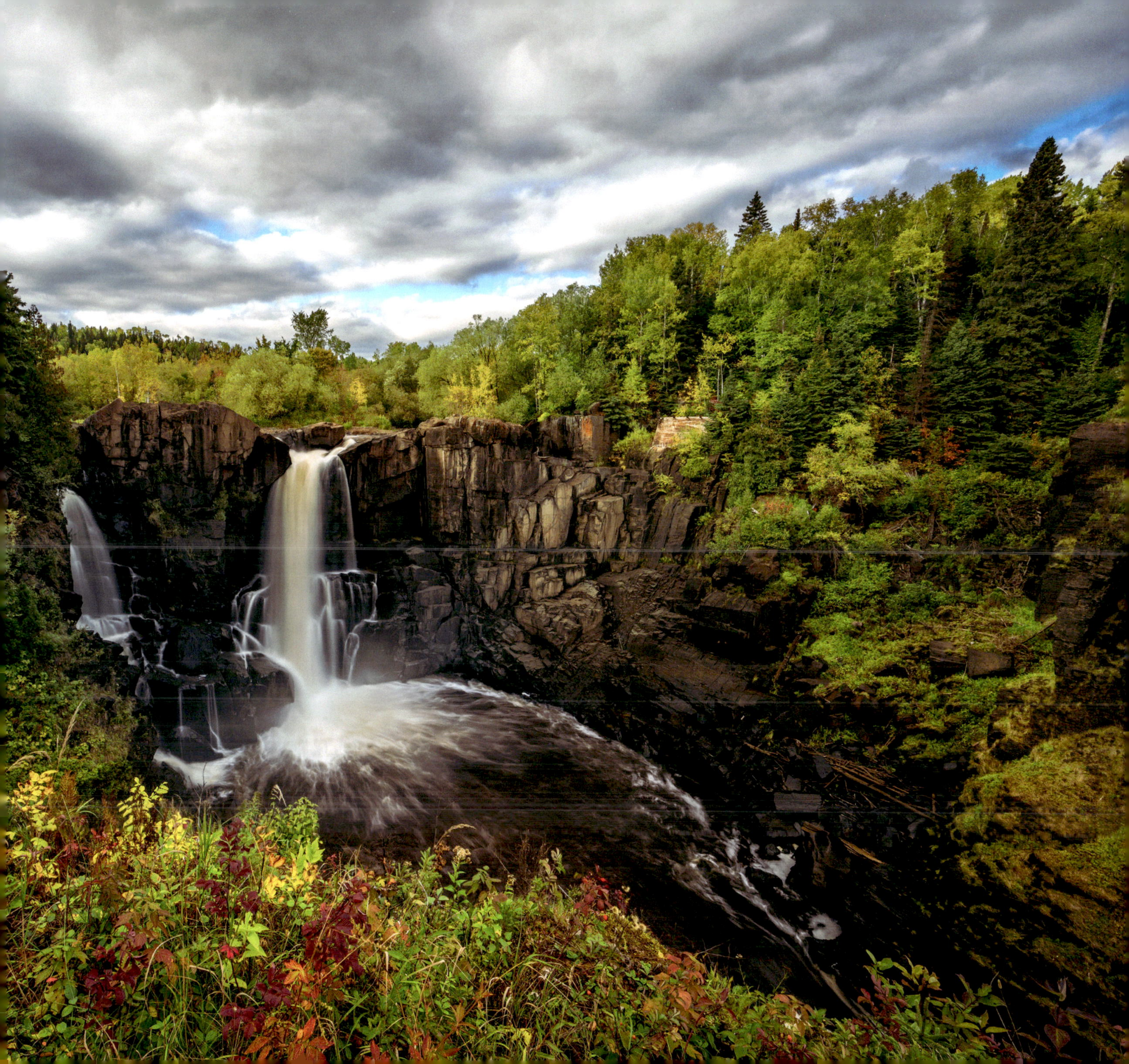

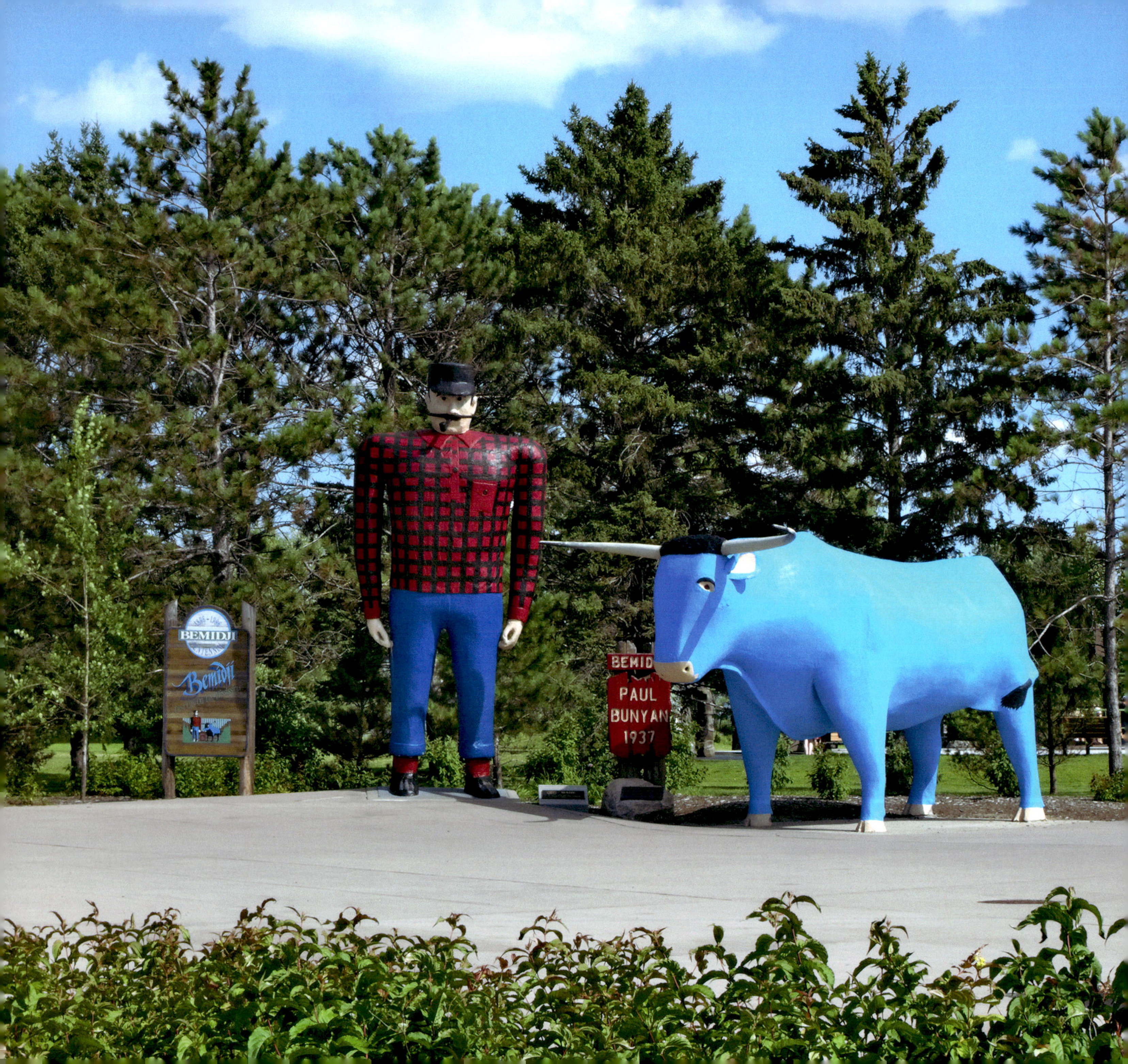
BEMIDJI
Bemidji
BEMID
PAUL
BUNYAN
1937

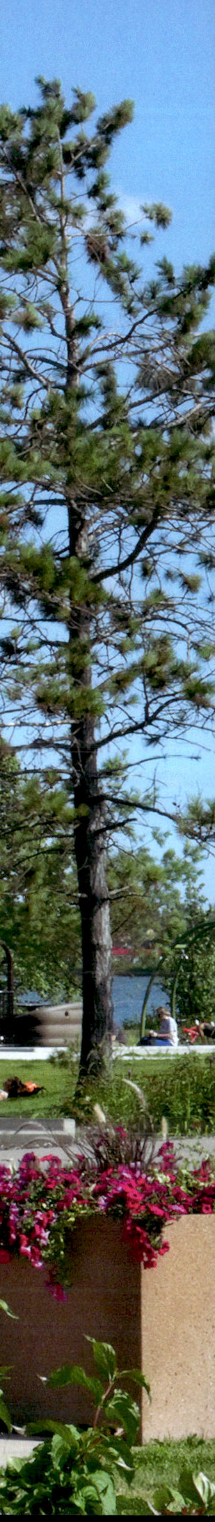

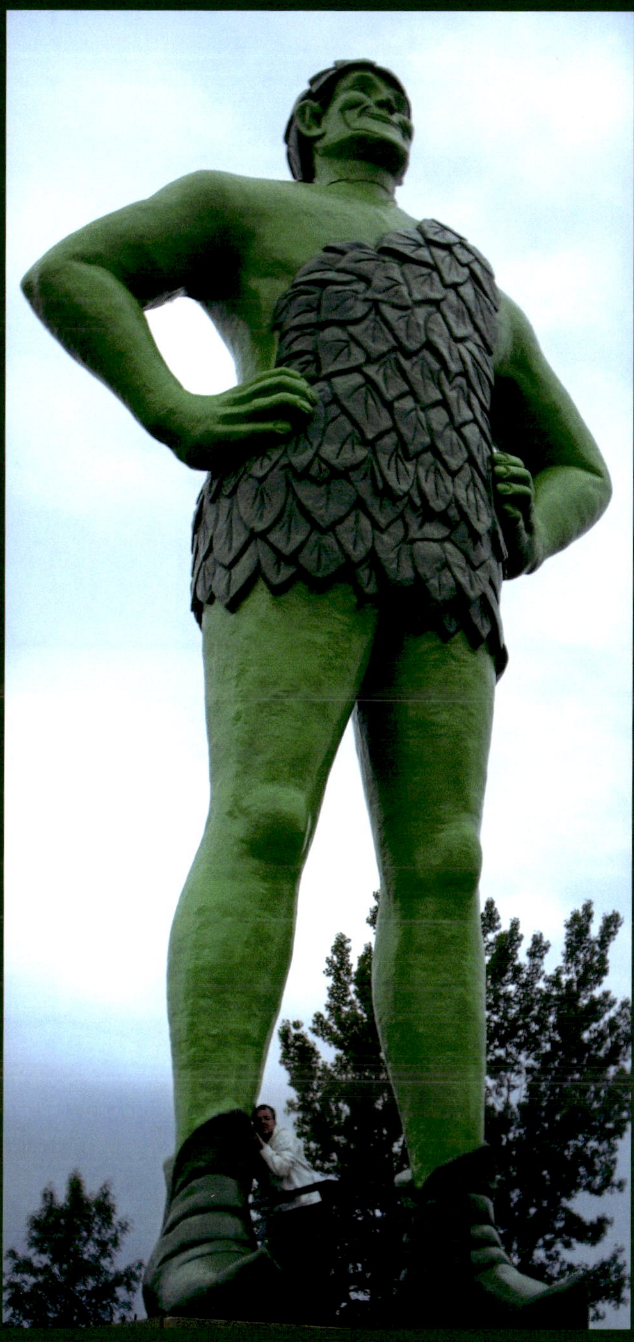

Left: In the town of Blue Earth, just off Interstate 90 at exit 119, the 55.5-foot fiberglass Jolly Green Giant statue tower's over a man standing between his feet.
JONATHUNDER/PUBLIC DOMAIN

Far left: Legendary Paul Bunyan and his Blue Ox, Babe, stand ready for photo ops at Paul Bunyan Park in Bemidji.
EDGAR LEE ESPE/SHUTTERSTOCK

Below: In the town of Red Wing, the Red Wing Museum's centerpiece is a size 638 ½ D Style 877 work boot. The "world's largest boot" was made in 2005 to commemorate the shoe company's 100th anniversary and is 20 feet long and 16 feet tall, weighing 2,300 pounds. ERICKSONLORI/PIXABAY

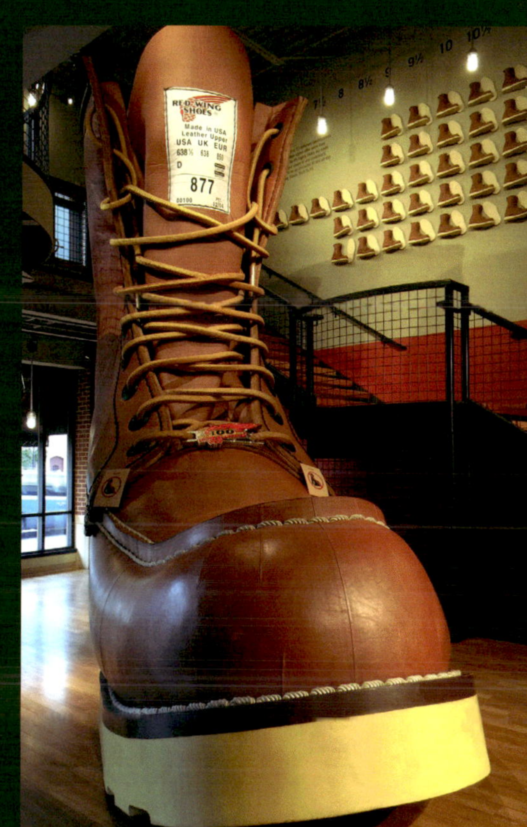

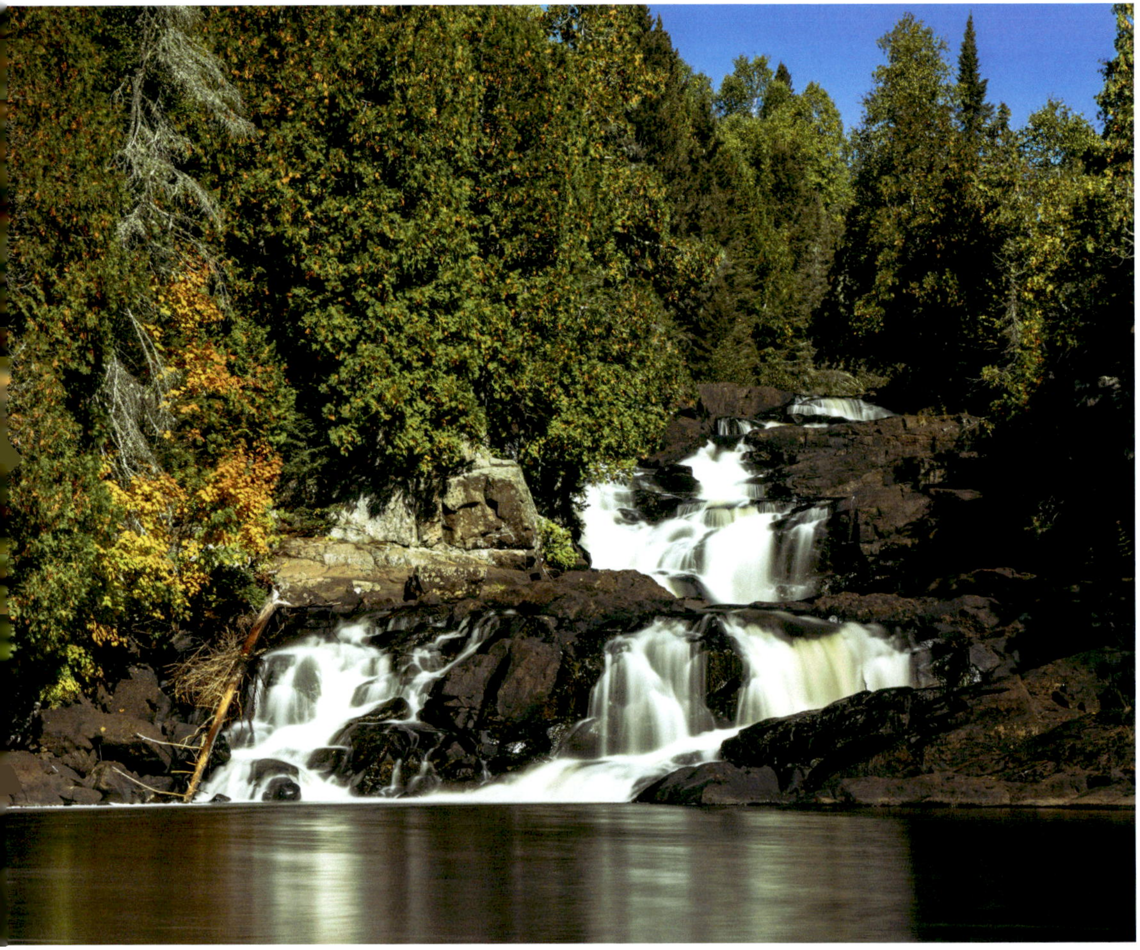

Above: Manitou Cascades churns tumble into a placid pool in George Crosby Manitou State Park along Lake Superior's North Shore. TOM UMPHREYS/UNSPLASH

Right: One-week-old marmot pups tentatively explore their world. These large rodents are widely known as groundhogs or woodchucks, the latter label based on their Algonquian name, *wuchak.* RALPH KATIEB/UNSPLASH

Far right: Plunging 63 feet, the High Falls of the Baptism River thunder within Tettegouche State Park. MAX FOSTER

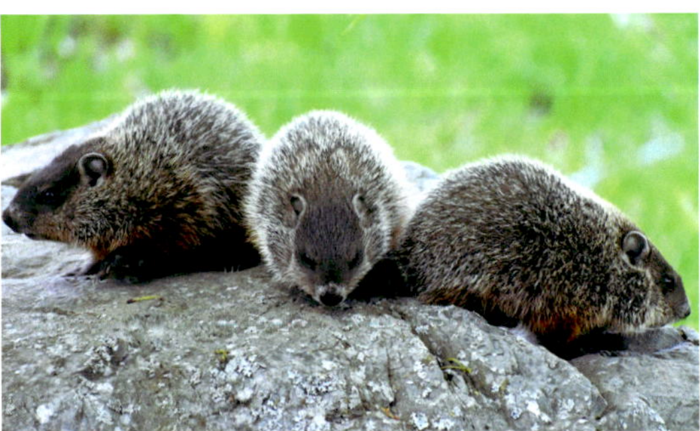

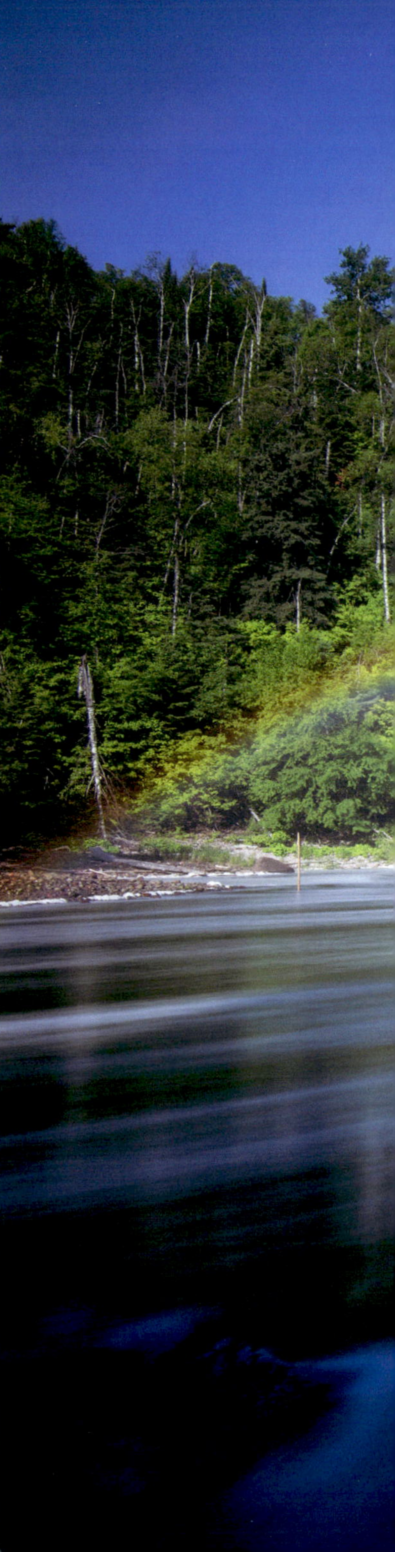

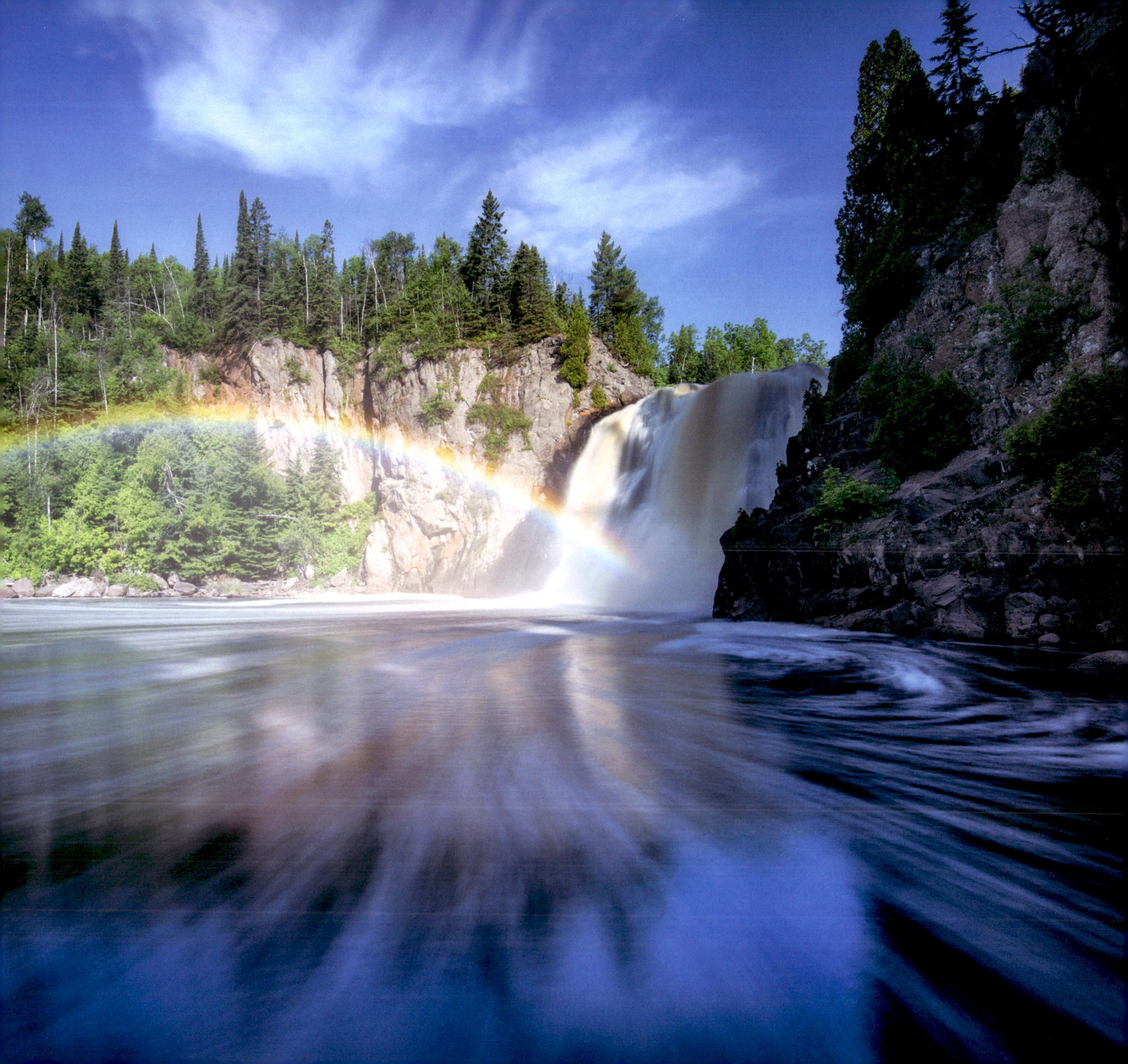

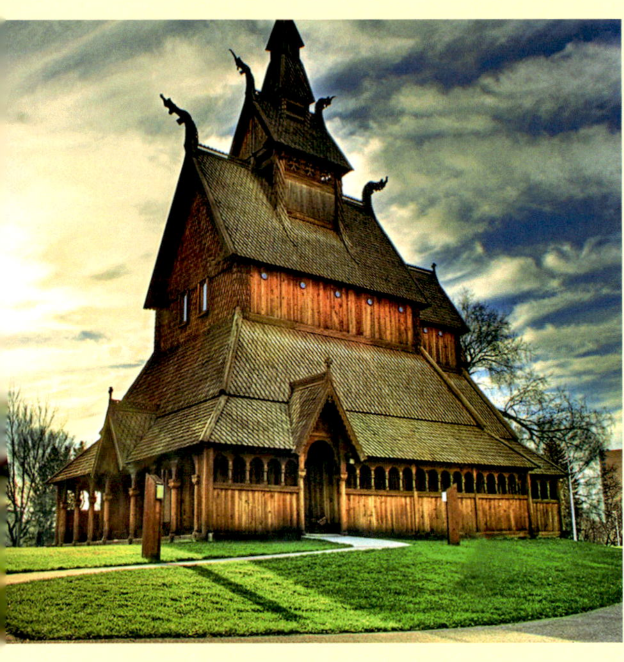

Above: Completed in 2001, this stave church, a replica of the 900-year-old Hopperstad Stave Church in Vik, Norway, celebrates Norse culture on the grounds of the Hjemkomst Center in Moorhead. ZACH HELLER/WIKIPEDIA

Right: Completed in 1895, the Basilica of Saint Stanislaus Kostkain in Winona features colorful stained glass windows and serves as the religious and cultural center of the local Polish community. TOM FISK/PEXELS

Facing page: Nestled among farm fields and woodlots on the outskirts of Hampton, about 30 miles south of St. Paul, Watt Munisotaram is the largest Buddhist temple in North America, founded by the Minnesota Cambodian Buddhist Society. TOM FISK/PEXELS

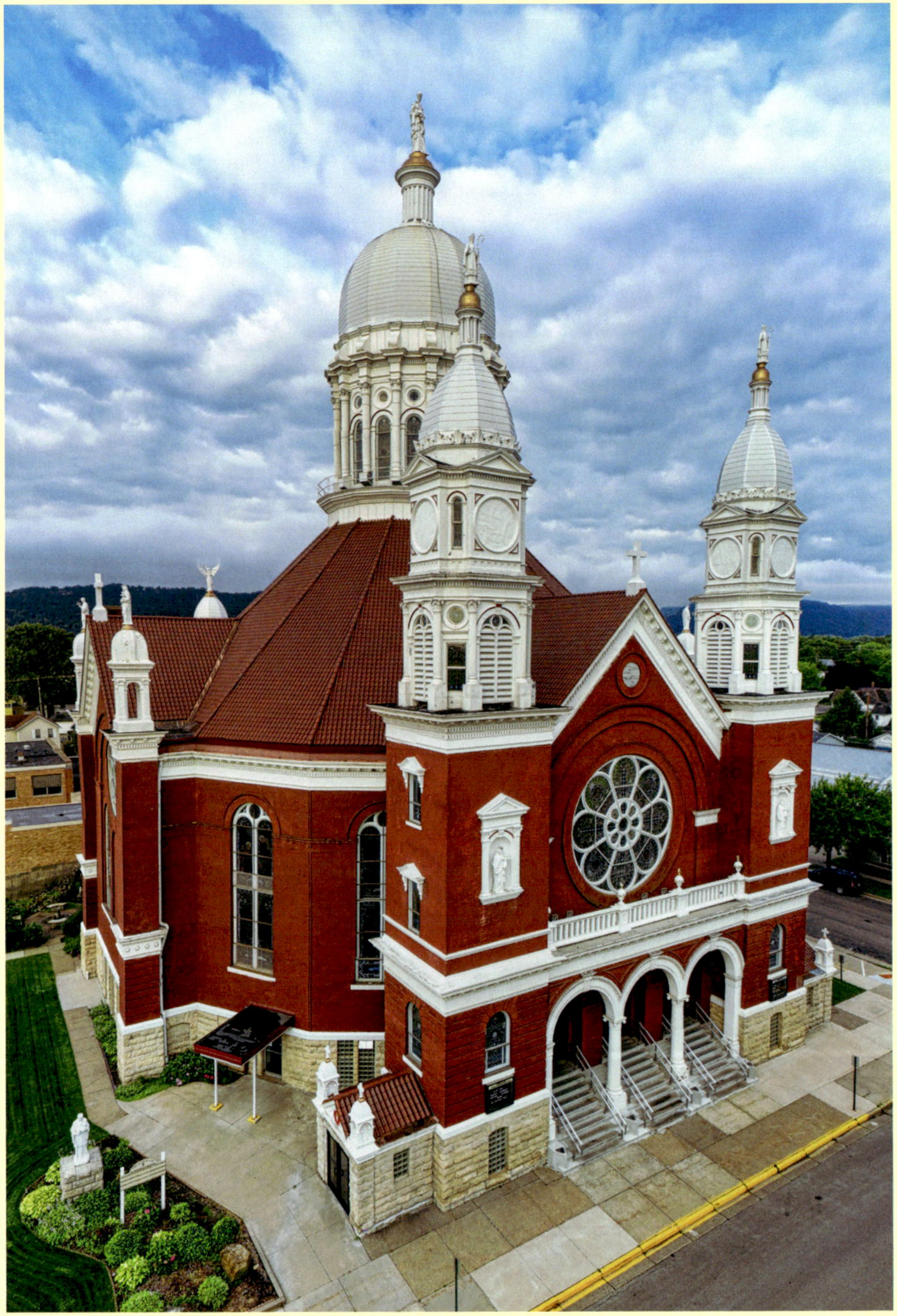

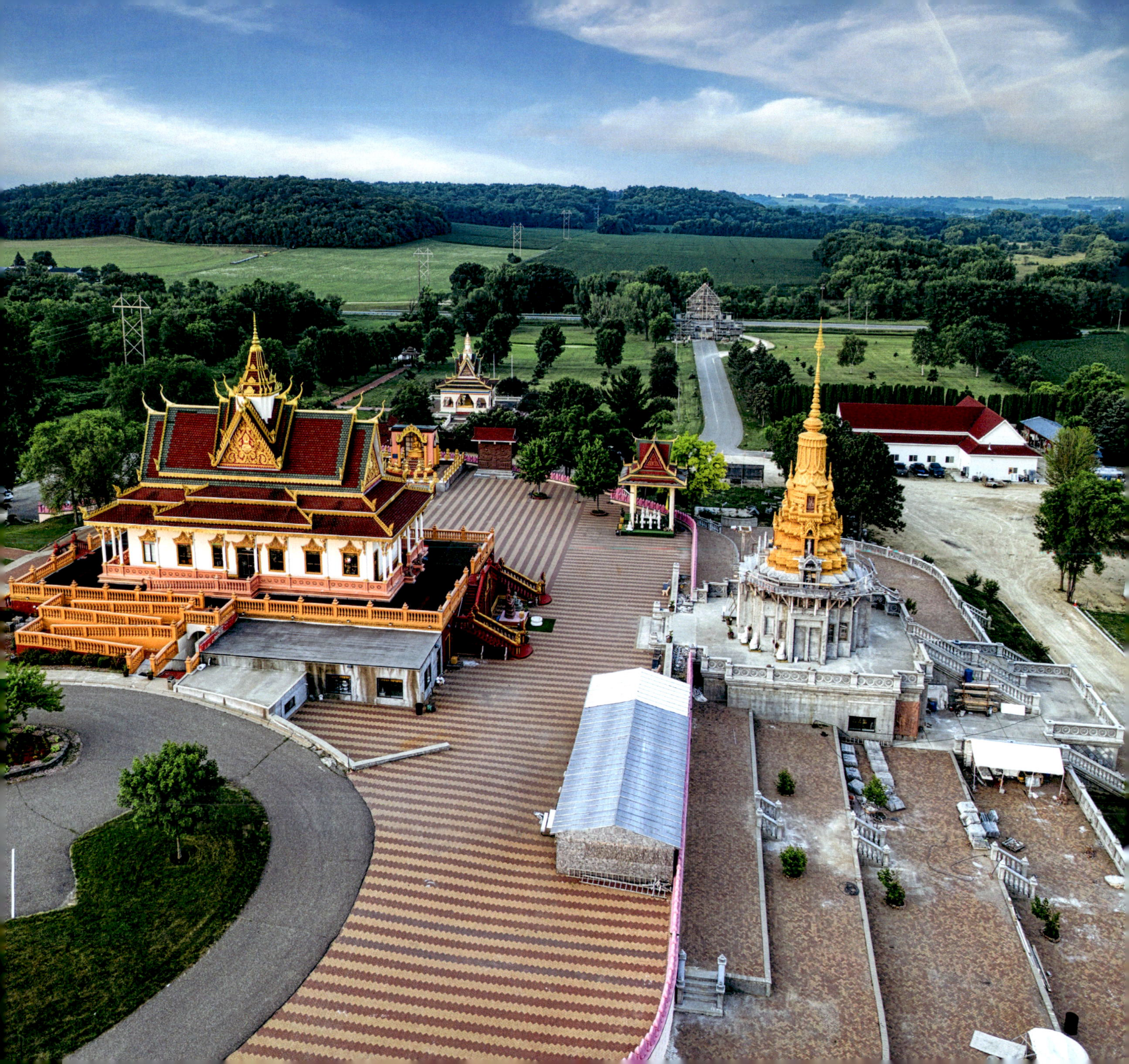

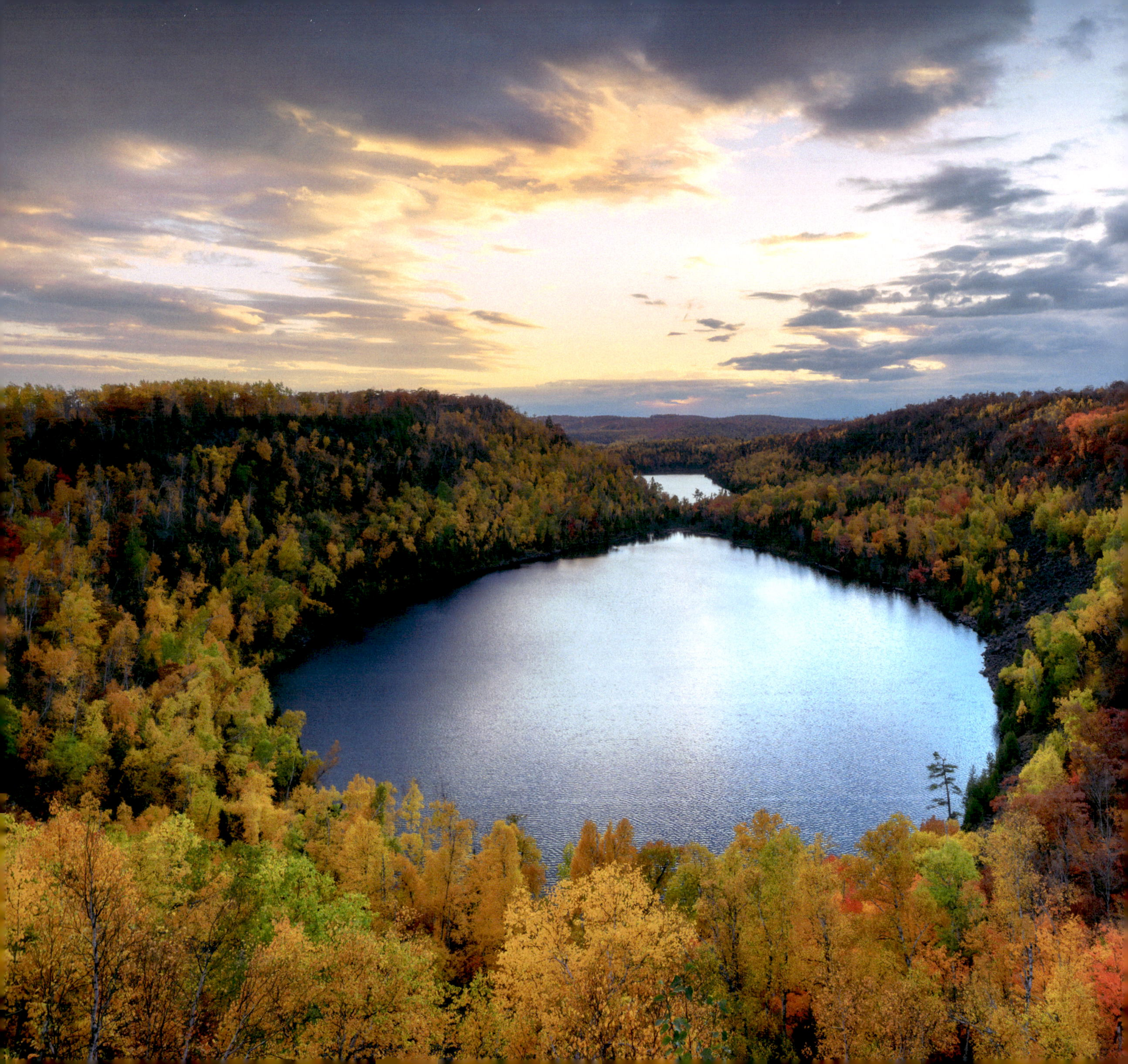

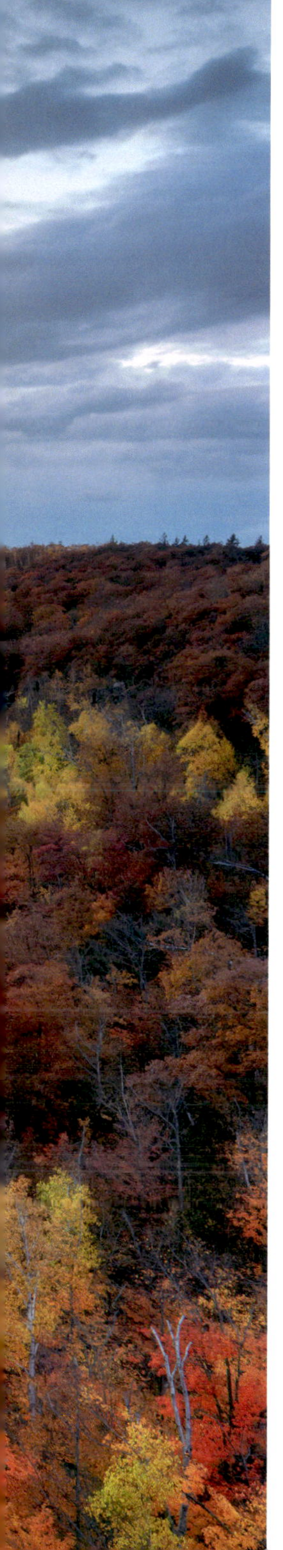

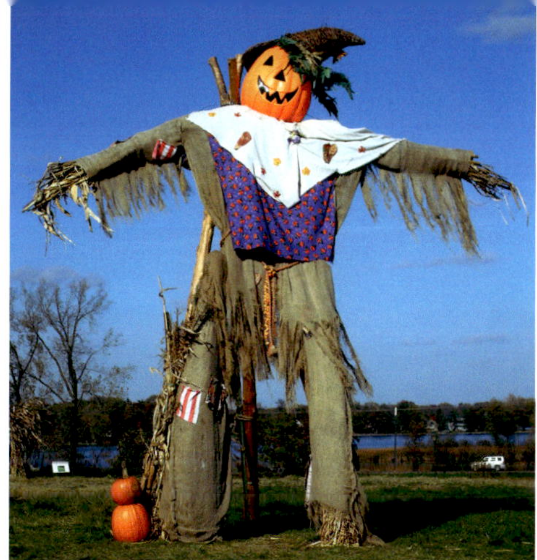

Left: A scarecrow stands tall at the 1,200-acre Minnesota Landscape Arboretum in Chaska, southwest of Minneapolis. Visitors explore display gardens, woodlands, and nationally recognized plant collections on miles of pathways. CGORDON8527/PIXABAY

Far left: Autumn hues ring Bear Lake (foreground) and its neighbor, Bean Lake, near Silver Bay. MAX FOSTER

Below: Not far downstream from the more famous Devil's Kettle, the Upper Falls of the Brule River cascade over volcanic rock in Judge CR Magney State Park north of Grand Marais. MAX FOSTER

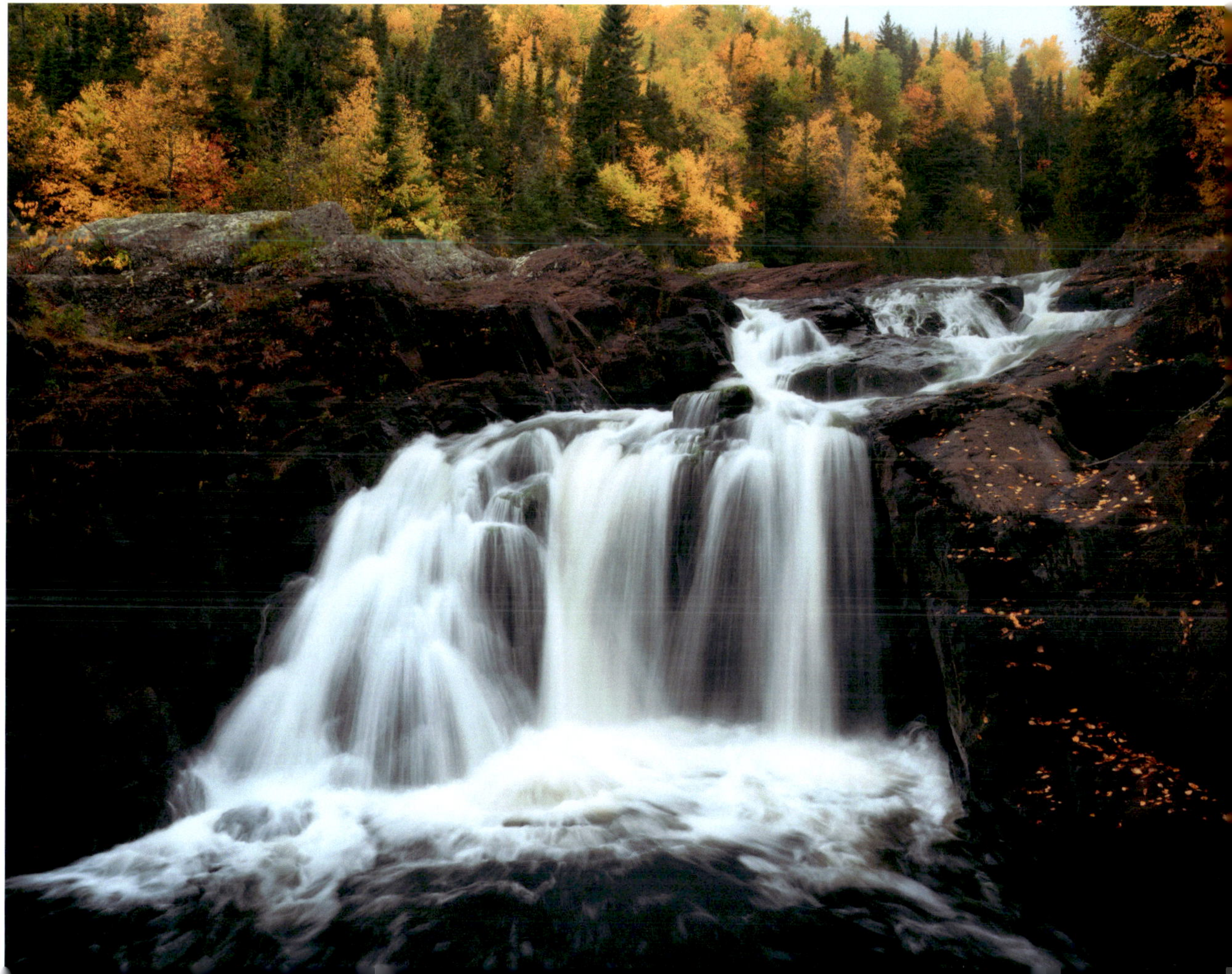

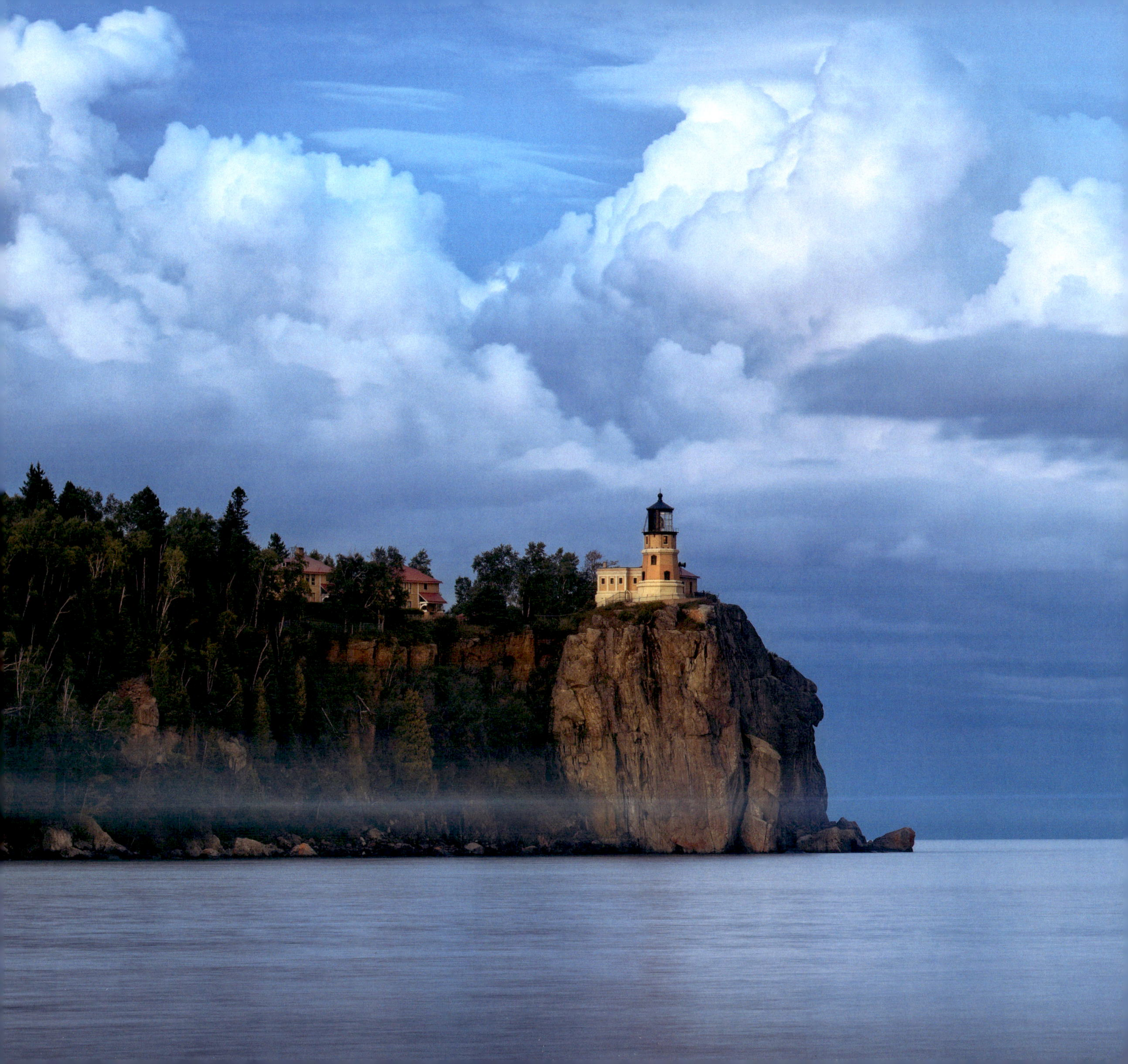

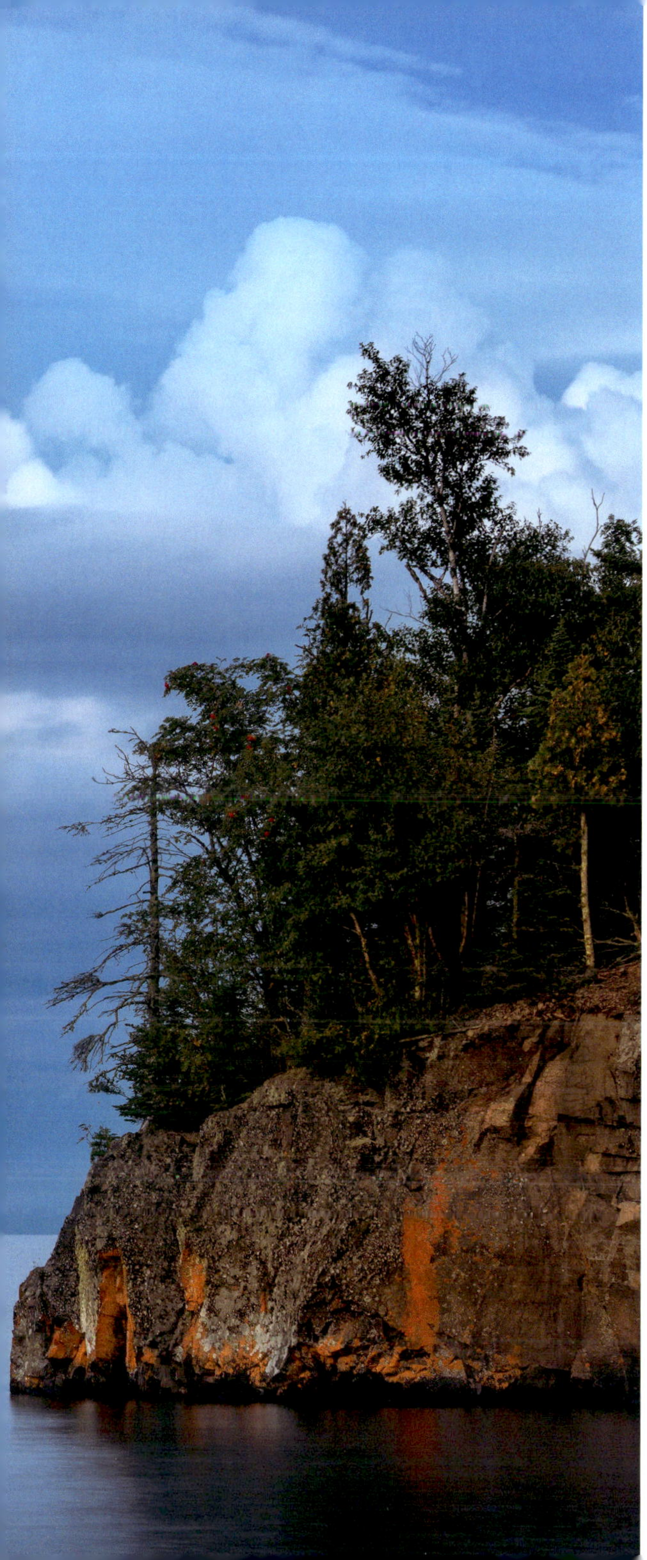

Left: From atop a 133-foot cliff on Lake Superior's North Shore, Split Rock Lighthouse guided ships from 1910 to 1969. A National Historic Landmark, the lighthouse is now the centerpiece of Split Rock Lighthouse State Park. MAX FOSTER

Below: The shoreline juts out into Lake Superior near the community of Beaver Bay, the oldest Euro-American settlement on the North Shore. MAX FOSTER

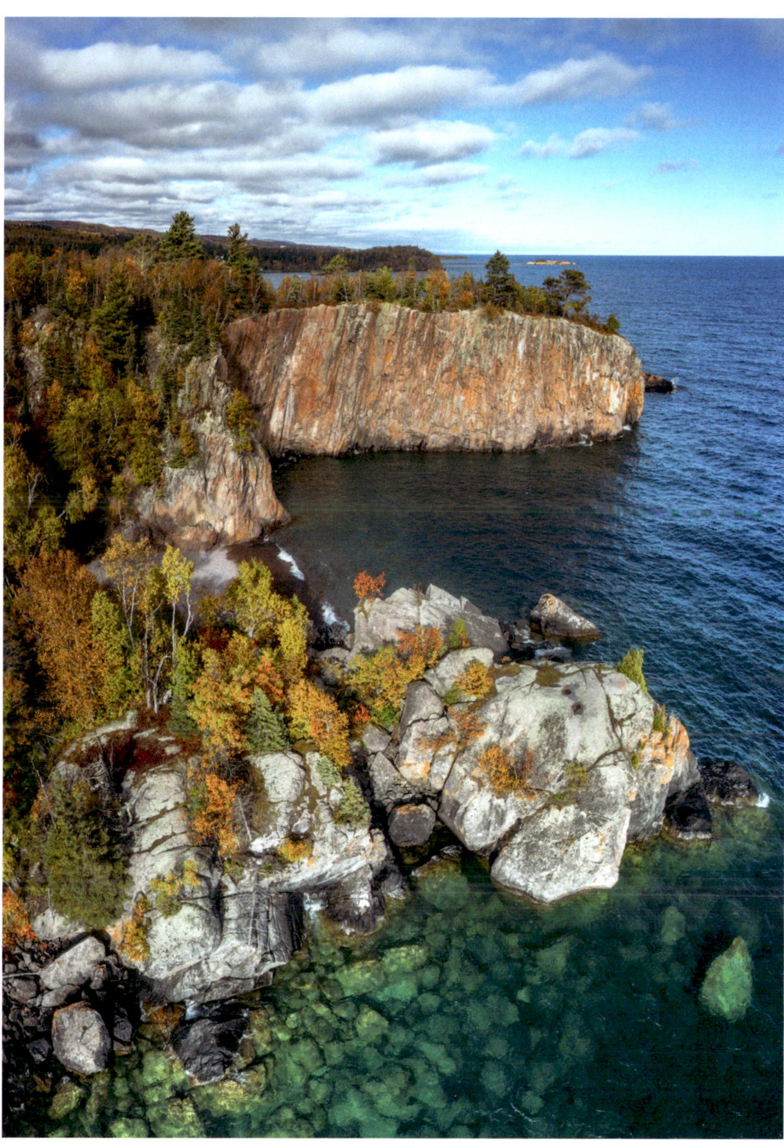

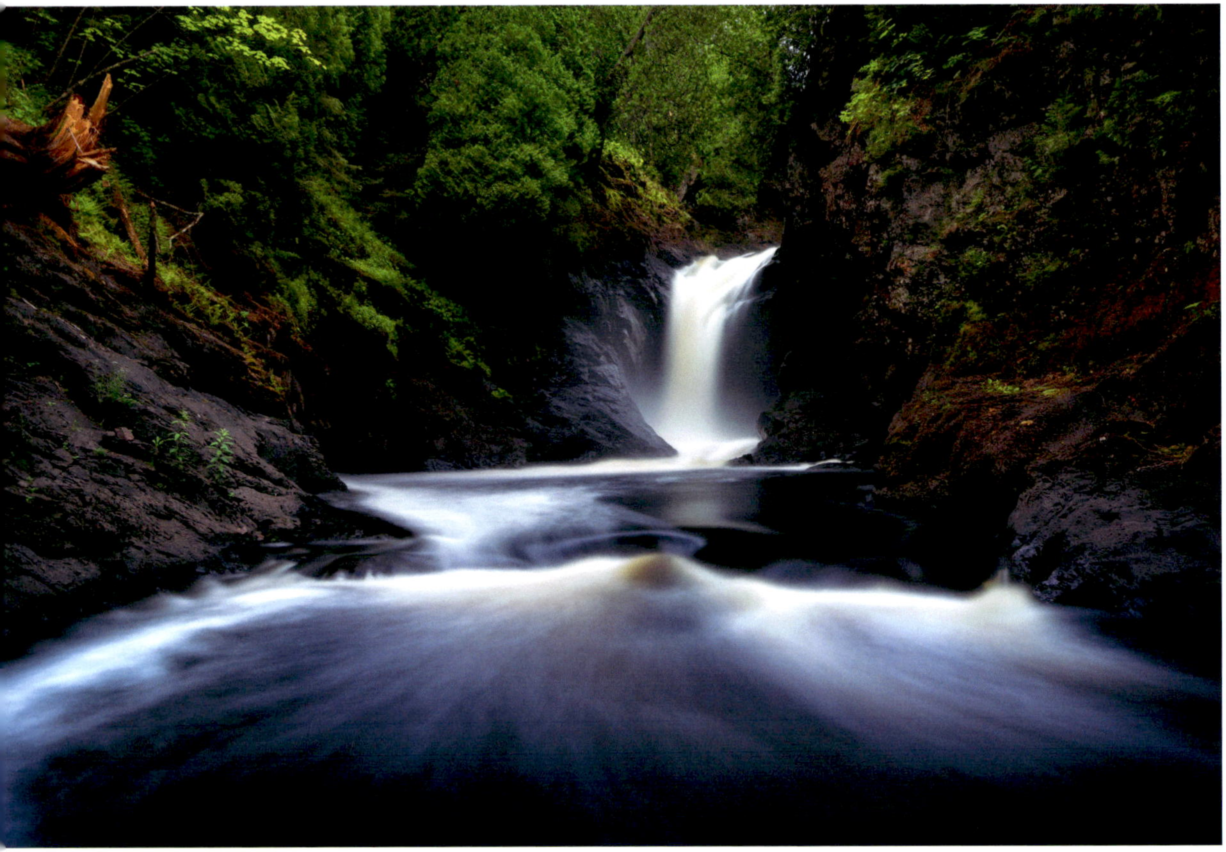

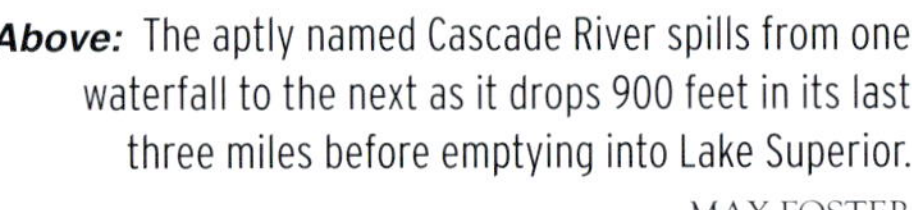

Above: The aptly named Cascade River spills from one waterfall to the next as it drops 900 feet in its last three miles before emptying into Lake Superior. MAX FOSTER

Right: The moose is Minnesota's largest wild animal. Adults like this bull can weigh more than 1,000 pounds and stand 6 feet tall at the shoulder. CC0/PUBLIC DOMAIN

Far right: The Manitou River churns tumble through a gorge of volcanic rock in George Crosby Manitou State Park. MAX FOSTER

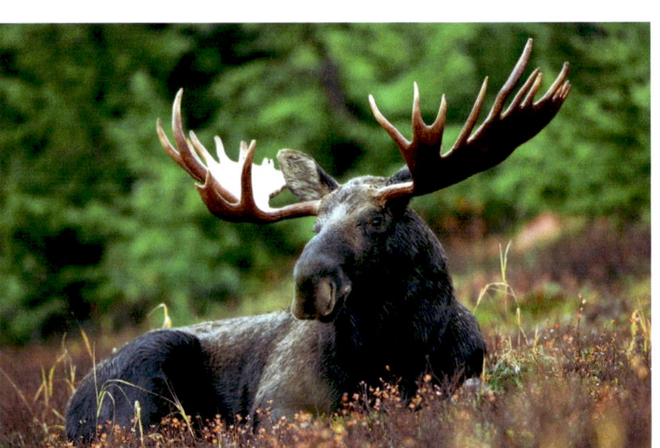

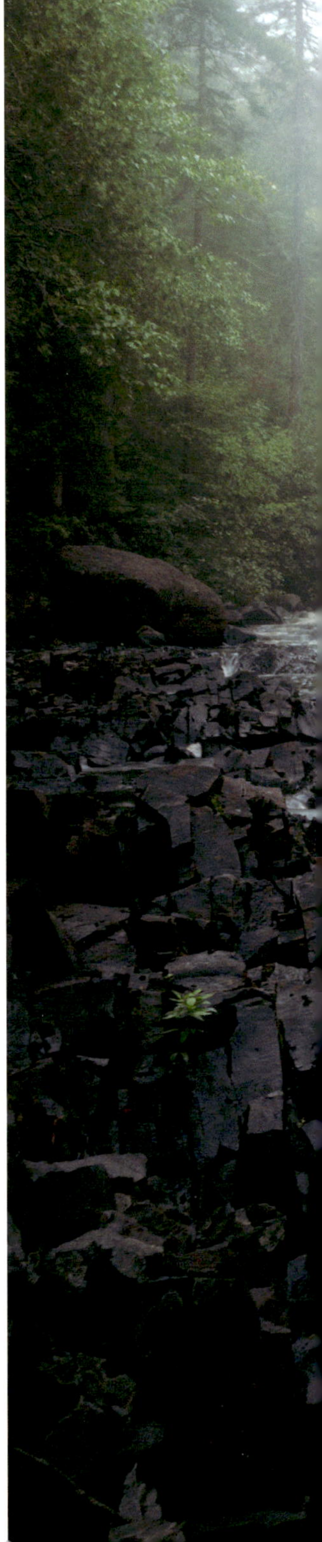

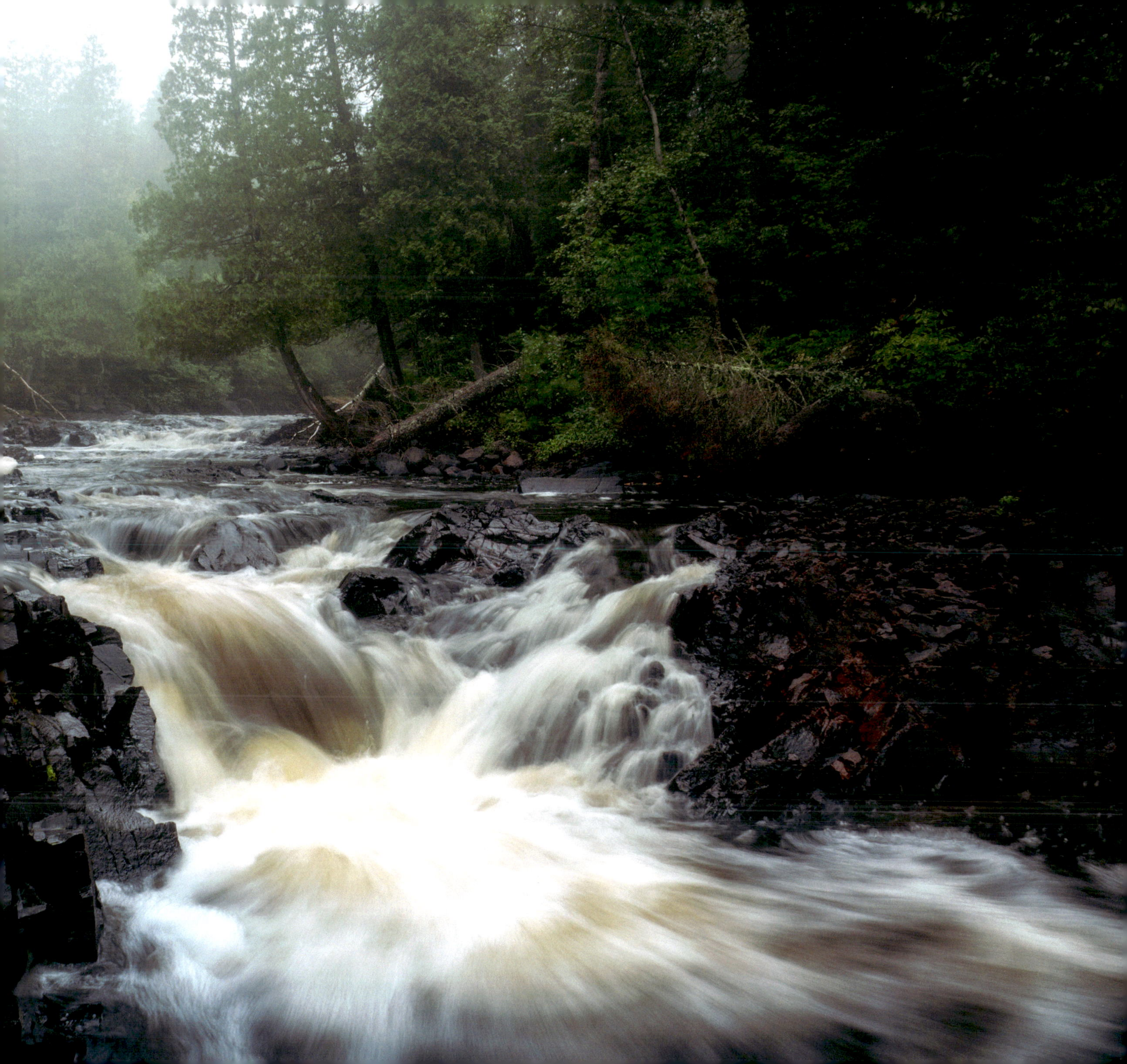

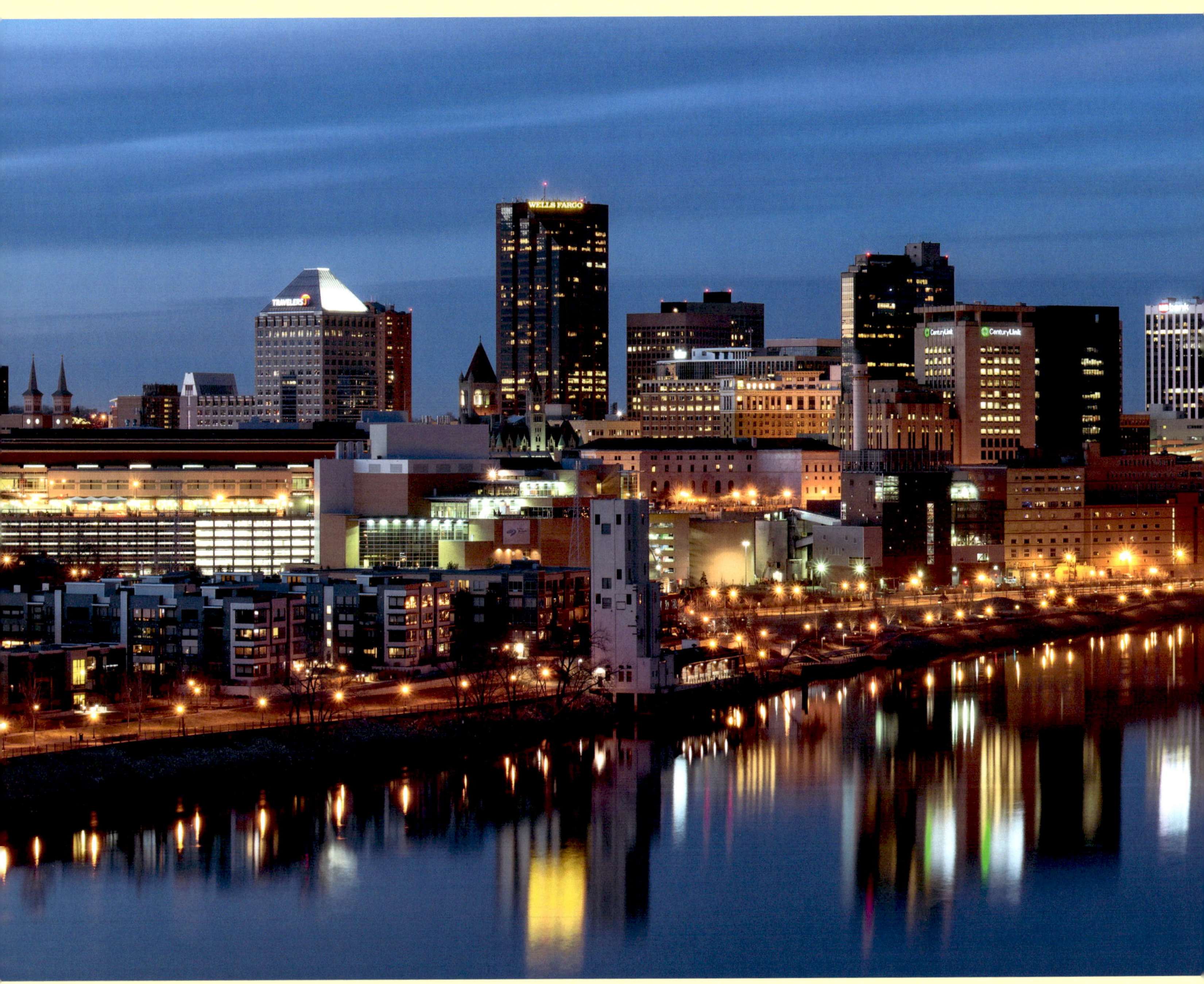
WELLS FARGO
TRAVELERS
CenturyLink
CenturyLink

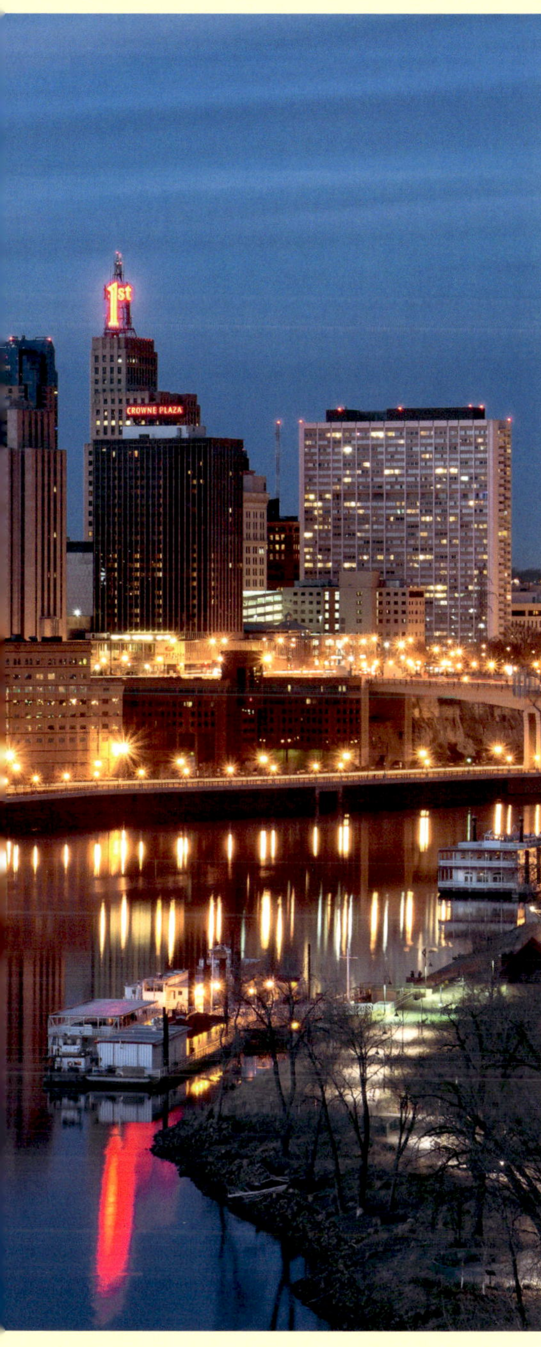

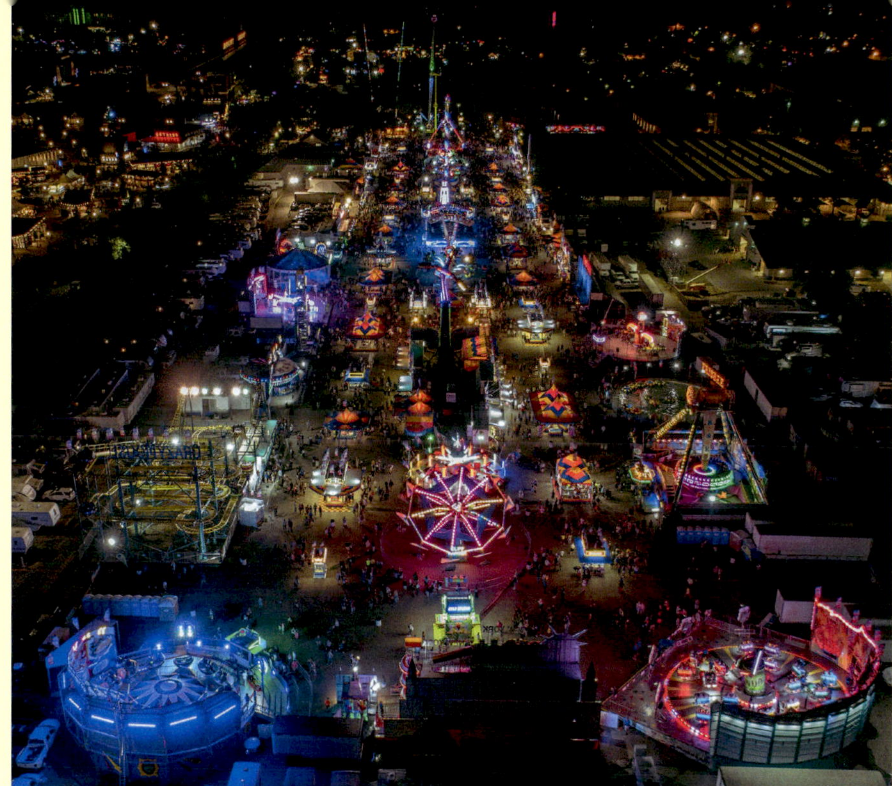

Above: Spanning 322 acres, the annual Minnesota State Fair is the largest in the country, attracting 2 million visitors over 12 days at summer's end. JACOB BOOMSMA/SHUTTERSTOCK

Left: From its beginnings as a Native settlement, then a U.S. military fort, St. Paul has grown to a diverse city of more than 300,000 people. MAX FOSTER

Below: River boat cruises on the Mississippi offer a way to see the St. Paul and Minneapolis waterfronts, along with lunch or dinner and stories of local history, culture, bird life, and more. One renovated towboat, now the Covington Inn, even serves as a permanently moored bed and breakfast. KRISTOPHER KETTNER/SHUTTERSTOCK

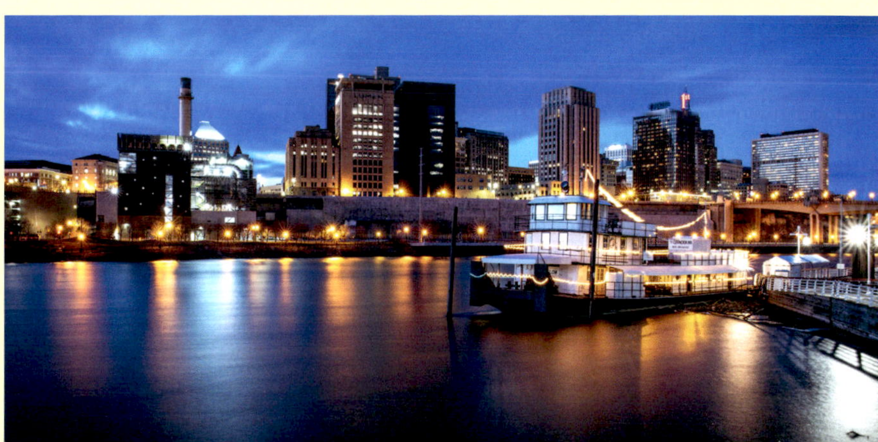

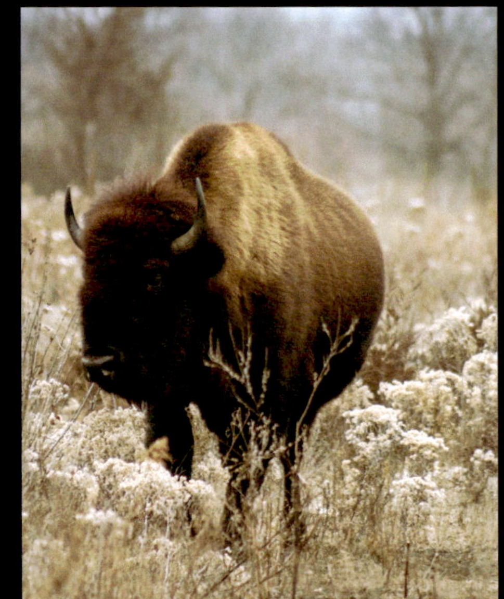

Right: Near Mankato, Minneopa State Park is home to a small bison herd on a 330-acre prairie enclosure. Visitors can view the animals from their cars along a road through the bison range. ZACHARY BECKMAN/UNSPLASH

Far right: Just before reaching Lake Superior, the Beaver River sluices through this rock-bound notch. MAX FOSTER

Below: Minnesota has always been home to gray wolves, also known as timber wolves, and today supports a stable population of roughly 3,000 wolves, mostly in the northeastern corner of the state. CRITTERBIZ/SHUTTERSTOCK

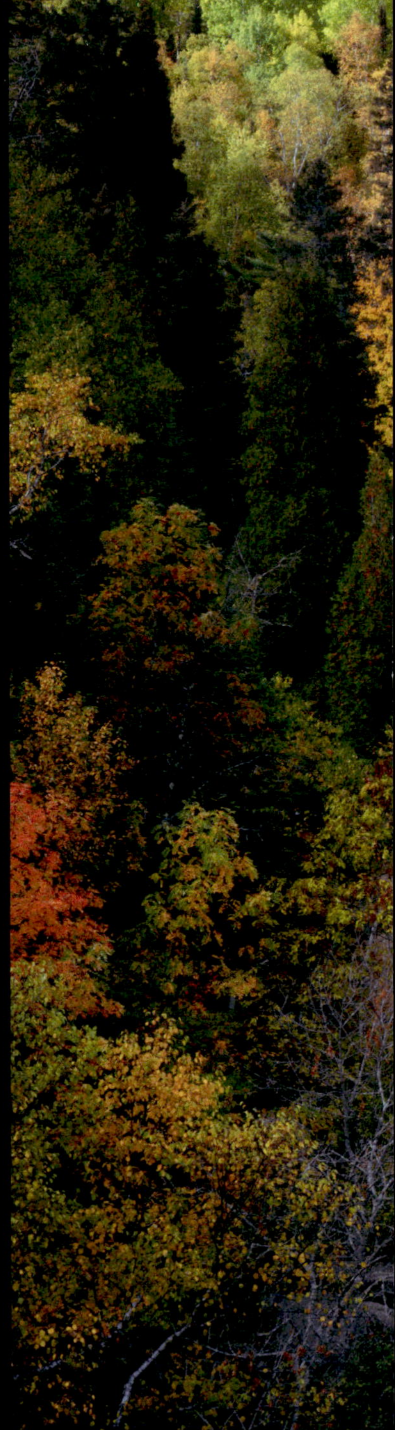

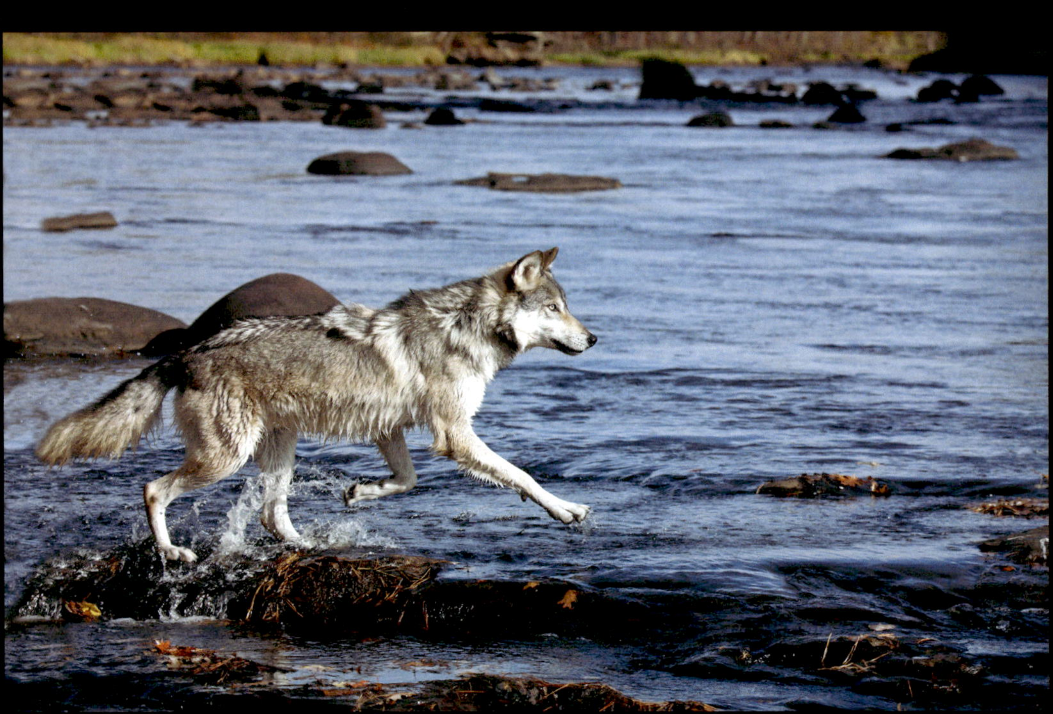

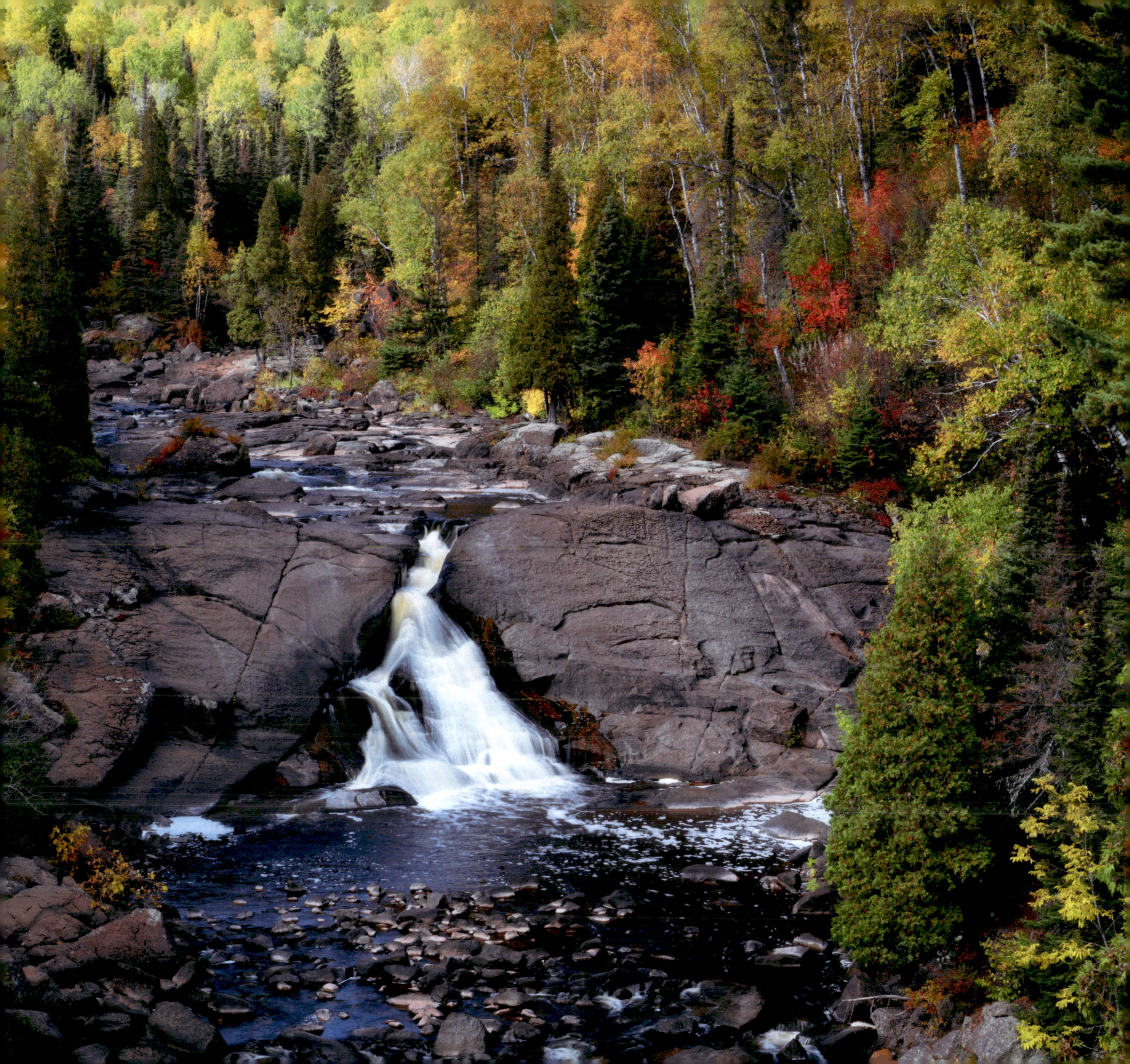

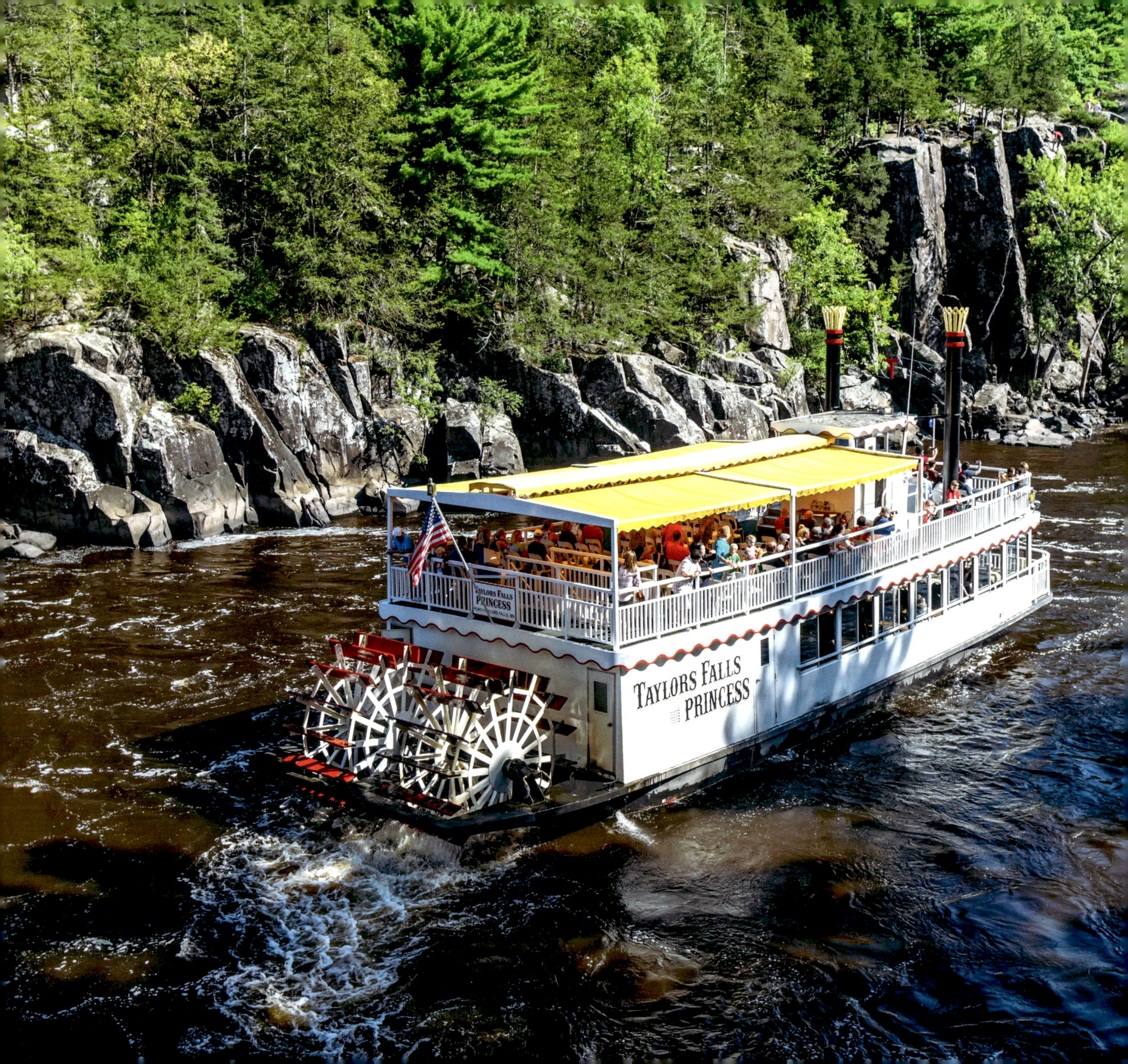
TAYLORS FALLS PRINCESS
TAYLORS FALLS PRINCESS

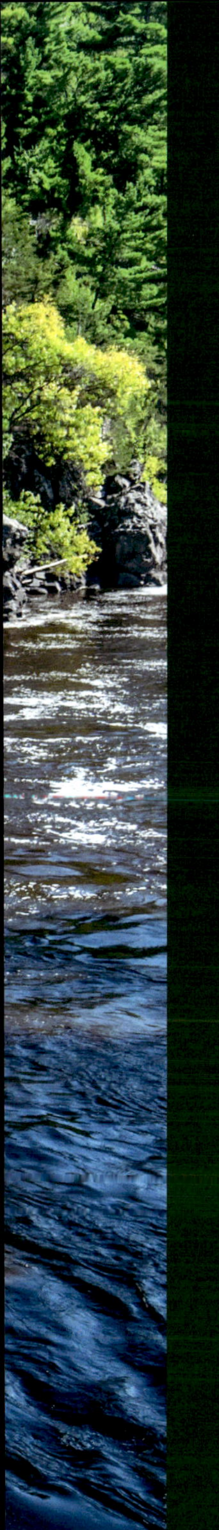

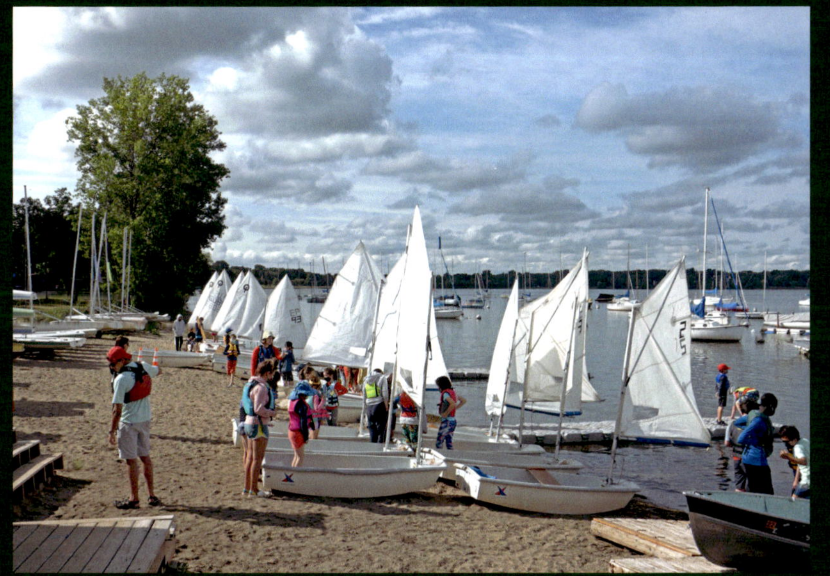

Left: Students at the Minneapolis Sailing Center on Lake Bde Maka Ska gather on the beach before launching. STEVE SKJOLD/SHUTTERSTOCK

Far left: Based on the Minnesota side in Taylors Falls, the *Taylors Falls Princess* sternwheeler plies the Dalles of the St. Croix River, a National Scenic Riverway. KEN WOLTER.SHUTTERSTOCK

Below: From May to September, the Lake Harriet Bandshell in Minneapolis hosts an incredible variety of concerts featuring music by indie bands, chamber and pop orchestras, and singer-songwriters. LINDA MCKUSICK/SHUTTERSTOCK

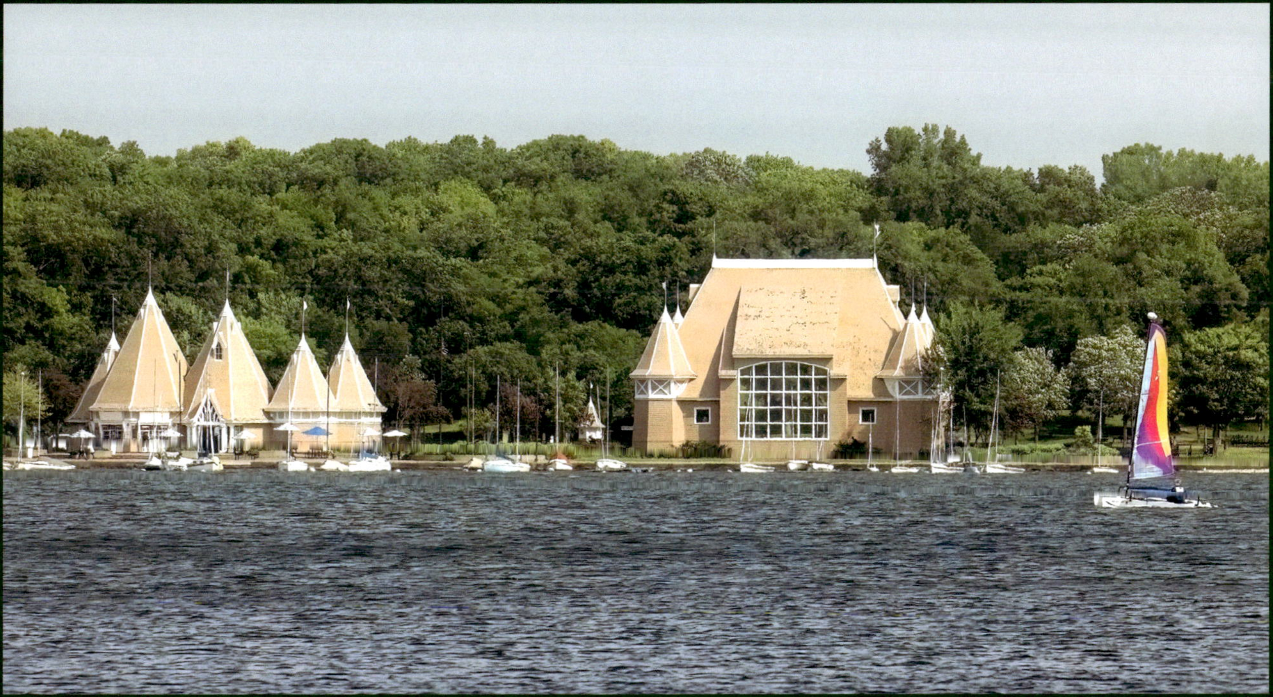

Right: Showcasing elements of French Renaissance and Classical design, the Cathedral of St. Paul also displays its Minnesotan heritage, with exterior walls of granite quarried in St. Cloud and interior walls clad in travertine from Mankato. CHINTLA/SHUTTERSTOCK

Far right: Outside, the world may be white, but indoors at the Como Park Zoo's Marjorie McNeely Conservatory in St. Paul, a midwinter flower show paints the sunken garden in warm, vibrant colors. TAMMIMILD/SHUTTERSTOCK

Below: Across from Rice Park in downtown St. Paul, the historic Landmark Center originally served as the federal post office, courthouse, and custom house for the Upper Midwest. Today the building is a center for art exhibitions, theater and dance performances, musical concerts, and other cultural events. EWY MEDIA/SHUTTERSTOCK

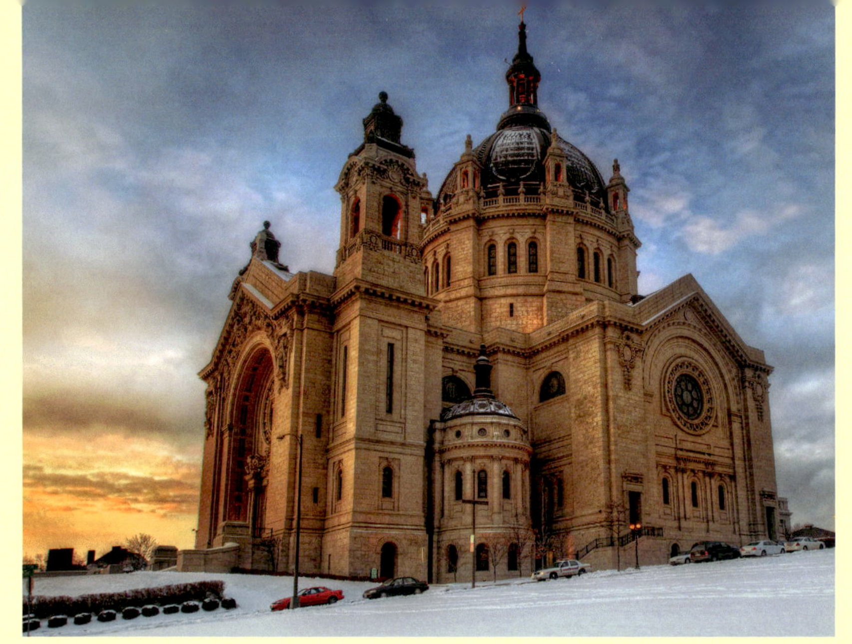

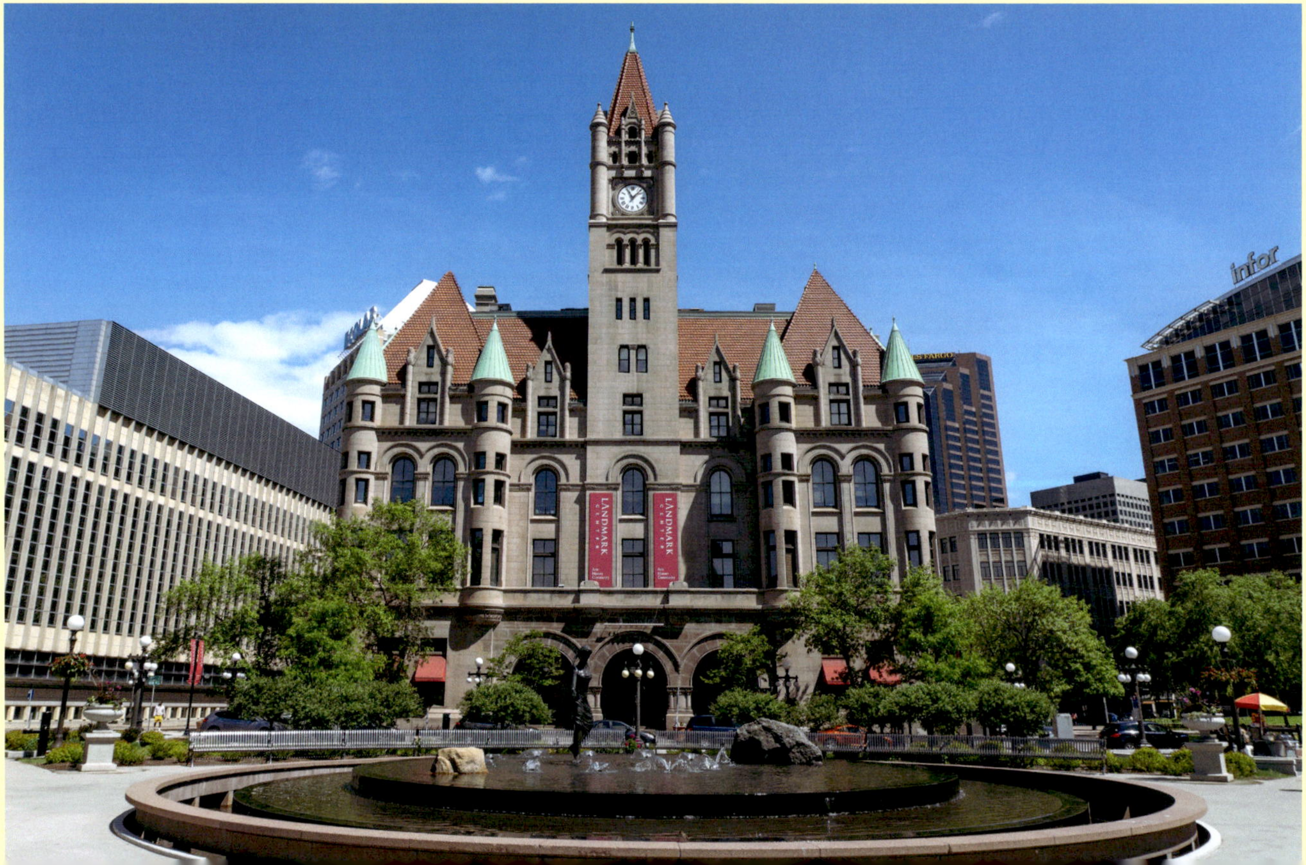

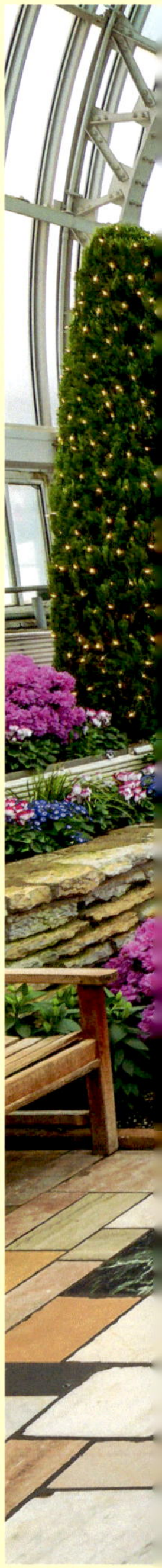

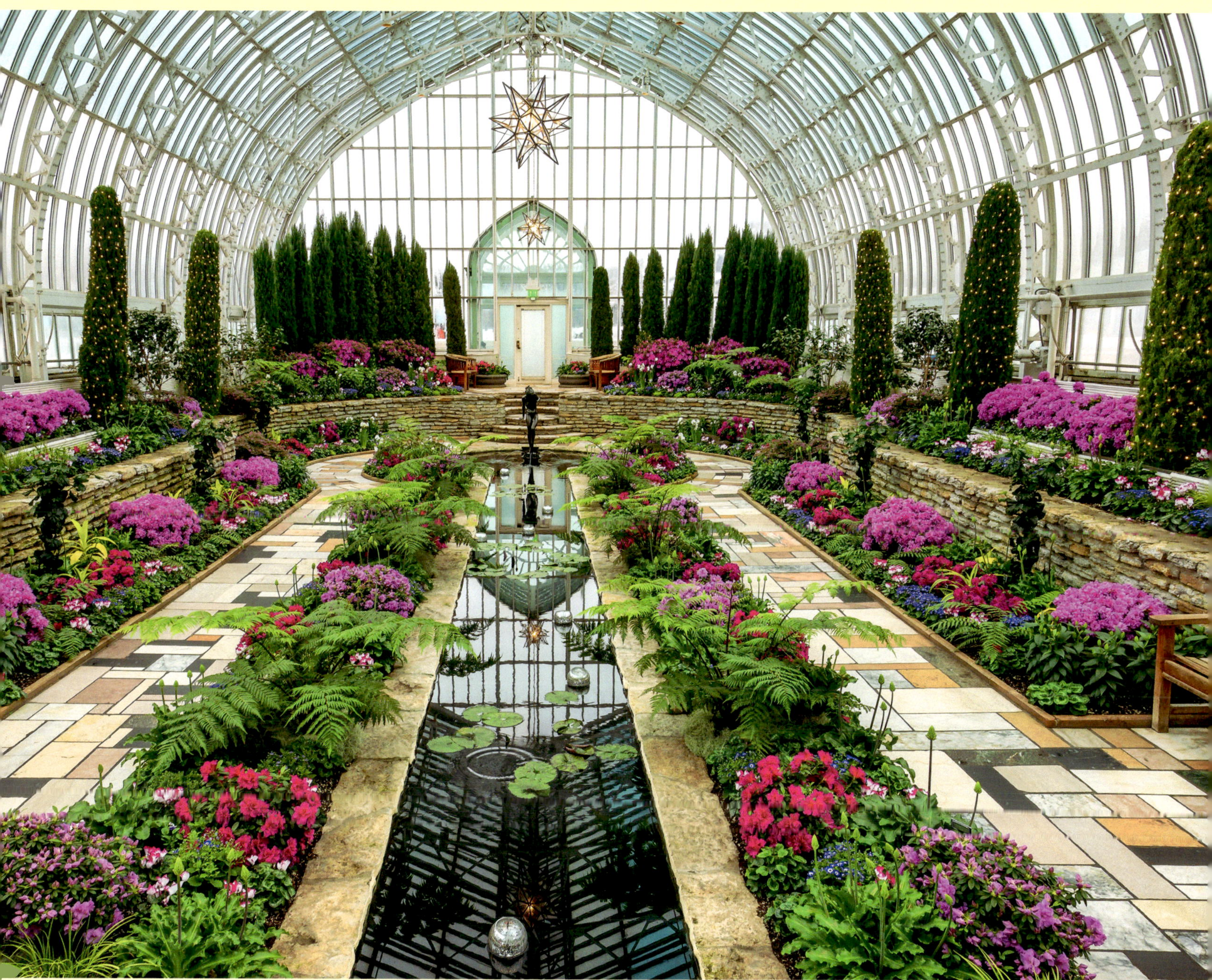

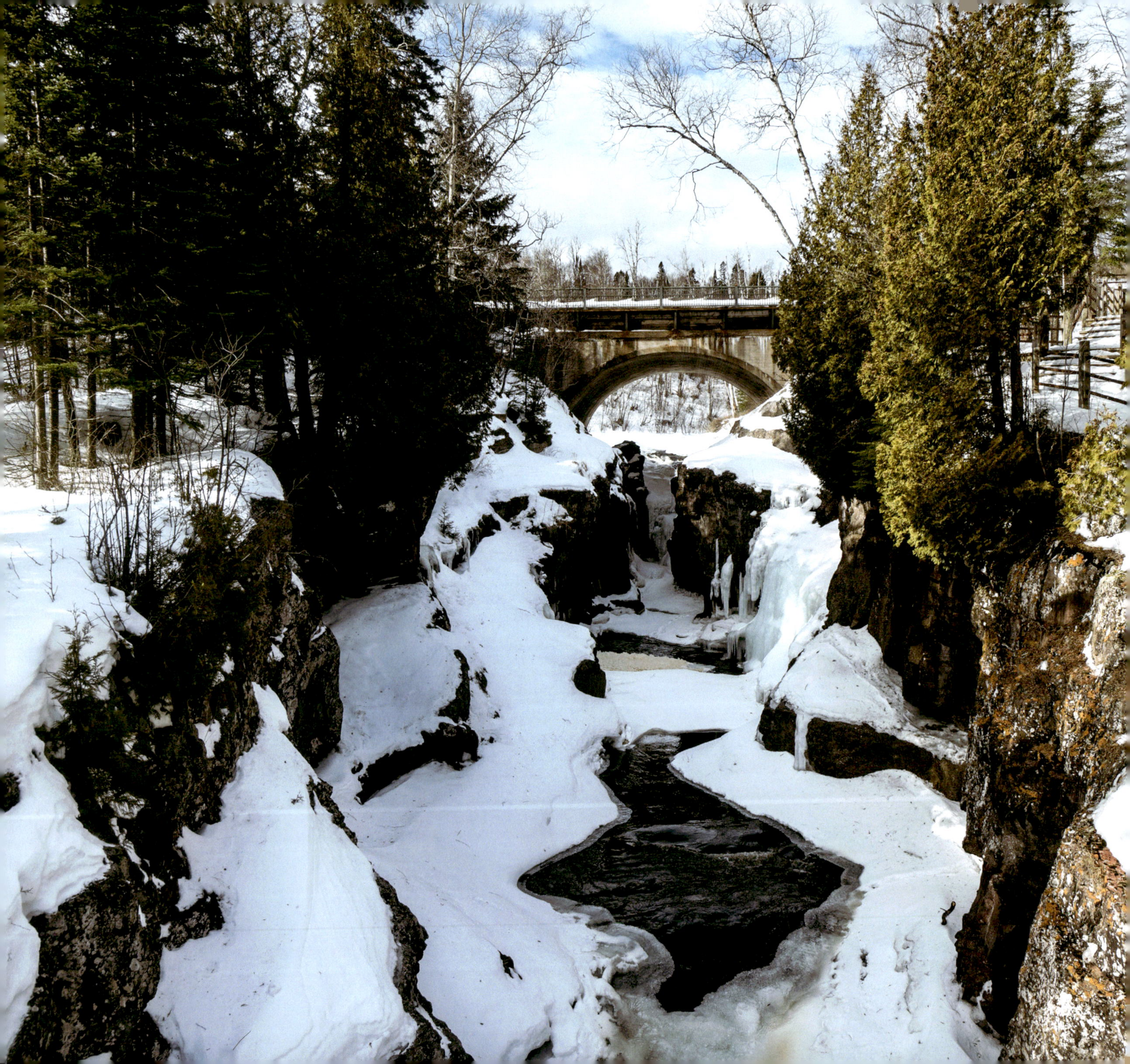

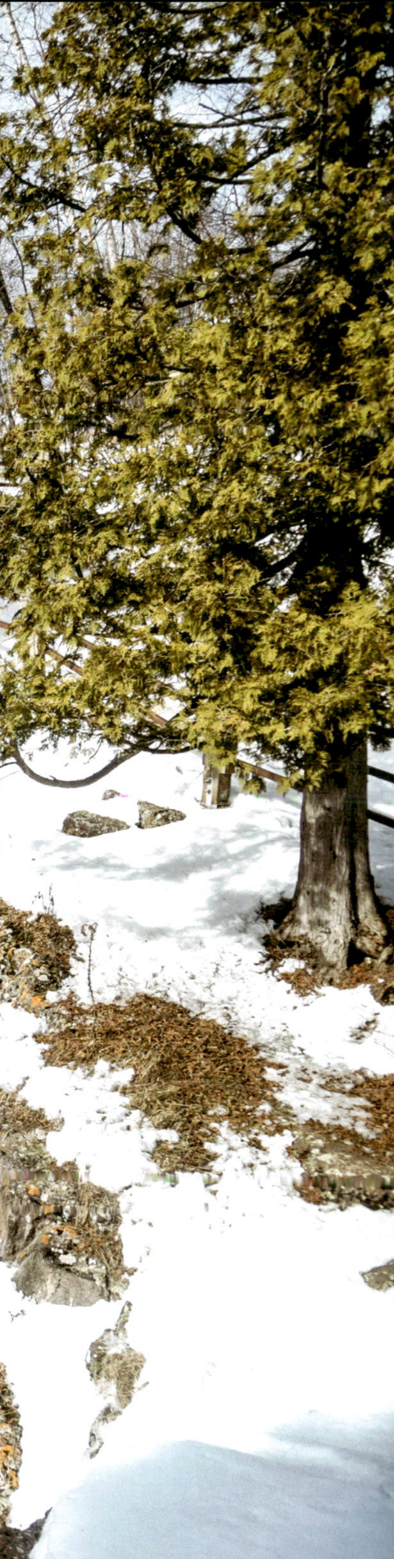

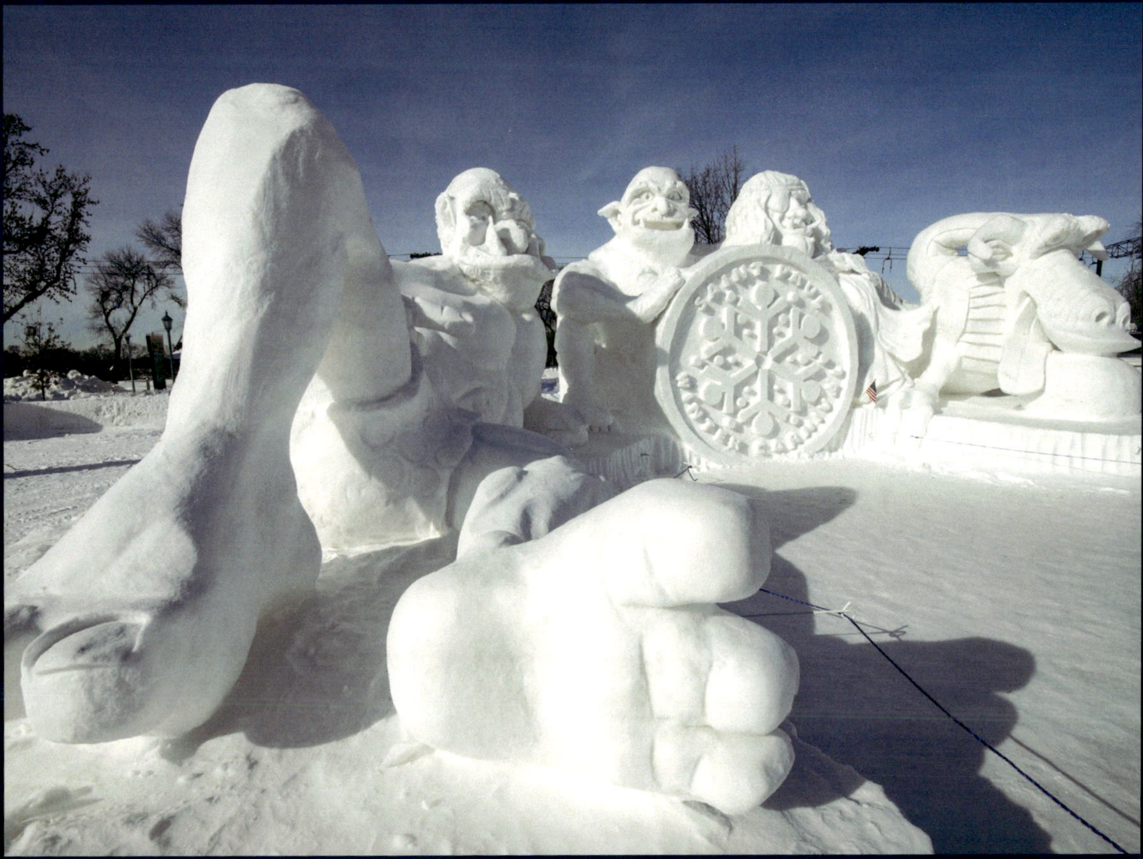

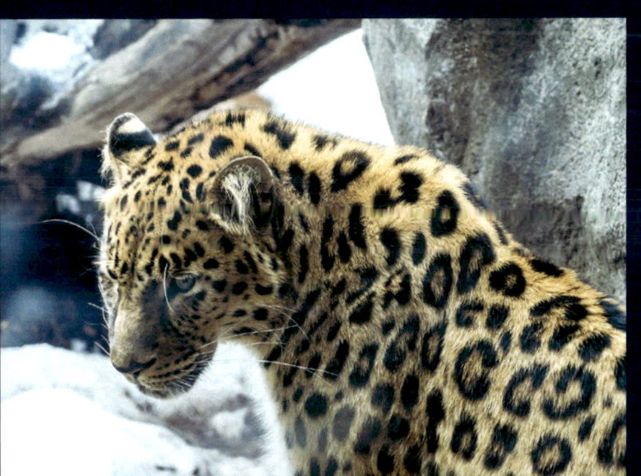

Above: Elaborate ice and snow sculptures are a popular attraction at the annual four-week-long St. Paul Winter Carnival, with events at Rice Park and the State Fairgrounds. PAUL GEILFUSS/SHUTTERSTOCK

Left: South of the Twin Cities in Apple Valley, the Minnesota Zoo is home to more than 4,000 animals representing more than 500 species from around the world, including this jaguar. REZAL SCHARFE/UNSPLASH

Far left: Temperance River State Park offers camping and hiking on trails along the deeply incised gorge of its namesake river. GOOD FREE PHOTOS

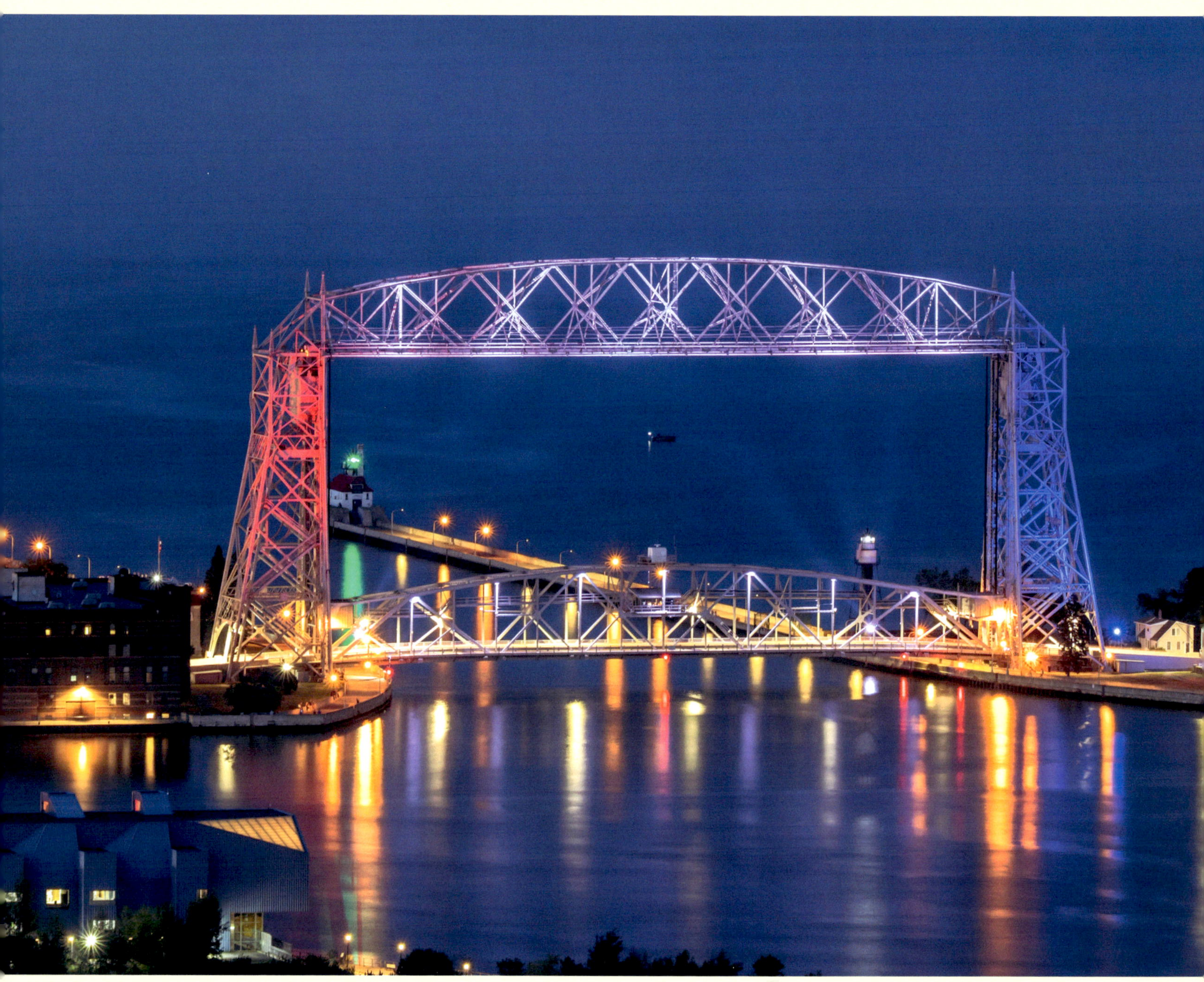

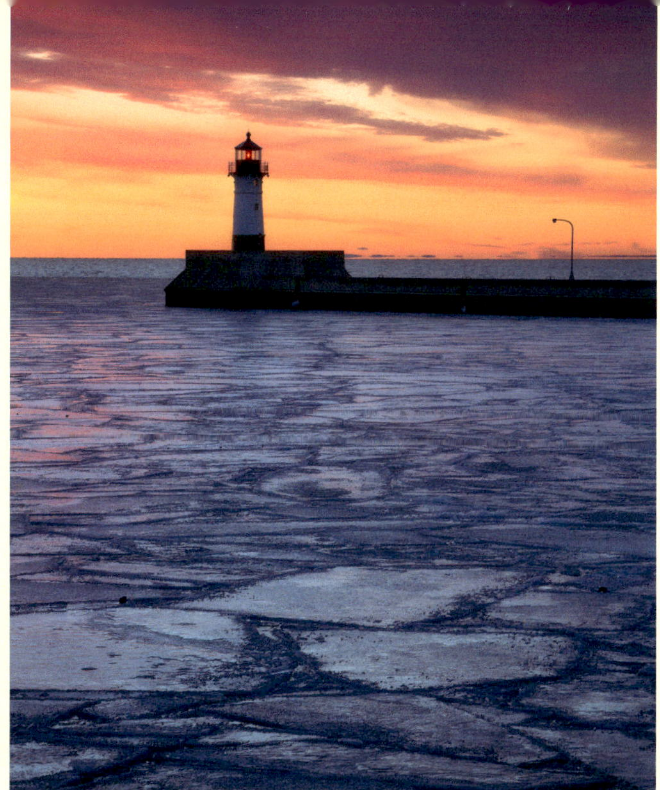

Left: Ice crowds against the North Breakwater at the Duluth Ship Canal. The lighthouse's red light flashes every 4 seconds and in clear conditions is visible for 13 miles. MAX FOSTER

Far left: Originally built in 1905 and modified in 1929, the Duluth Aerial Lift Bridge spans the Duluth Ship Canal. The roadway can be lifted between the towers to a height of 135 feet in about one minute, allowing lake freighters and other ships to pass beneath. Here the span is lit in red, white, and blue for the Fourth of July. SAM WAGNER/SHUTTERSTOCK

Below: A steady or "fixed" green light in the Duluth South Breakwater Outer Lighthouse guides ships from Lake Superior to the Duluth Ship Canal. MAX FOSTER

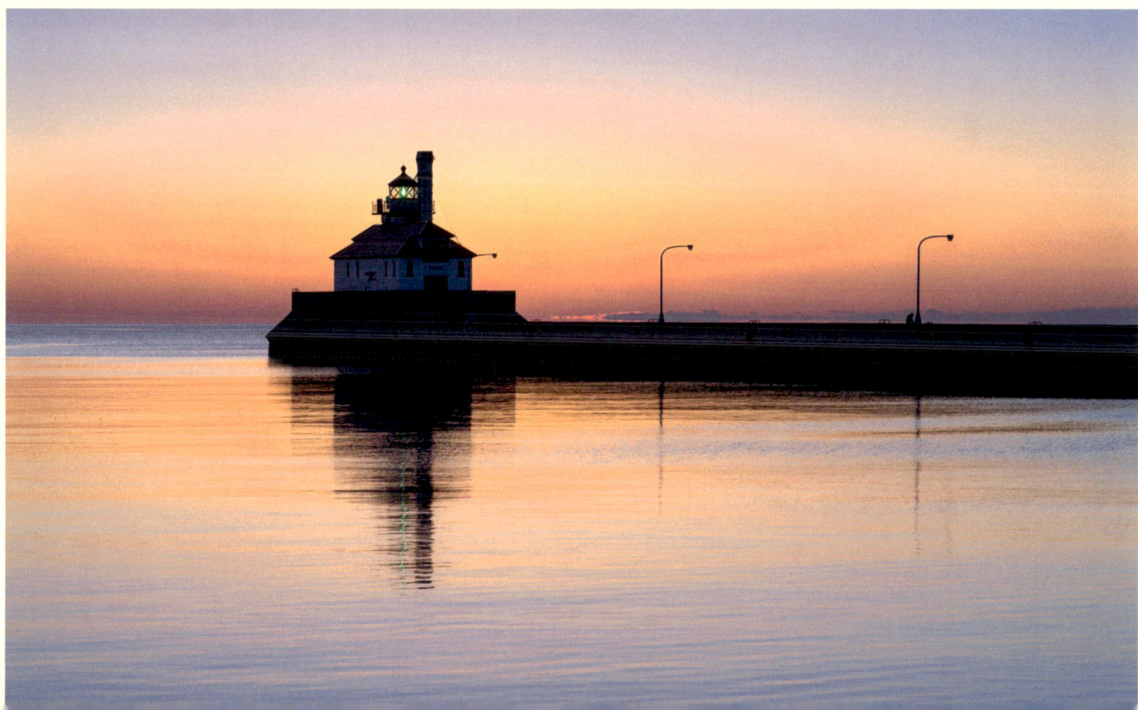

Right: Denizen of the North Woods, gray squirrels cache nuts and other food to carry them through long winters. ROBIN LYON/UNSPLASH

Far right: Fall colors carpet the 65-mile Border Route Trail that traverses the Boundary Waters Canoe Area Wilderness. MAX FOSTER

Below: A palette of autumn hues dapples the understory of a birch grove in Superior National Forest. MAX FOSTER

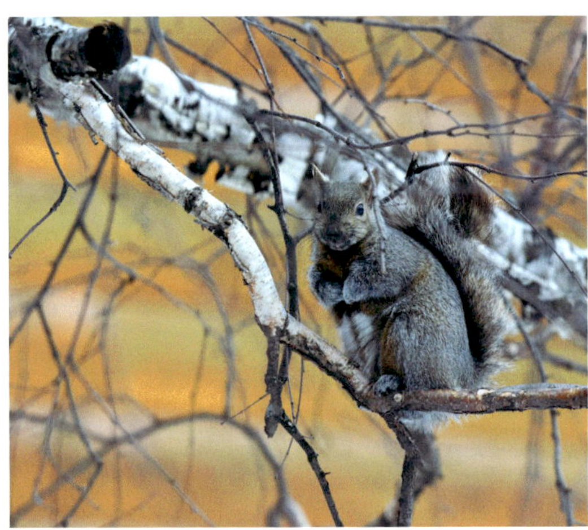

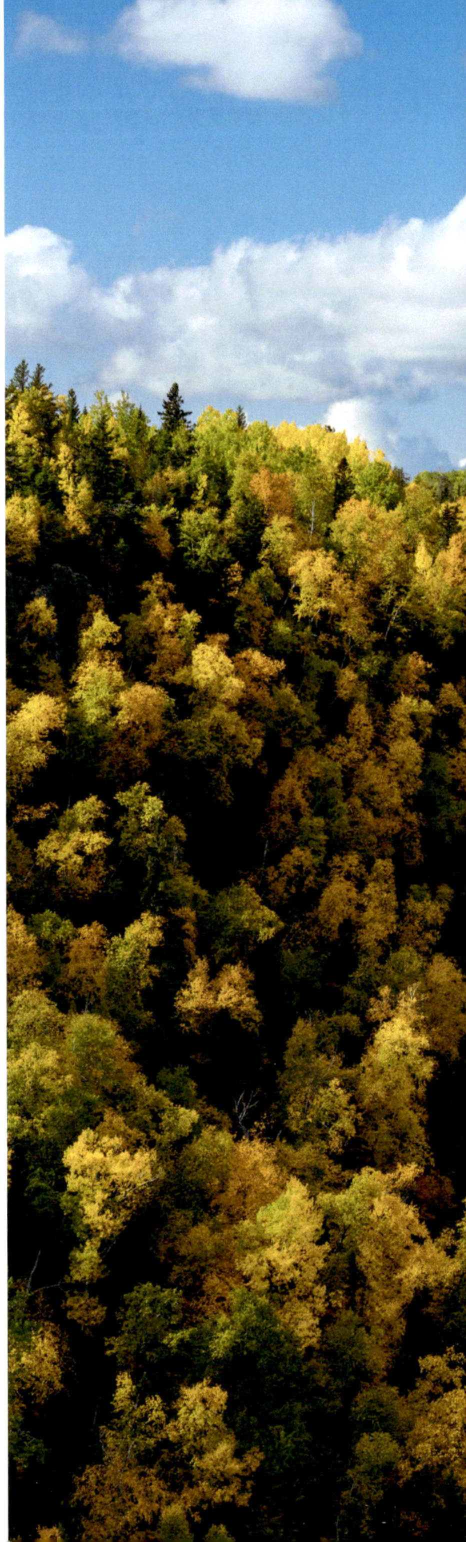

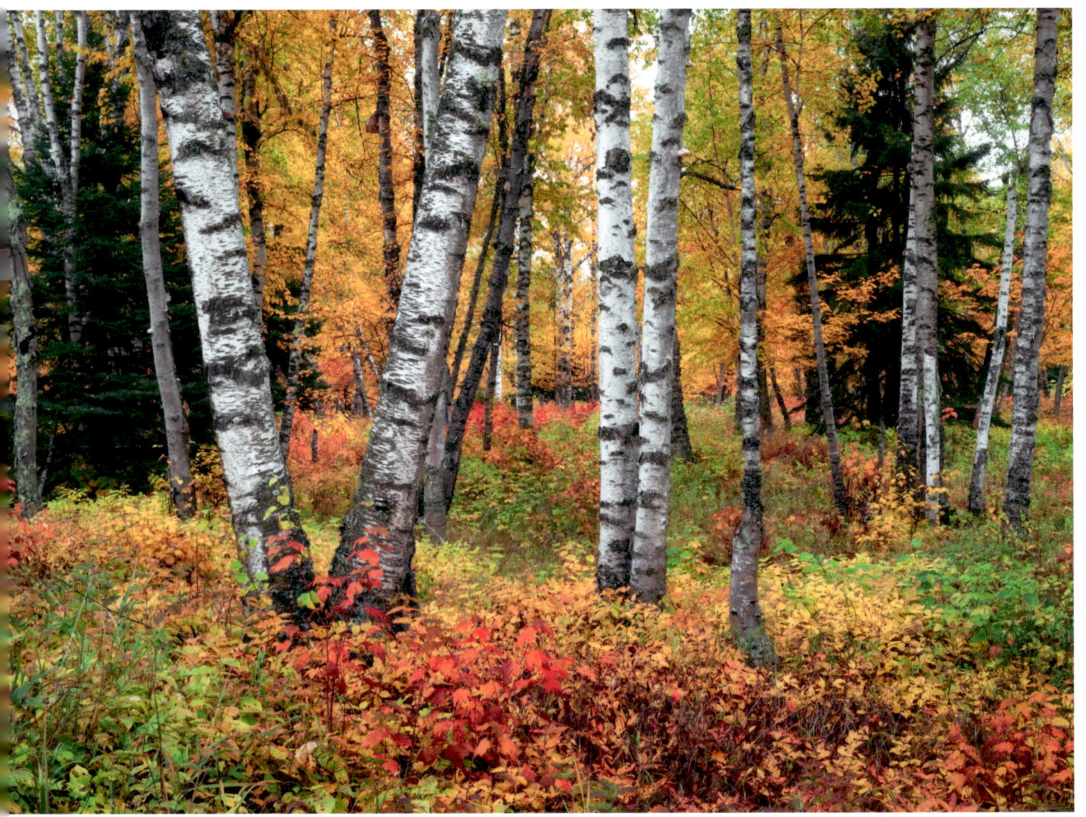

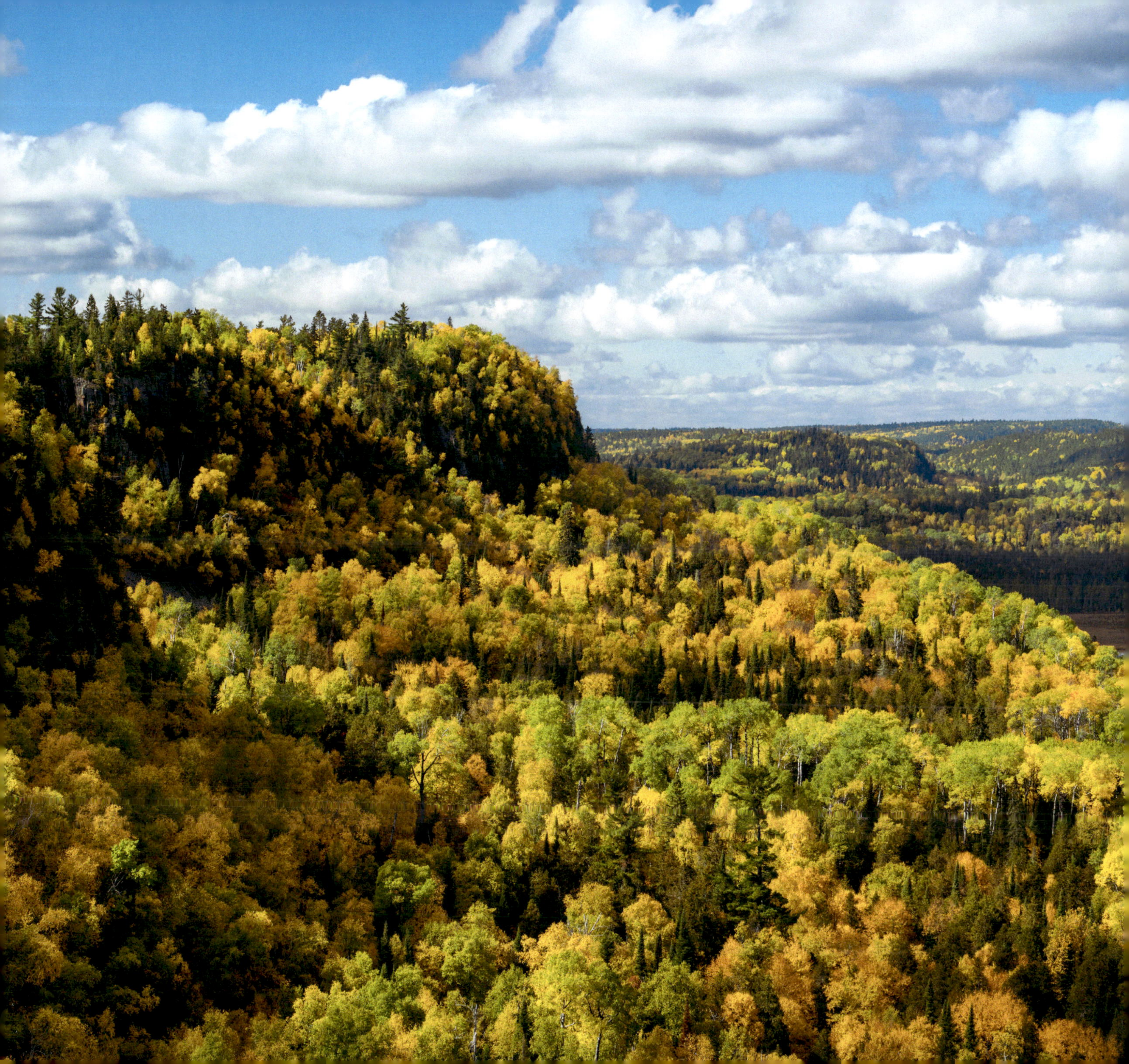

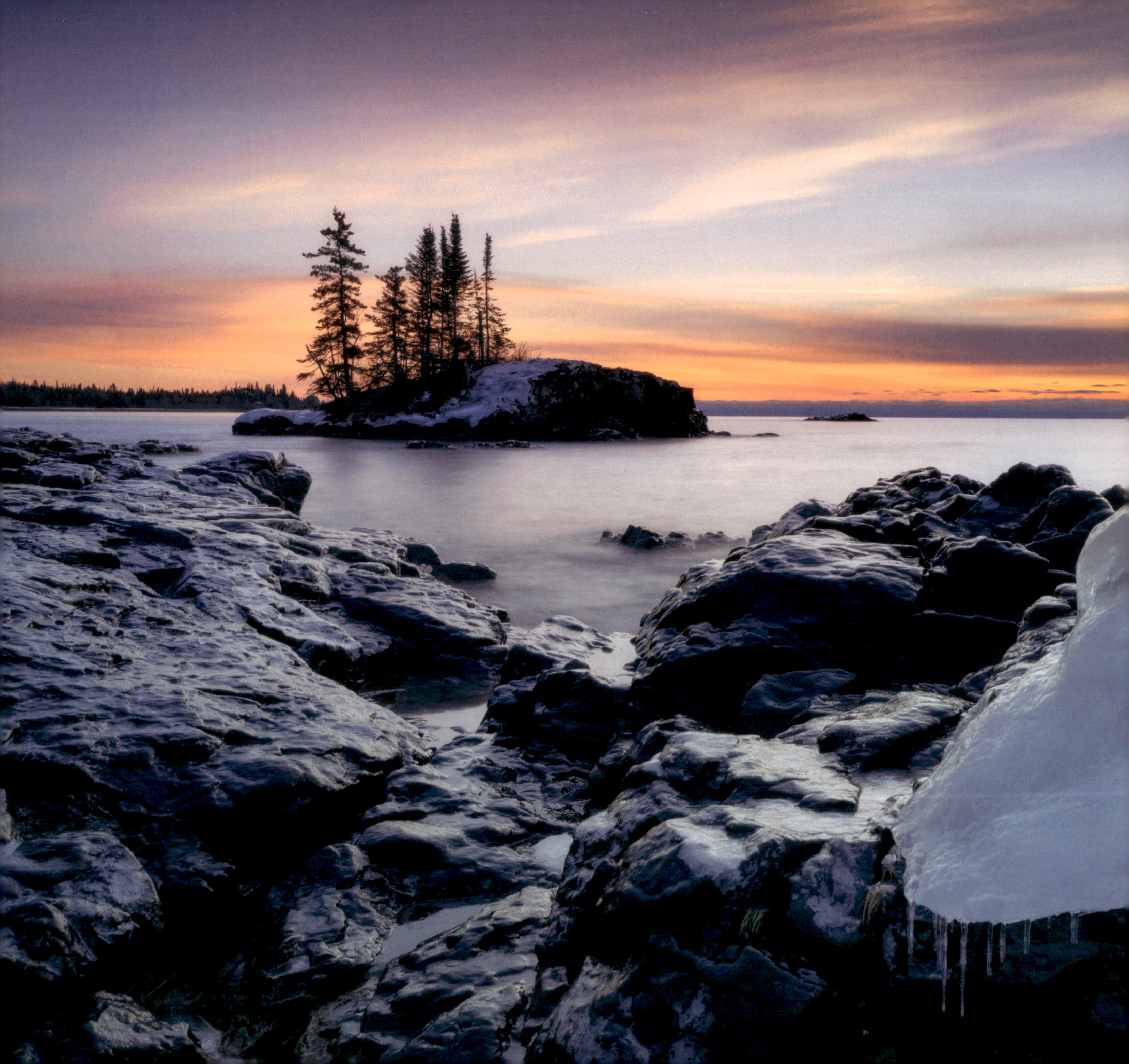

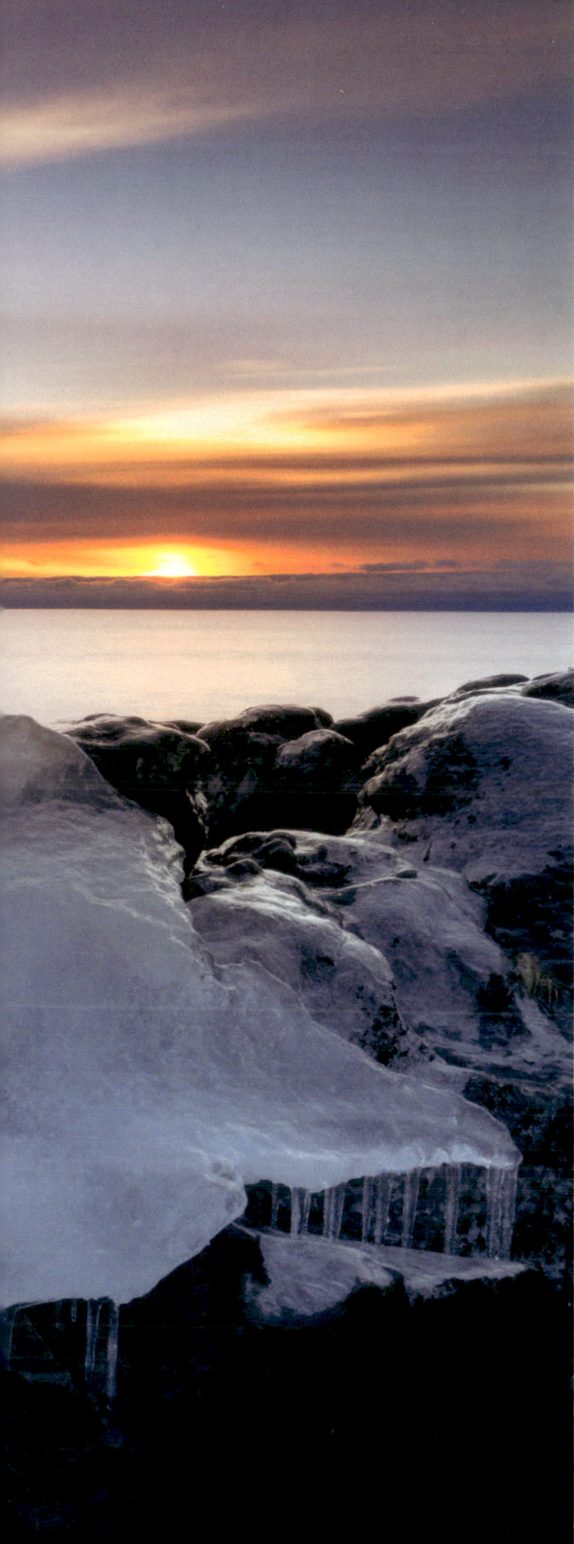

Left: Winter clads the Tombolo in an icy grip along the North Shore. The tiny island is tied to the mainland by a narrow isthmus of sand deposited by wave action. MAX FOSTER

Below: Part of Tettegouche State Park, the volcanic cliffs of Palisade Head provide stunning views of Lake Superior and the North Shore. MAX FOSTER

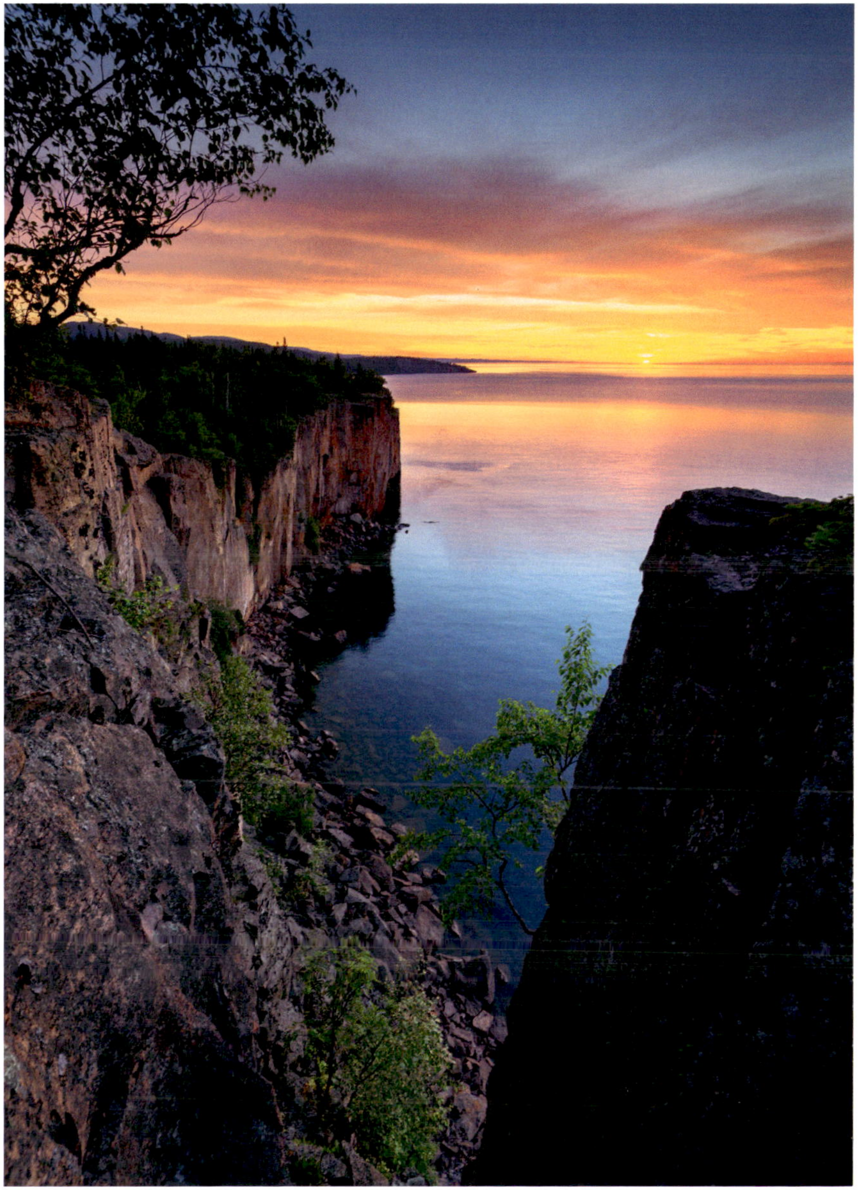

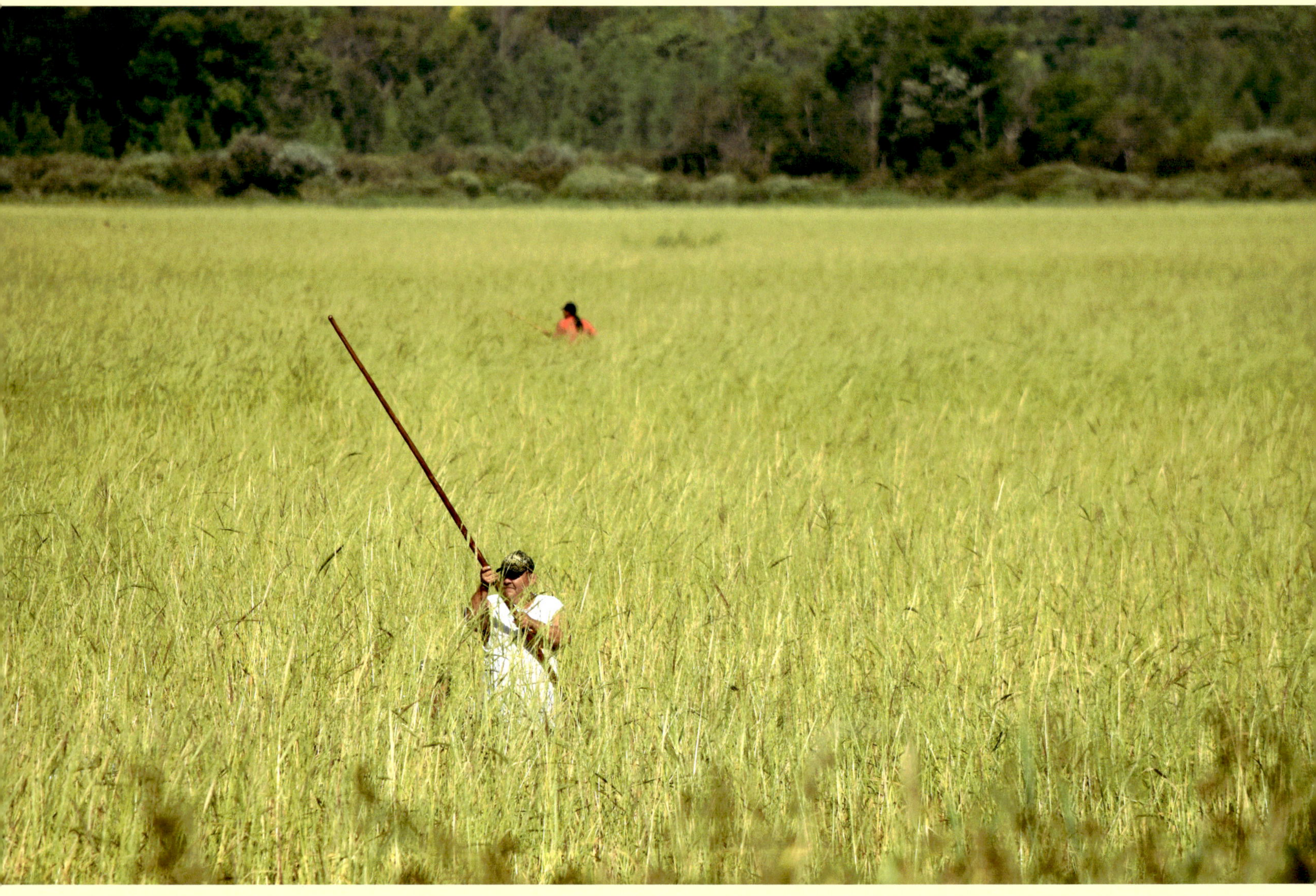

Above: Minnesota is the top U.S. producer of wild rice, which grows naturally in the many shallow lakes and is also cultivated on rice farms. U.S. ARMY CORPS OF ENGINEERS/ WIKIMEDIA COMMONS

Facing page, top: On the bank of the Mississippi River in downtown Wabasha, this life-size statue depicts Wapahasha II holding a cedar sprig, a Dakota sign for his people to listen to his important message. STEVE HEAP/SHUTTERSTOCK

Facing page, bottom left and right: The Mahkato Wacipi, or powwow, on the third full weekend in September is an annual gathering of Dakota people for dancing, singing, and reconnecting with old friends. The three-day event takes place at Dakota Wokiksuye Makoce (Land of Memories) Park in Mankato. KARLA CASPARI/SHUTTERSTOCK

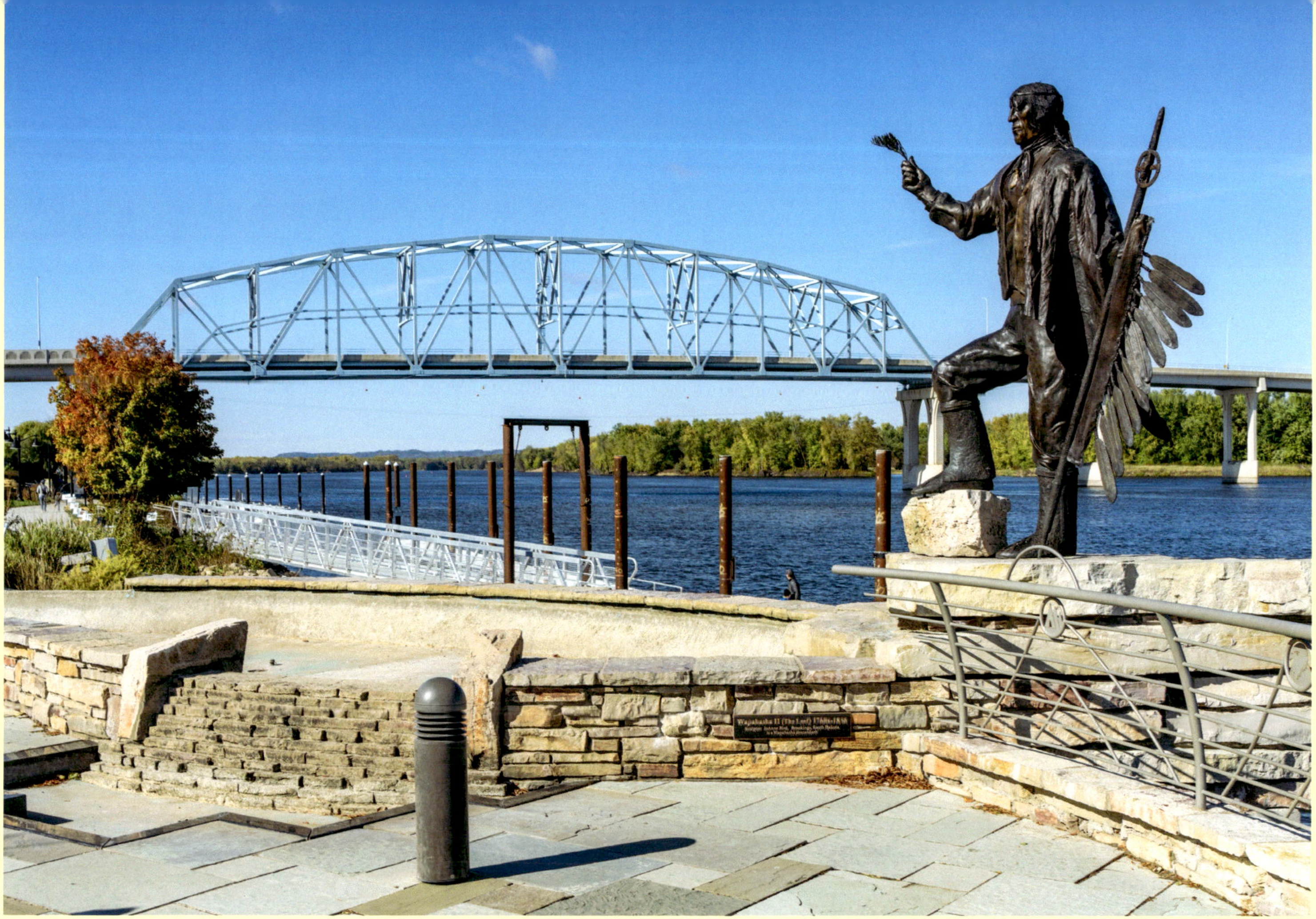

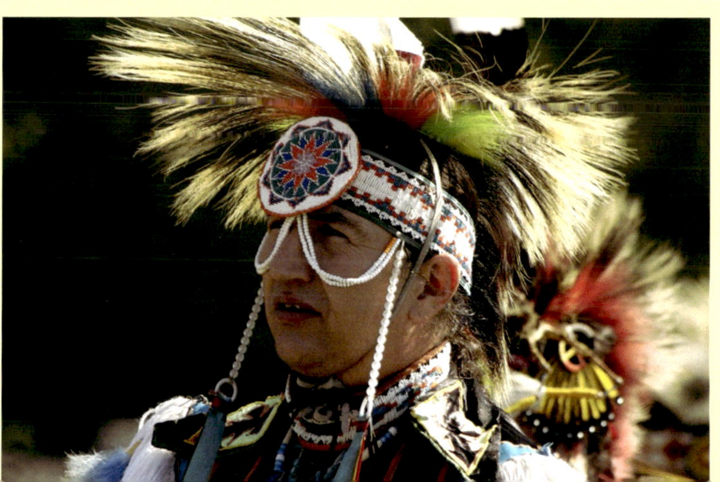

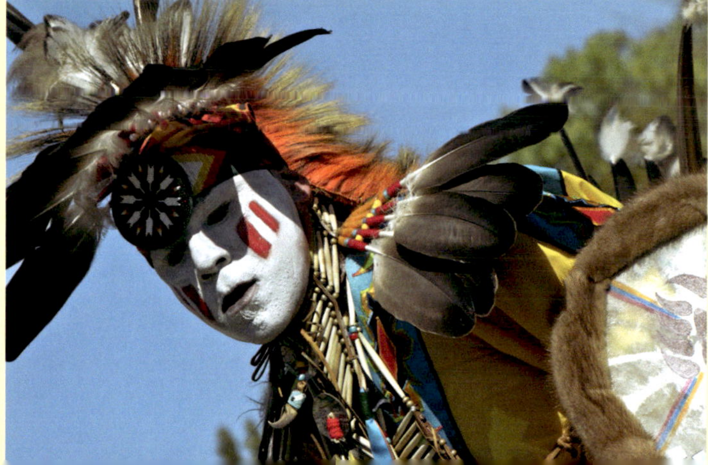

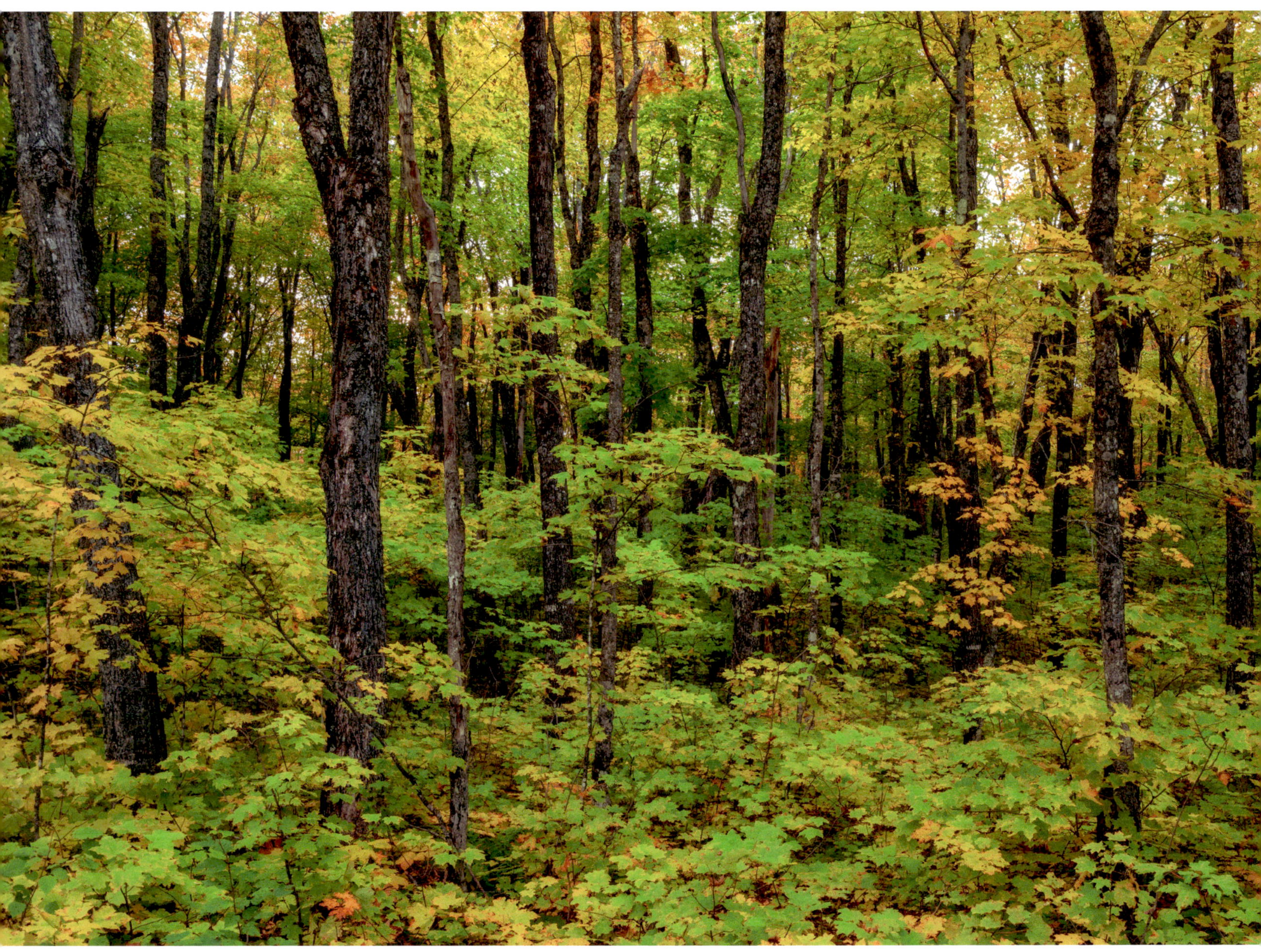

Above: Midway along the North Shore, the 720-acre Lutsen Scientific and Natural Area harbors one of the largest remaining stands of old-growth northern hardwood forest in Minnesota. MAX FOSTER

Facing page: From the Kadunce River State Wayside on Highway 61 north of Grand Marais, a 0.6-mile trail leads to a lush, deep gorge and several small waterfalls. MAX FOSTER

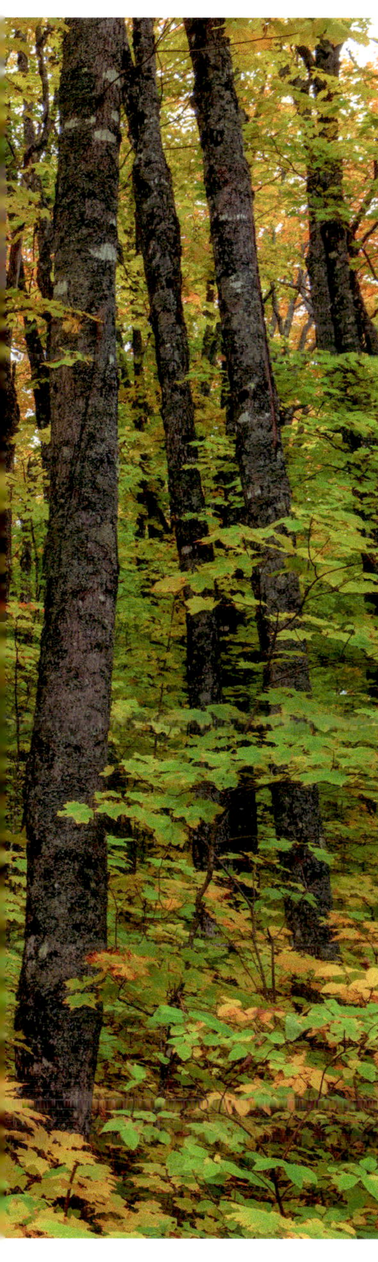

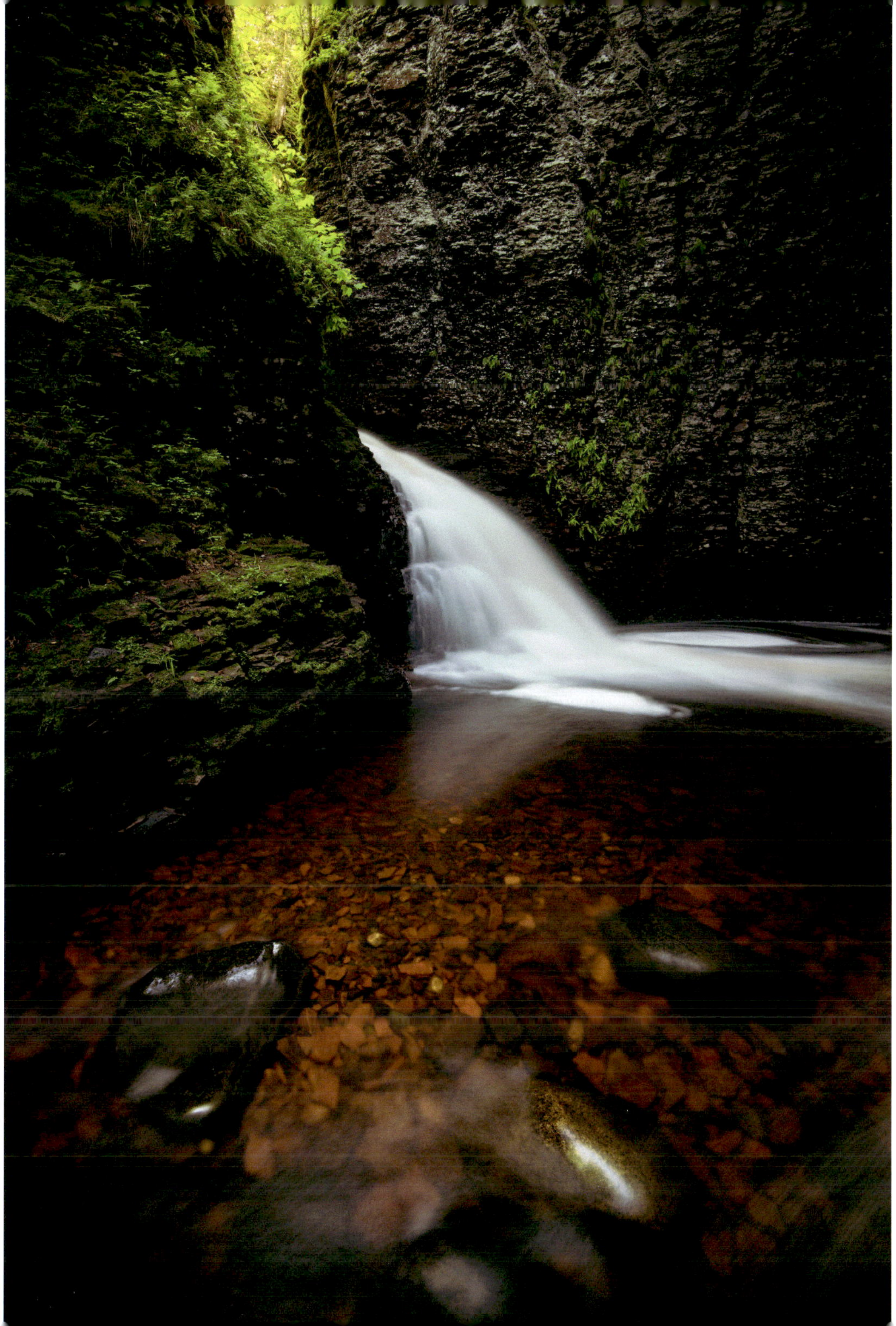

Right: History comes alive at the Minnesota History Center in St. Paul, with hands-on exhibits, thought-provoking programs, and live performances. GOOD FREE PHOTOS

Far right: Downtown Minneapolis glimmers during a summer sunset. MAX FOSTER

Below: The Minneapolis downtown skyline echoes the past with the Municipal Building's green copper roof and rose granite clock tower, and heralds the future with the curved glass façade of the nearby Fifth Street Towers. ARTAXERXES_LONGHAND/ SHUTTERSTOCK

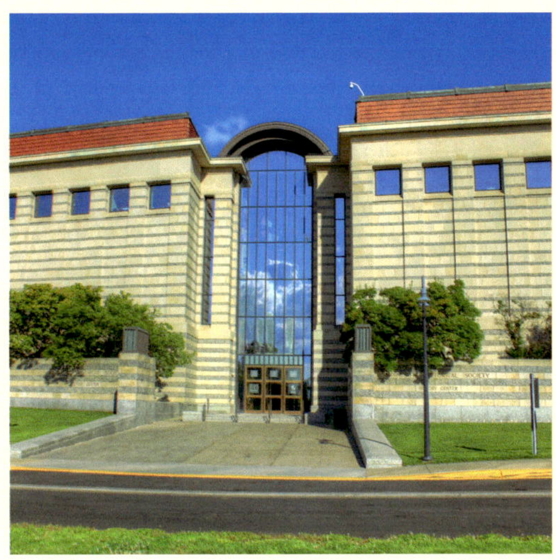

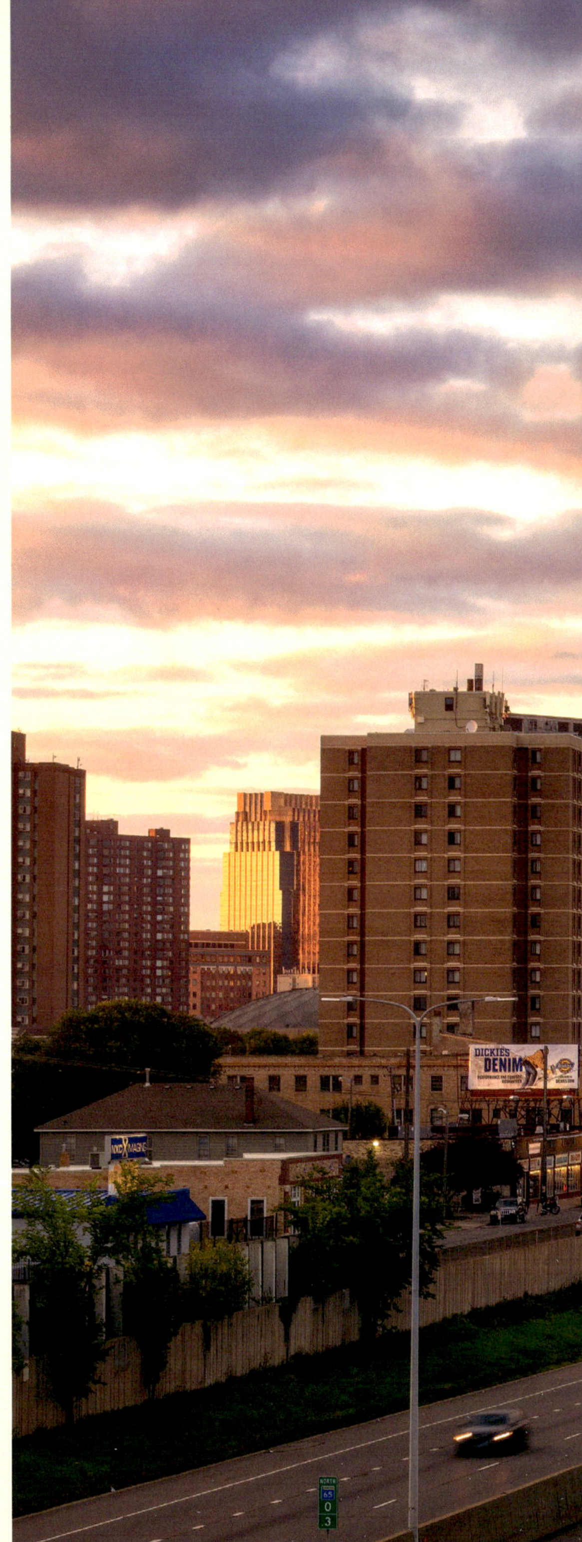

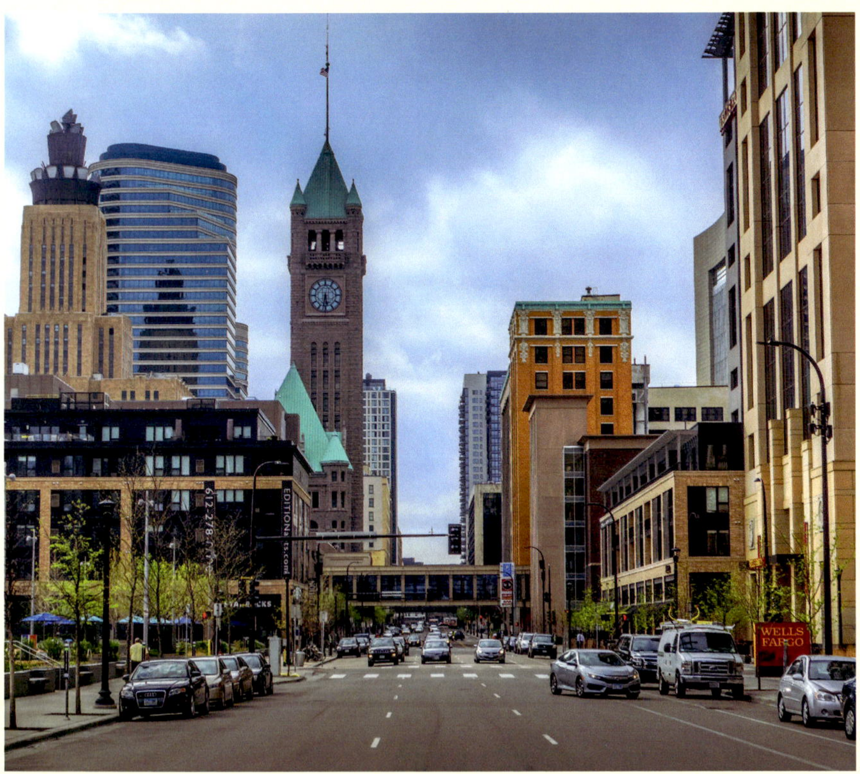

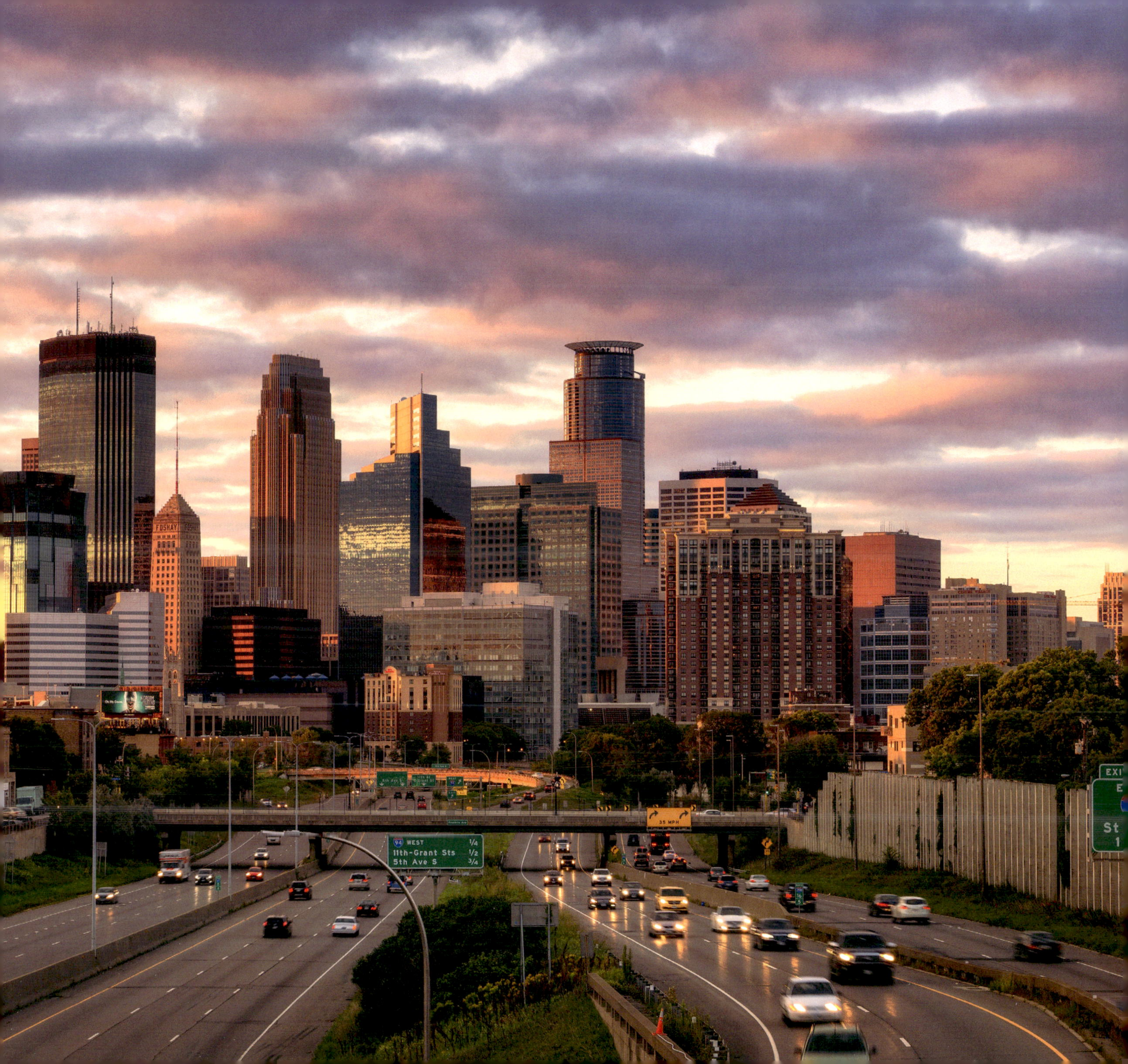
FOSHAY
94 WEST 1/4
11th-Grant Sts 1/2
5th Ave S 3/4
35 MPH

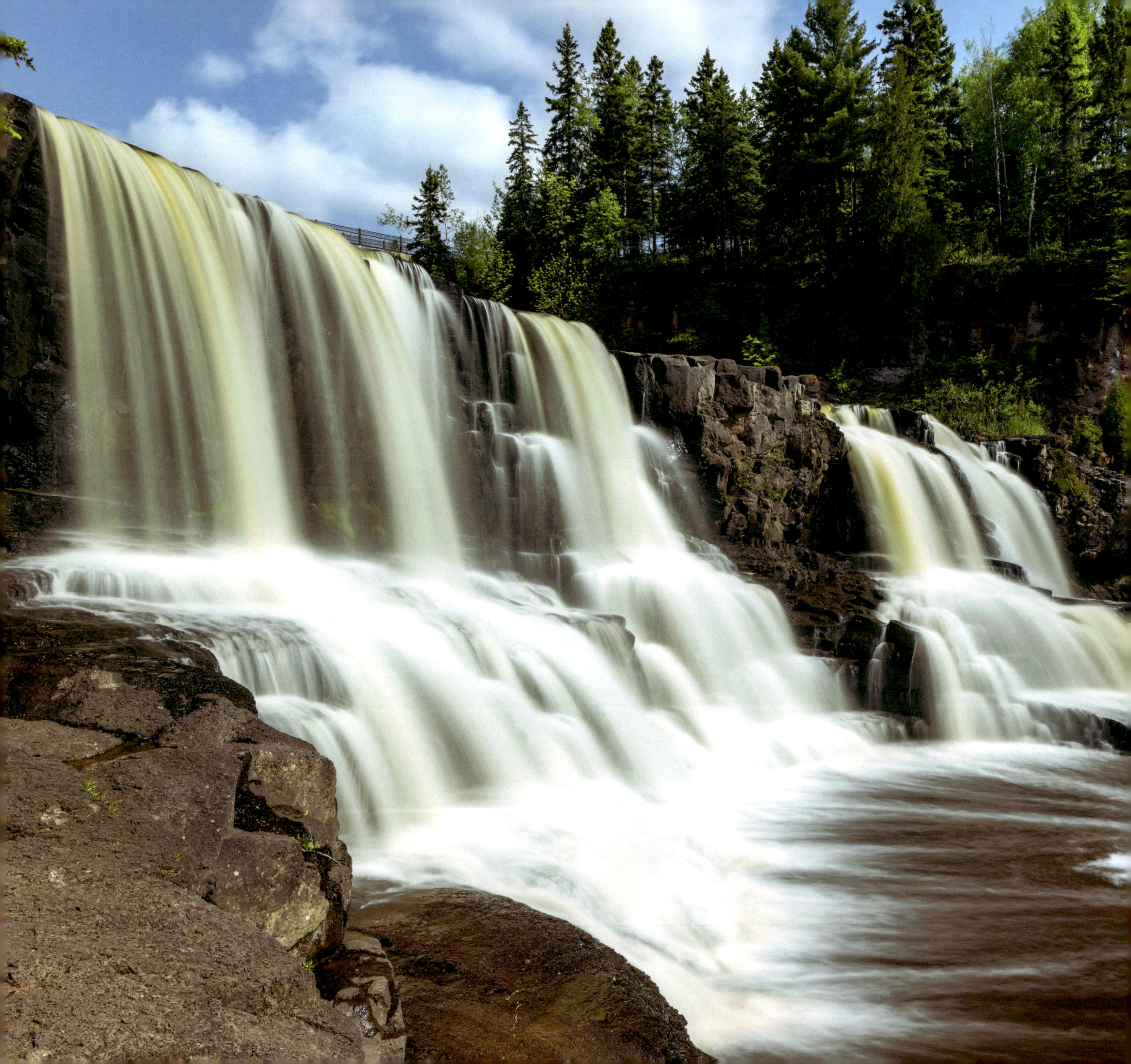

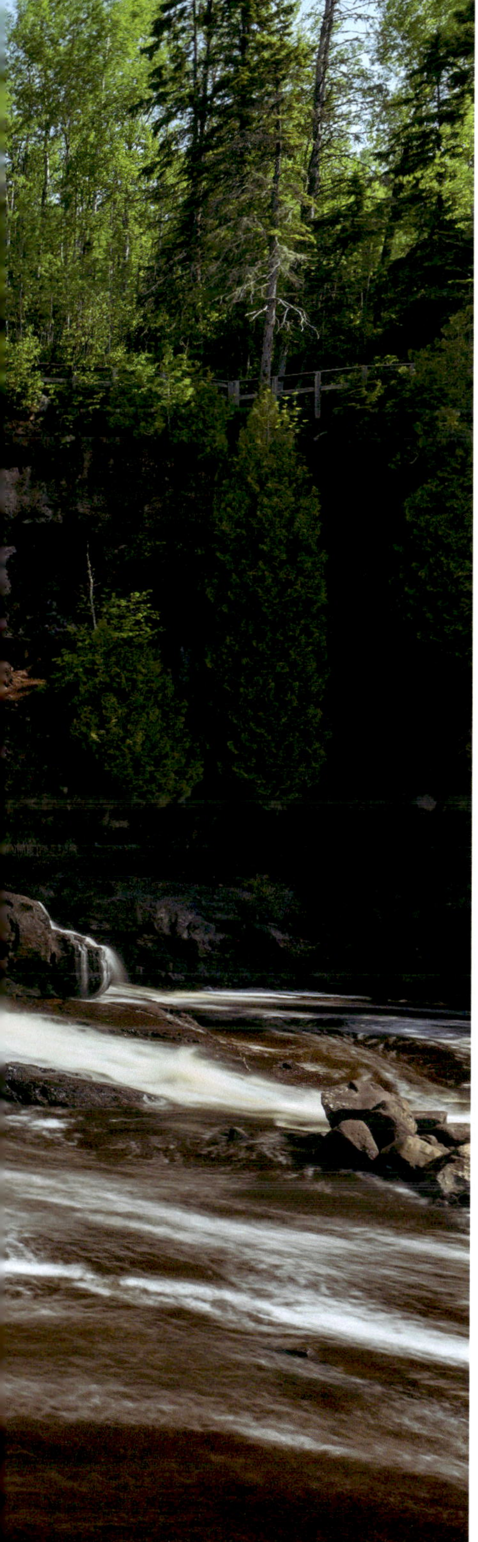

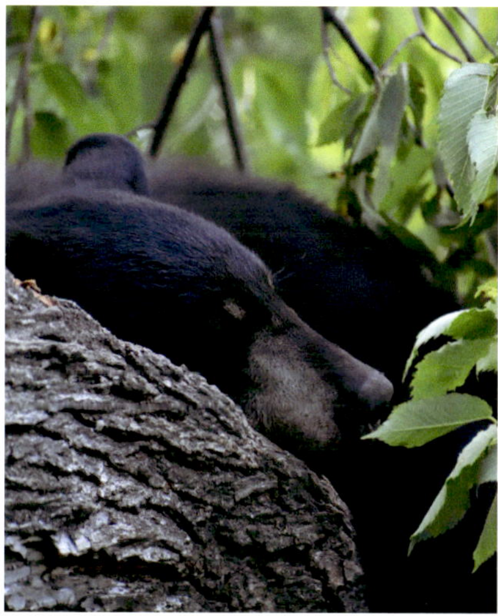

Left: Savoring the abundance, a black bear catches a midday nap. JONATHAN MILLER/PIXABAY

Far left: Just below Highway 61, Gooseberry Falls splashes over multiple ledges in its namesake state park. JOHN BRUESKE/SHUTTERSTOCK

Below: River scouring reveals gnarled tree roots below Gooseberry Falls. MAX FOSTER

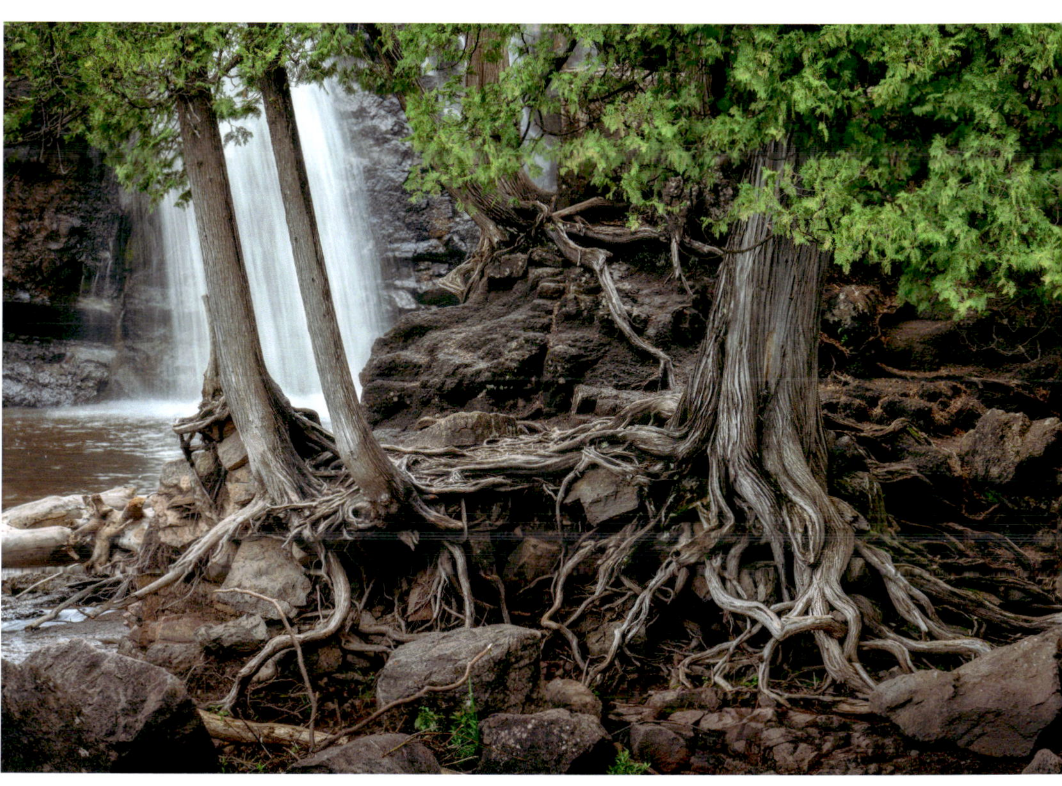

Right: The longest continually operating lighthouse in Minnesota has been guiding ships into Lake Superior's Agate Bay at Two Harbors since 1892. 12019/PIXABAY

Far right: About half a mile southwest of Split Rock Lighthouse, tiny Ellingson Island anchors one end of Little Two Harbors cove. Accessible by kayak or wading, the island is off limits from March 1 to August 1 to protect wildlife. MAX FOSTER

Below: On the north pier of the Duluth Ship Canal, next to the Aerial Lift Bridge, the Lake Superior Maritime Visitor Center offers engaging exhibits and programs on Great Lakes shipping and the wreck of the Edmund Fitzgerald. This retired tugboat rests out front, in Canal Park. GOOD FREE PHOTOS

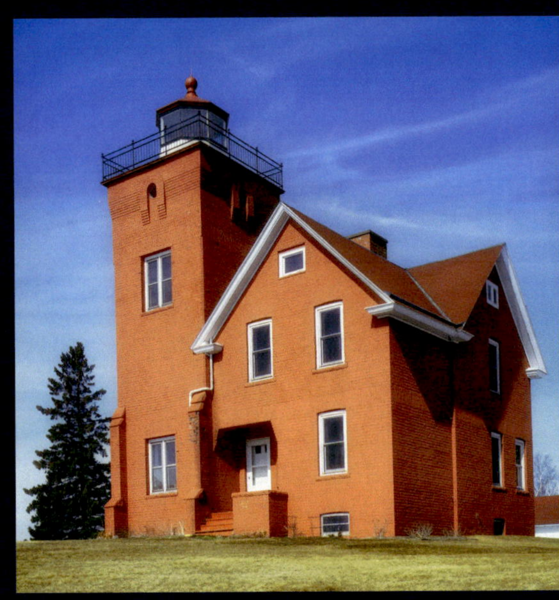

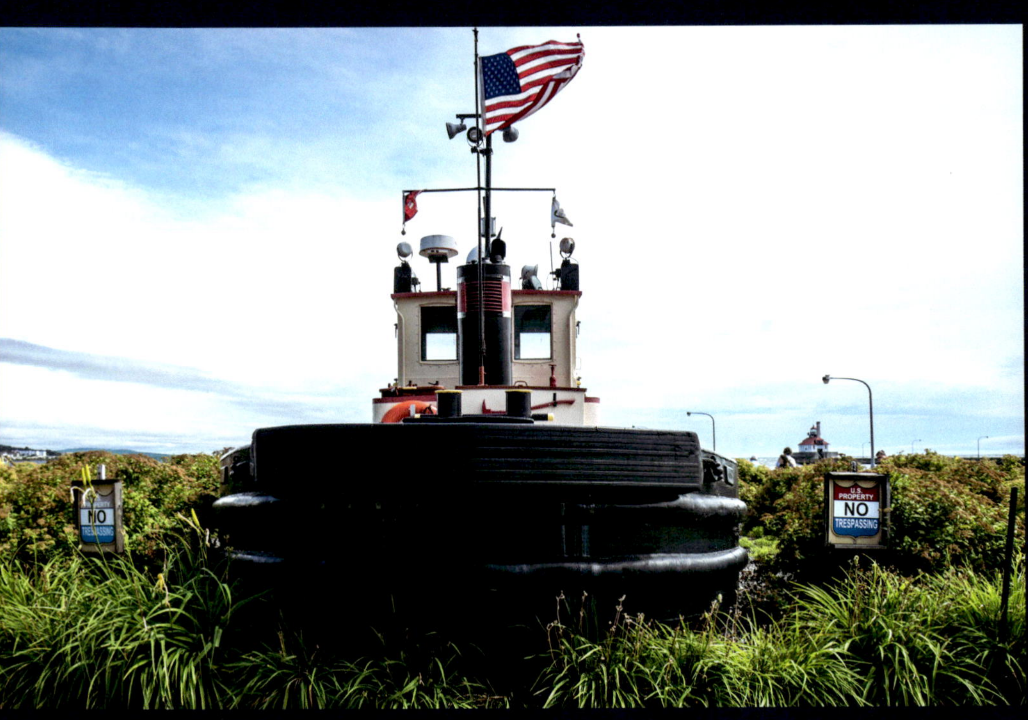

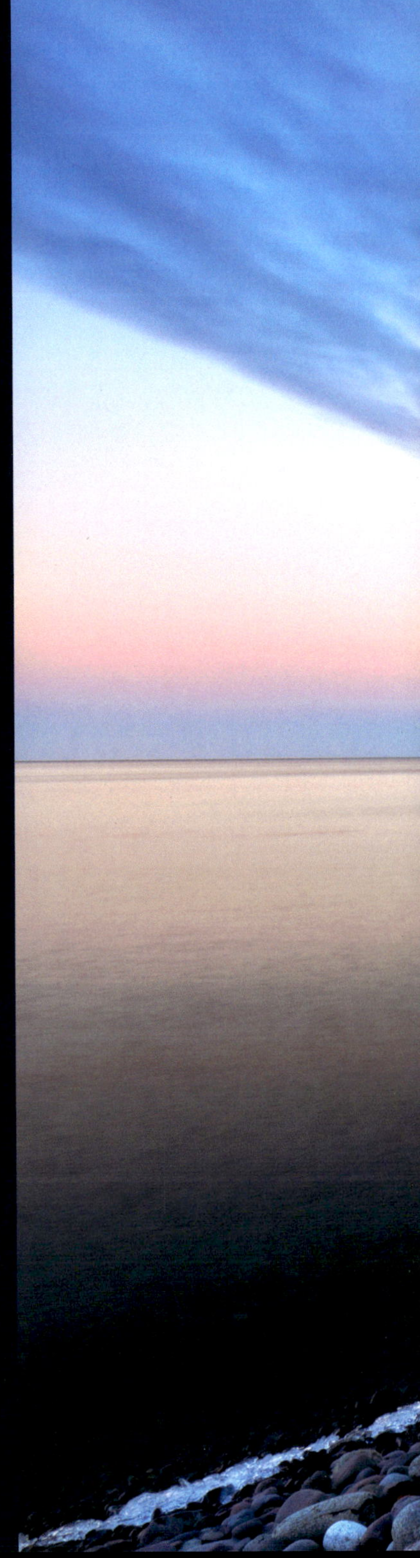

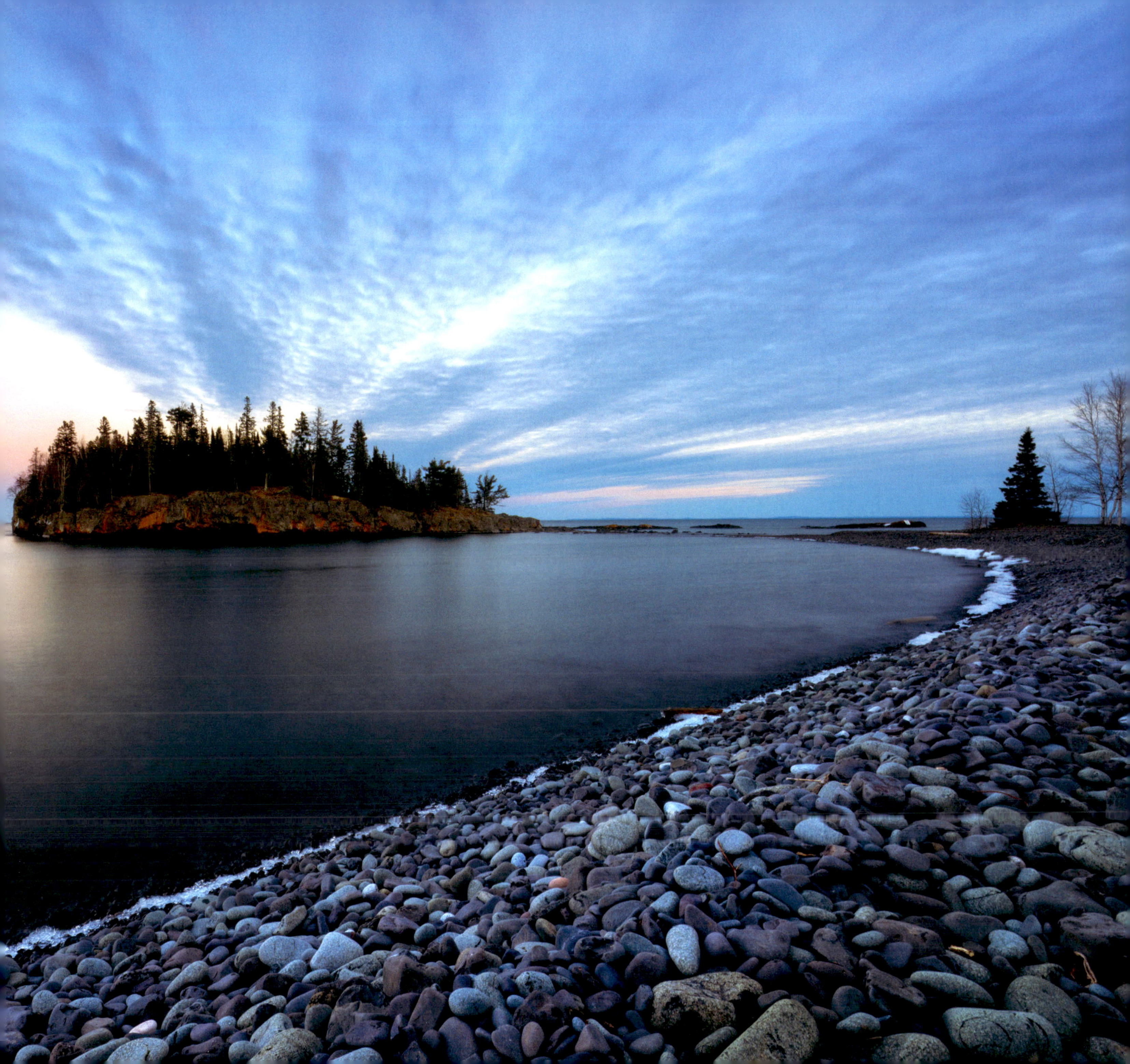

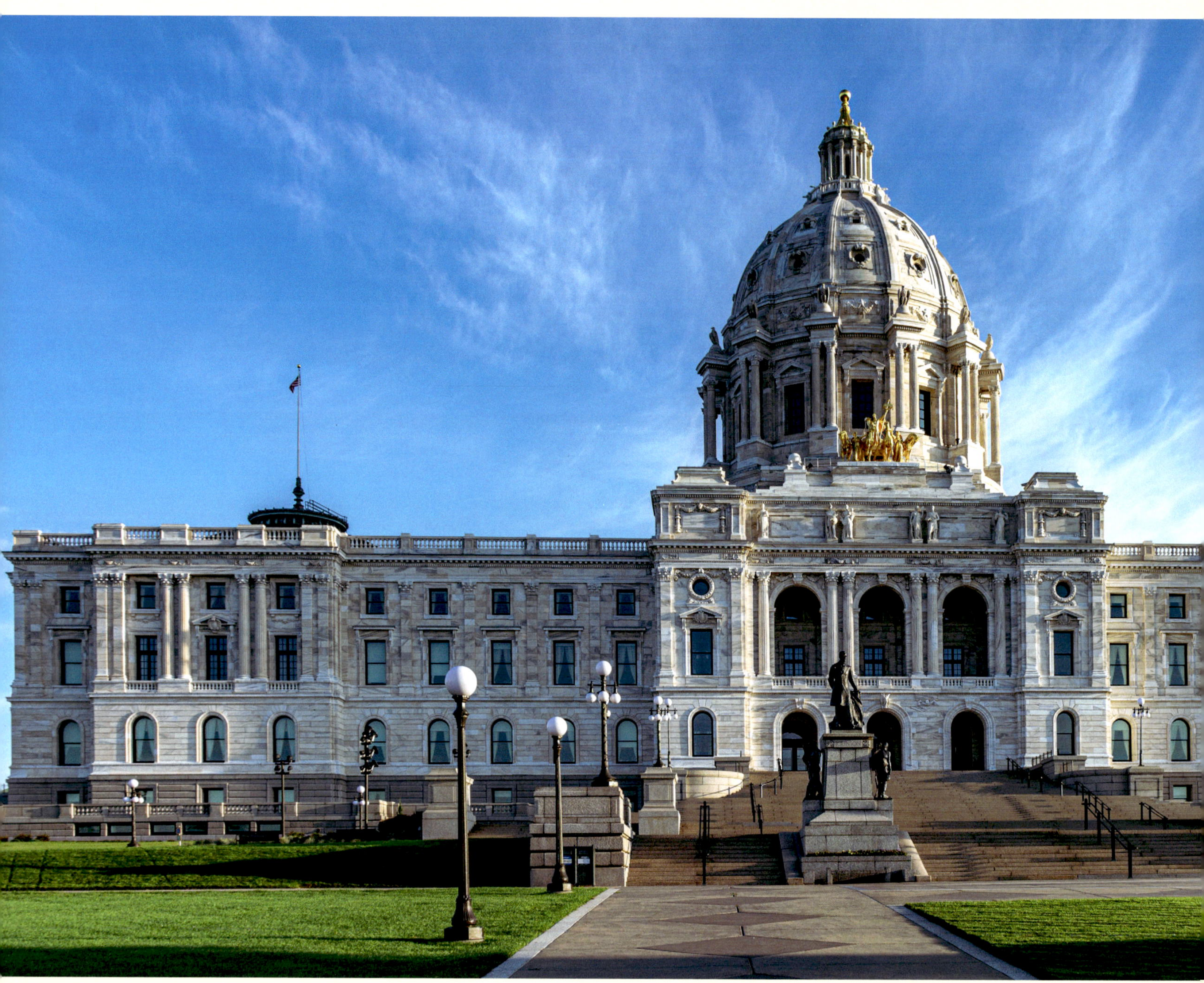

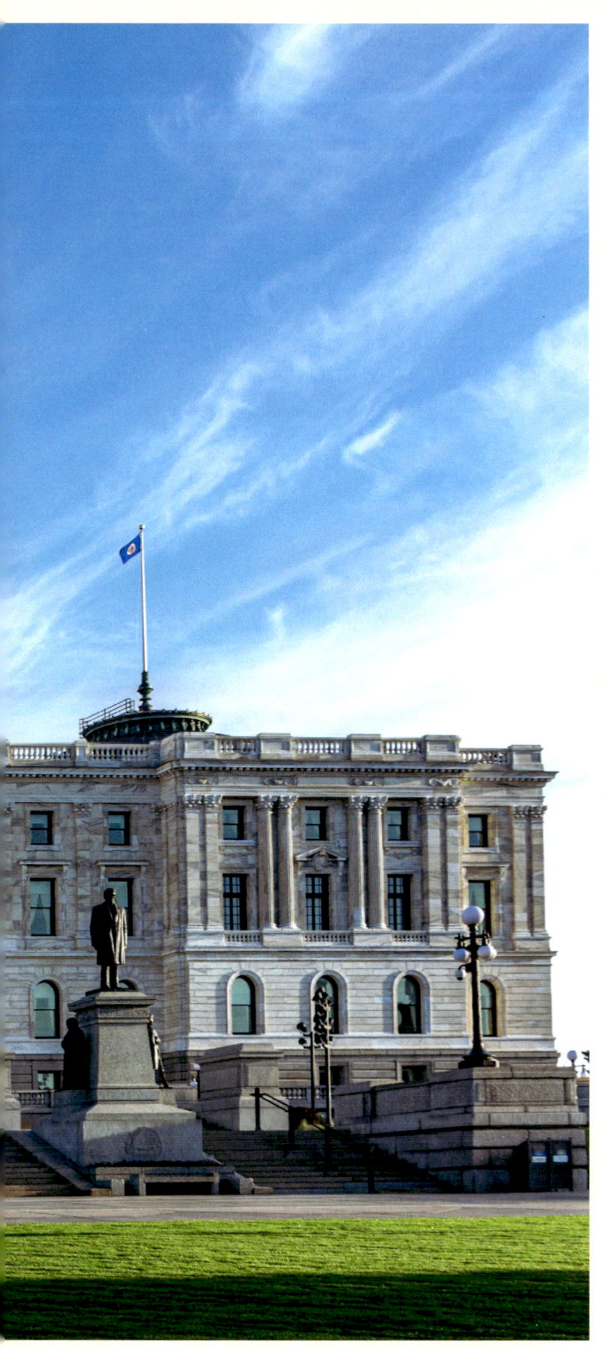

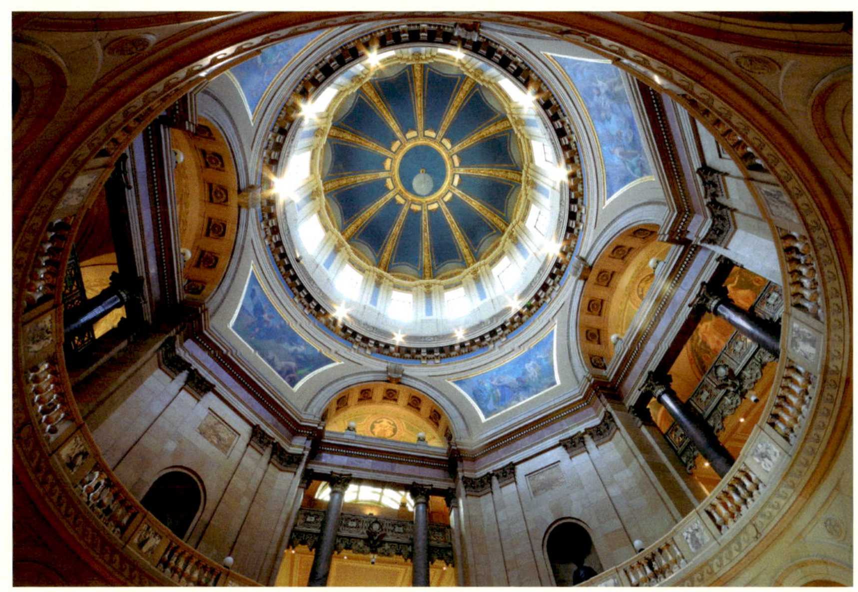

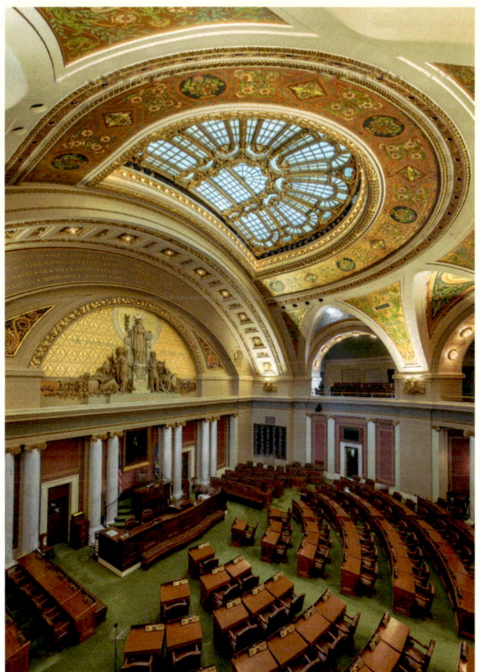

Above: The State Capitol dome soars 220 feet above ground level, with the interior rotunda ceiling 142 feet above the "L'Étoile du Nord" or The Star of the North, set in the floor. IMG_191/ SHUTTERSTOCK

Left: Regular House sessions are held in the Minnesota House of Representatives Chamber, as are joint sessions of the state legislature. NAGEL PHOTOGRAPHY/ SHUTTERSTOCK

Far left: First opened in 1905, the State Capitol in St. Paul underwent a comprehensive four-year restoration, completed in 2017, to clean and repair the marble and St. Cloud granite exterior, as well as revitalize interior spaces, artwork, skylights, and elevators. RANDY RUNTSCH/SHUTTERSTOCK

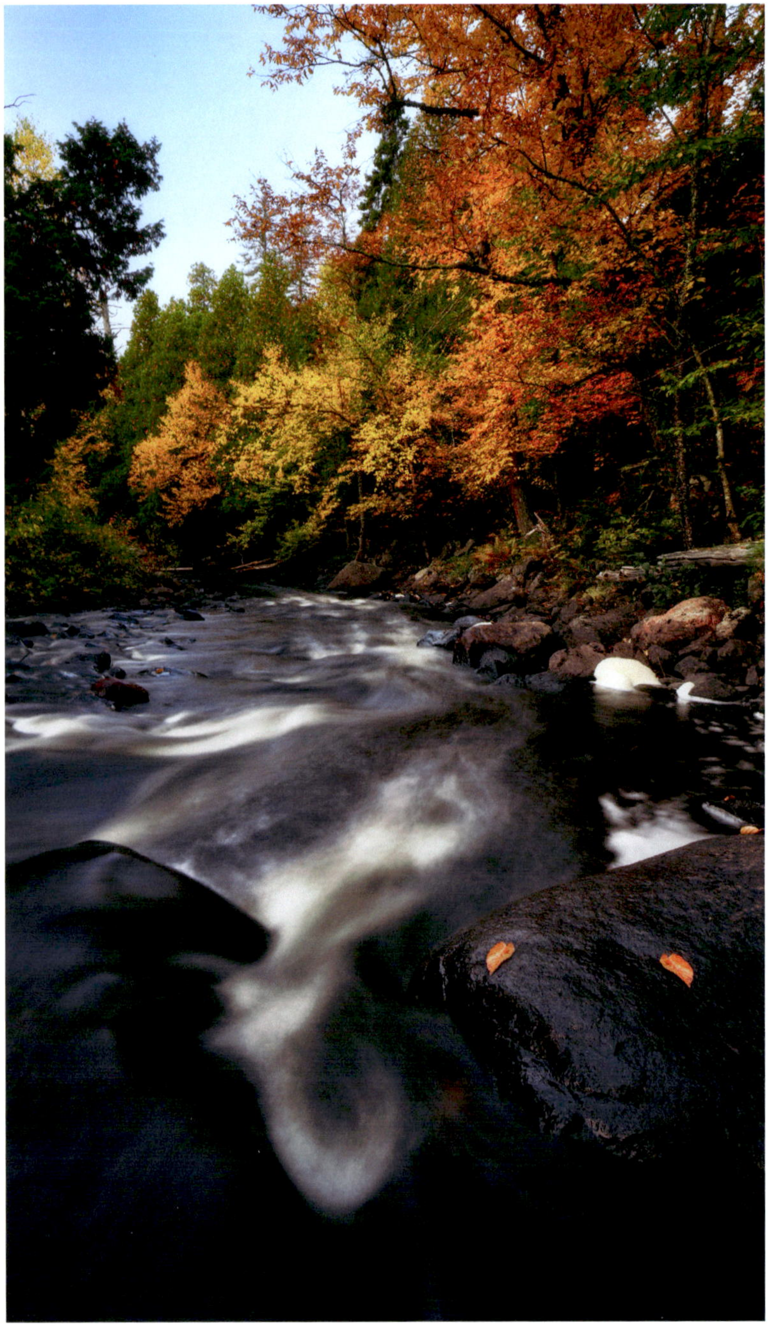

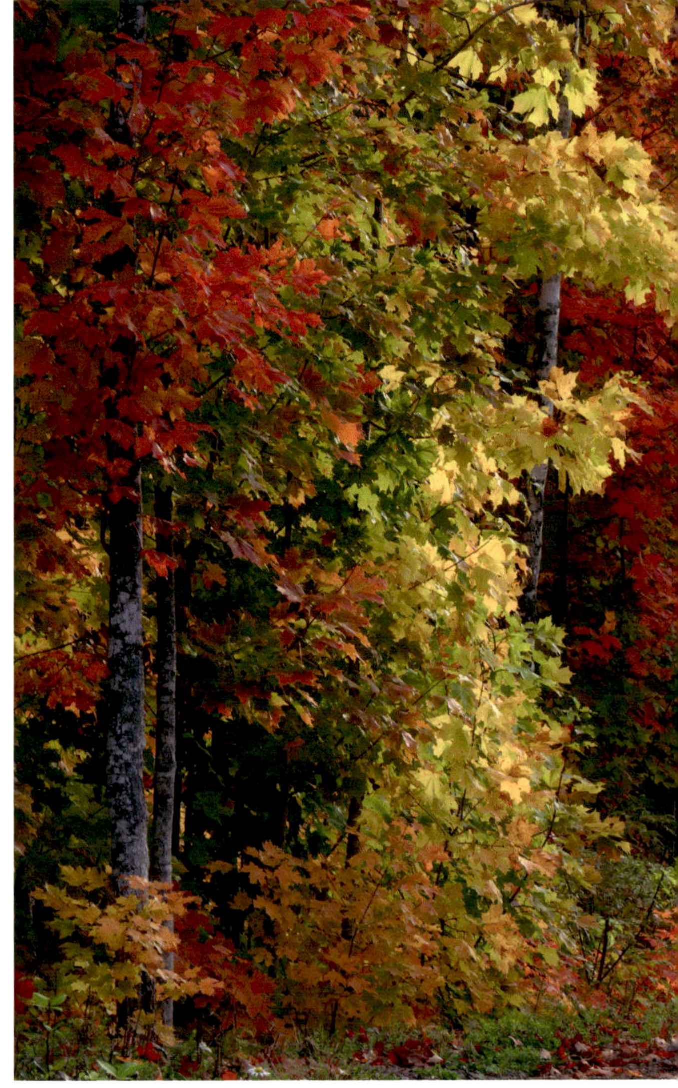

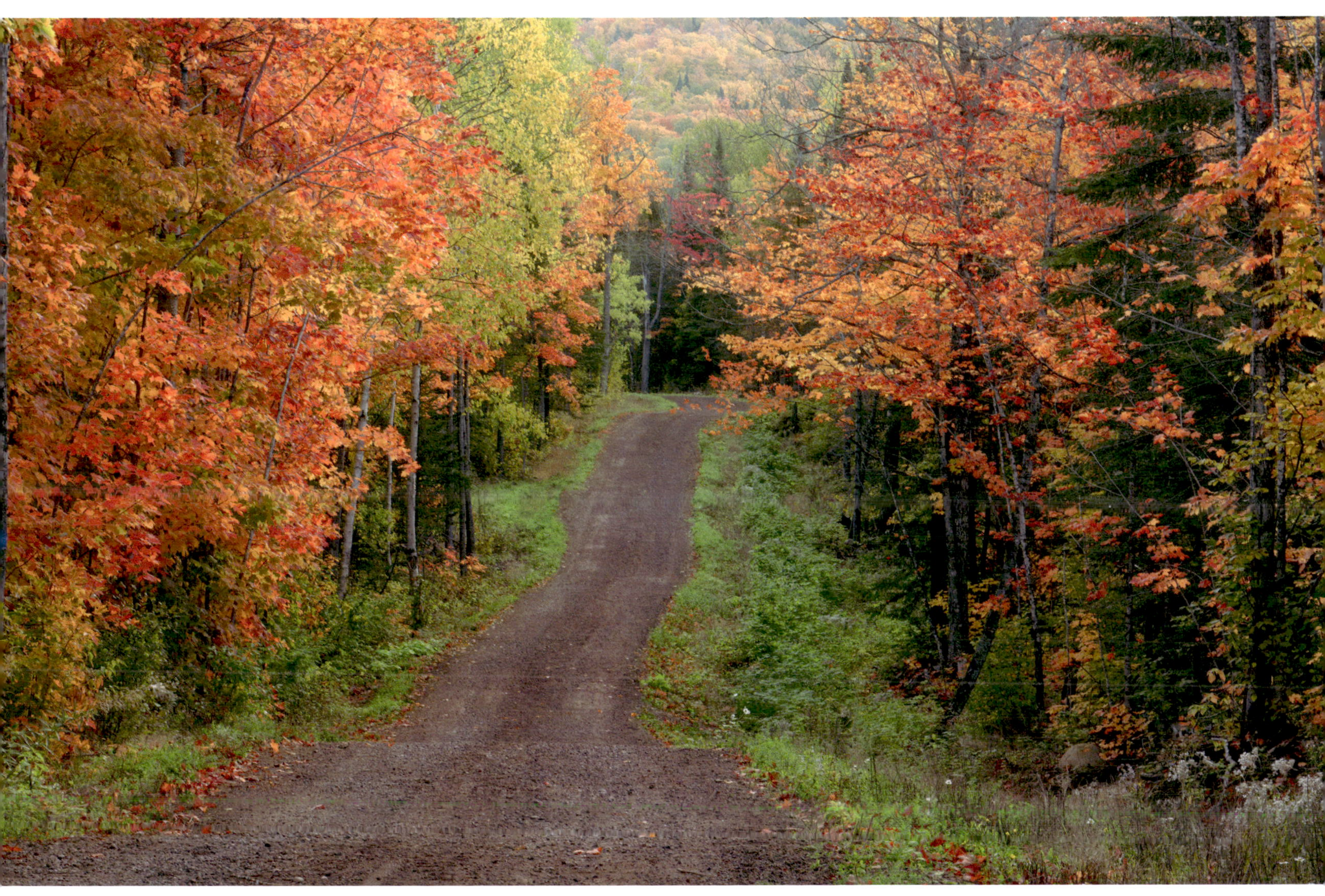

Above: A back road threads between brilliant multihued maples in Cook County at the state's northeastern tip. MAX FOSTER

Facing page: On a bright fall day, the Manitou River races downstream toward its Lake Superior destination. MAX FOSTER

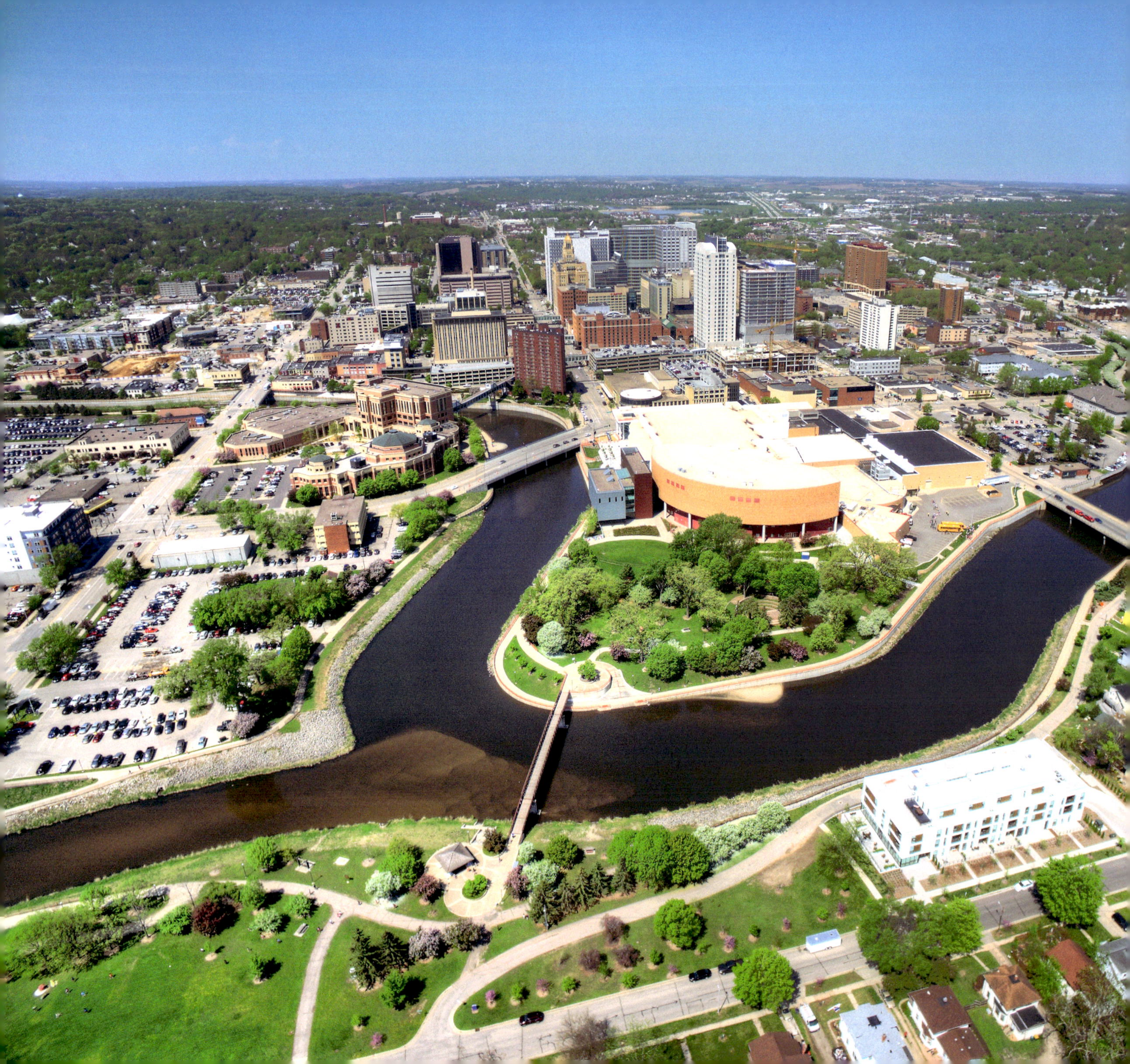

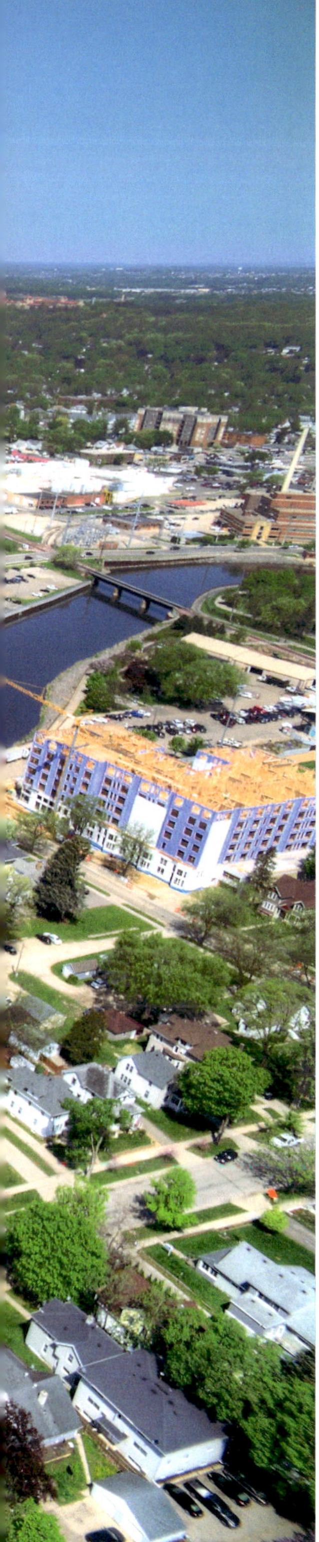

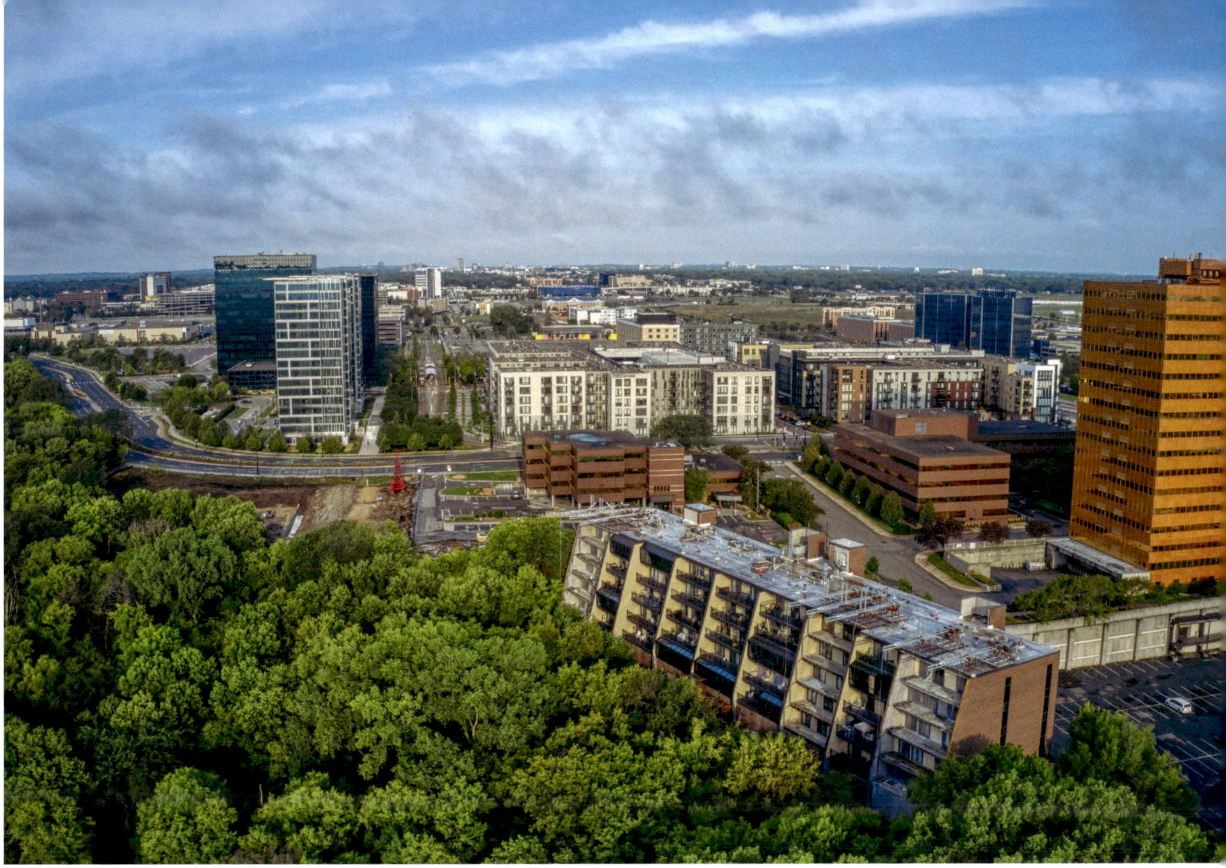

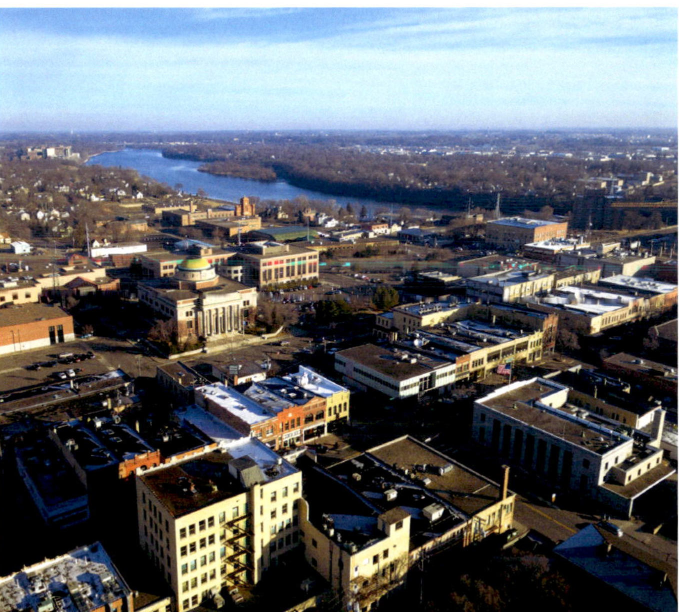

Above: Minnesota's fourth-largest city, Bloomington is home to numerous corporate headquarters and also the Mall of America, with more than 500 stores and almost 3 million square feet of retail space. JACOB BOOMSMA/ SHUTTERSTOCK

Left: In 2019, St. Cloud won three first place awards from the International Awards for Liveable Communities. ANH LUU/ SHUTTERSTOCK

Far left: Rochester, home to the world-renowned Mayo Clinic, is a city of bridges, hugging the west bank of the South Fork of the Zumbro River. JACOB BOOMSMA/ SHUTTERSTOCK

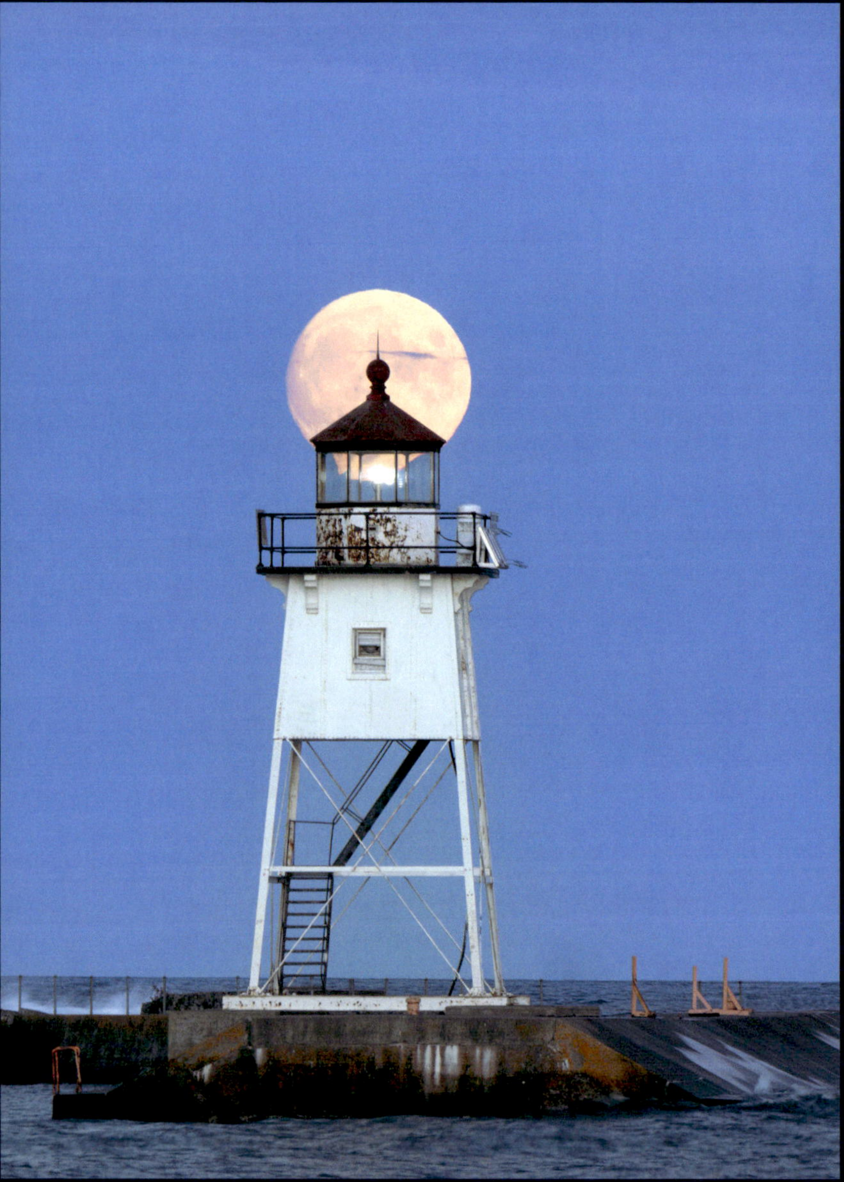

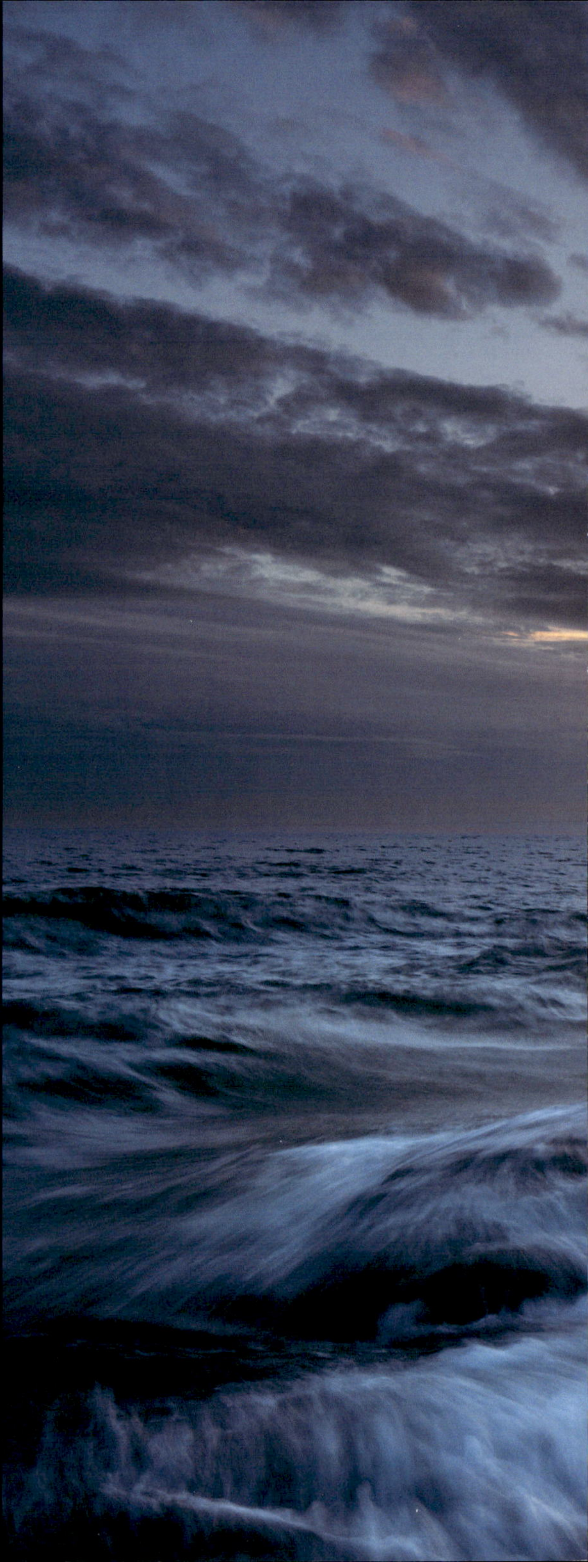

Above: Perched on the north breakwater at the entrance to the harbor, the Grand Marais light was first lit in 1922. MAX FOSTER

Right: Lake Superior waves meet volcanic bedrock near Grand Marais. MAX FOSTER

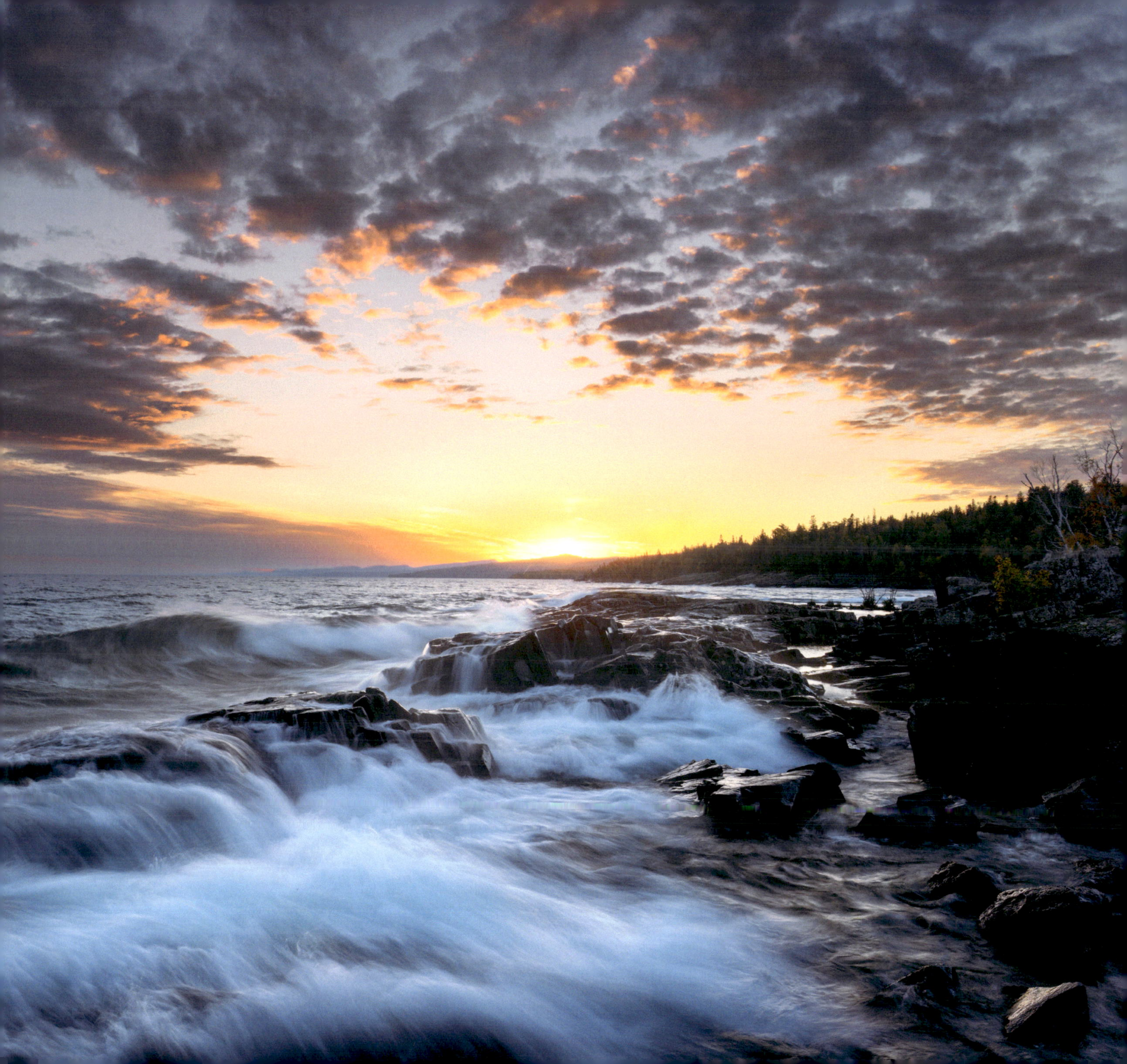

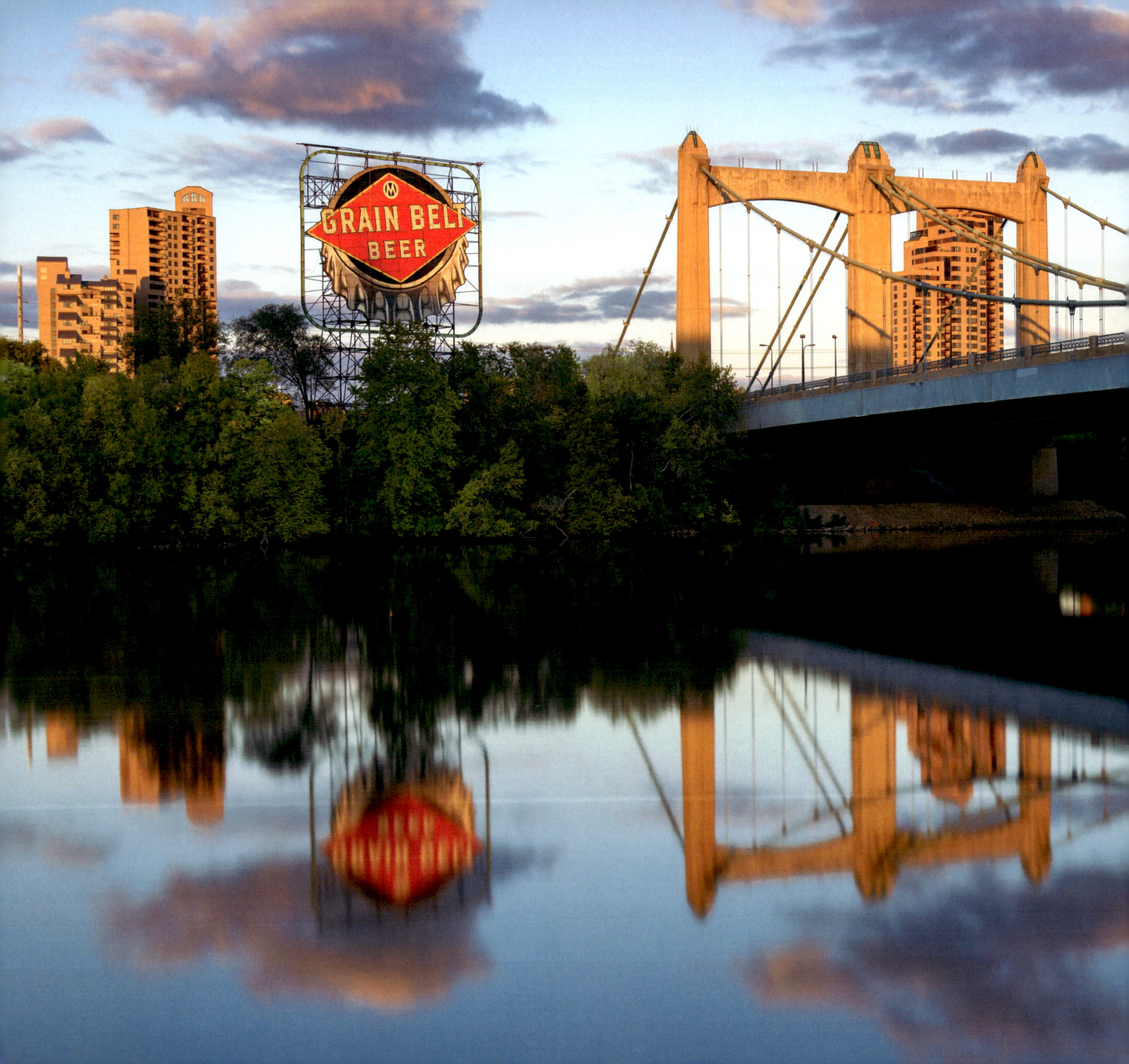
GRAIN BELT
BEER

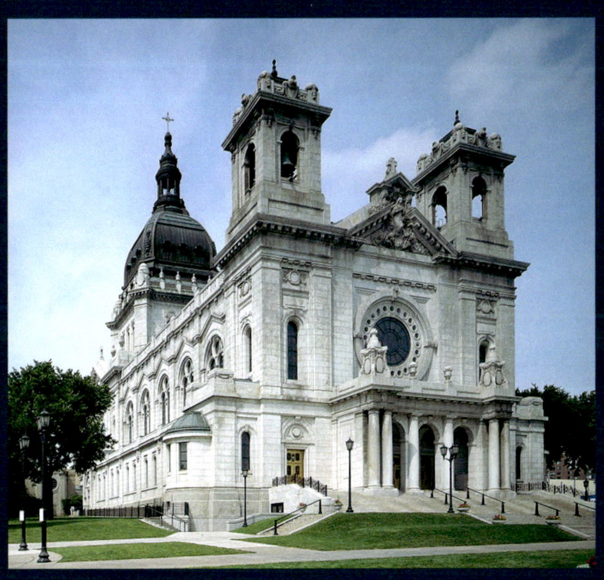

Left: The Beaux-Arts Basilica of Saint Mary in Minneapolis is renowned for its architecture and beautiful stained glass windows, and also for the organ's powerful Herald Trumpet tuba-scale stop that rumbles like prairie thunder. CAROL HIGHSMITH/ PICRYL

Far left: Brewed since the 1890s, Grain Belt beer remains a favored Minnesota beverage. The 48-foot-high sign was first installed in 1941 in downtown Minneapolis. It now resides on Nicollet Island by the Hennepin Avenue Bridge. MAX FOSTER

Below: The Walker Art Center and municipal park and recreation board cooperatively run the 11-acre Minneapolis Sculpture Garden, which houses 40 permanent art installations, including the Spoonbridge and Cherry, a sculptural fountain designed by Claes Oldenburg and Coosje van Bruggen. MAX FOSTER

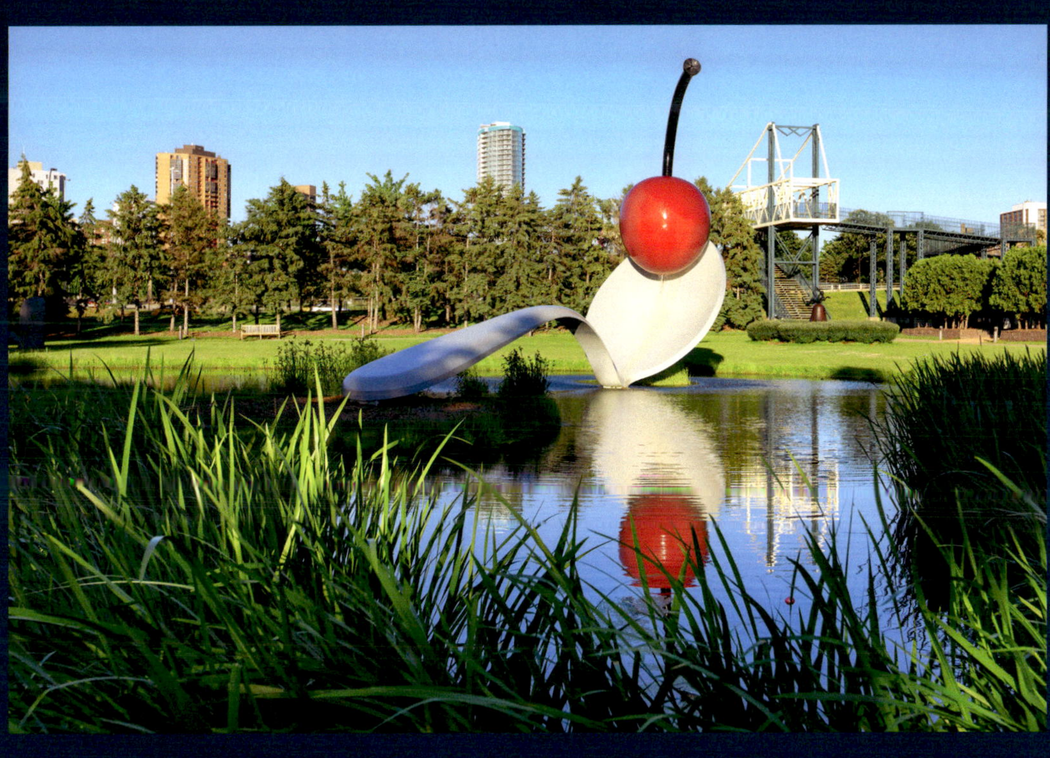

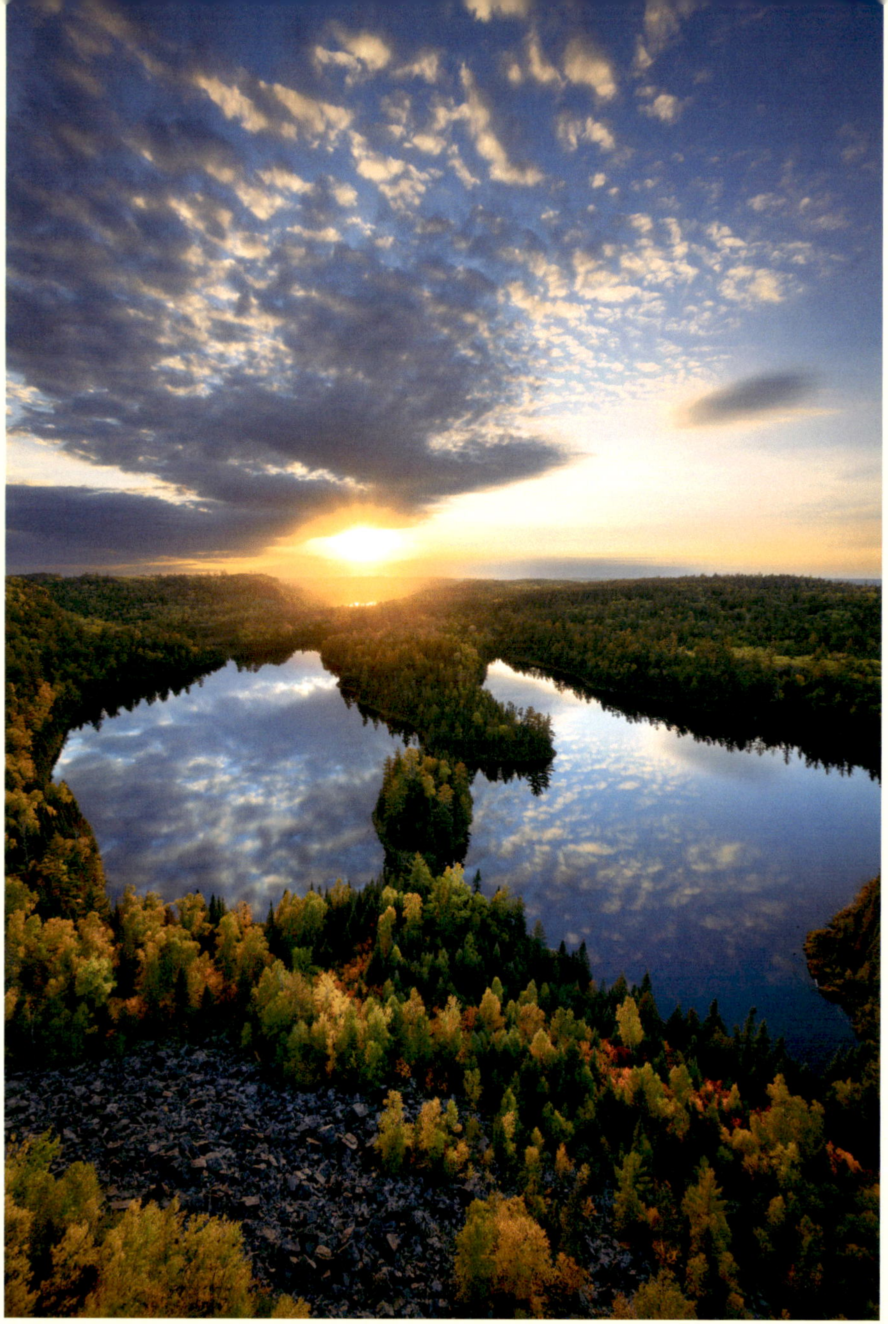

Above: A North Woods sunset paints Twin Lakes in Superior National Forest. MAX FOSTER

Right: The Oberg Mountain Trail leads to several overlooks, including one with this stunning vista of autumn forest and shimmering Lake Superior. MAX FOSTER

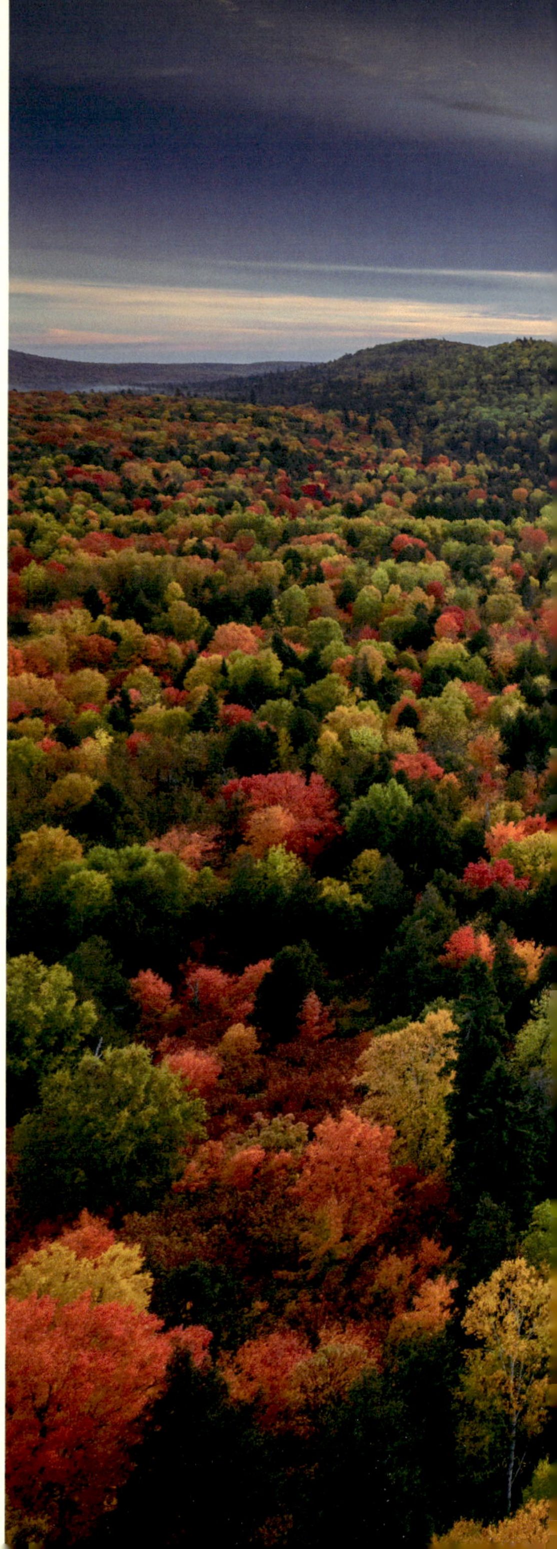

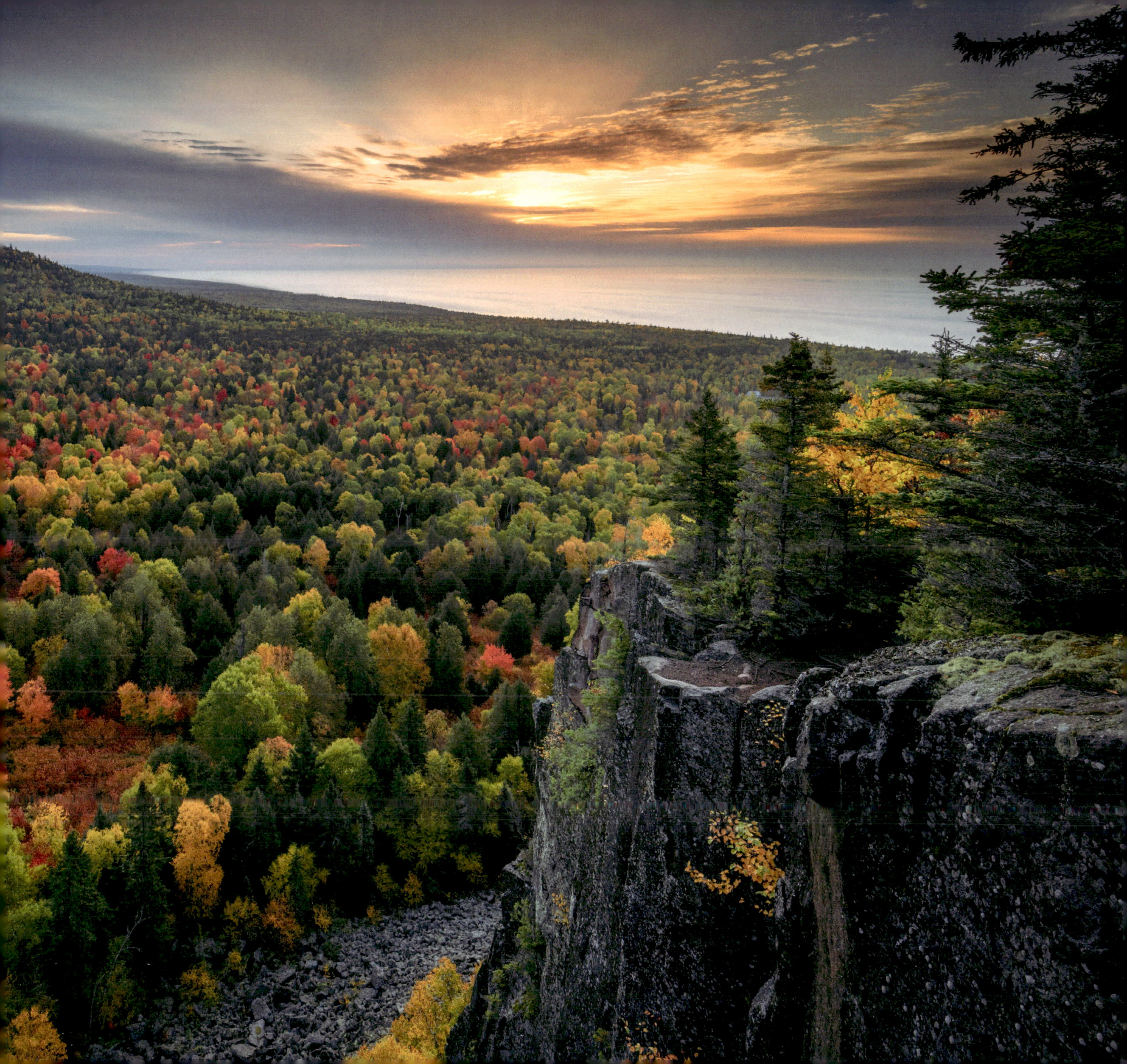

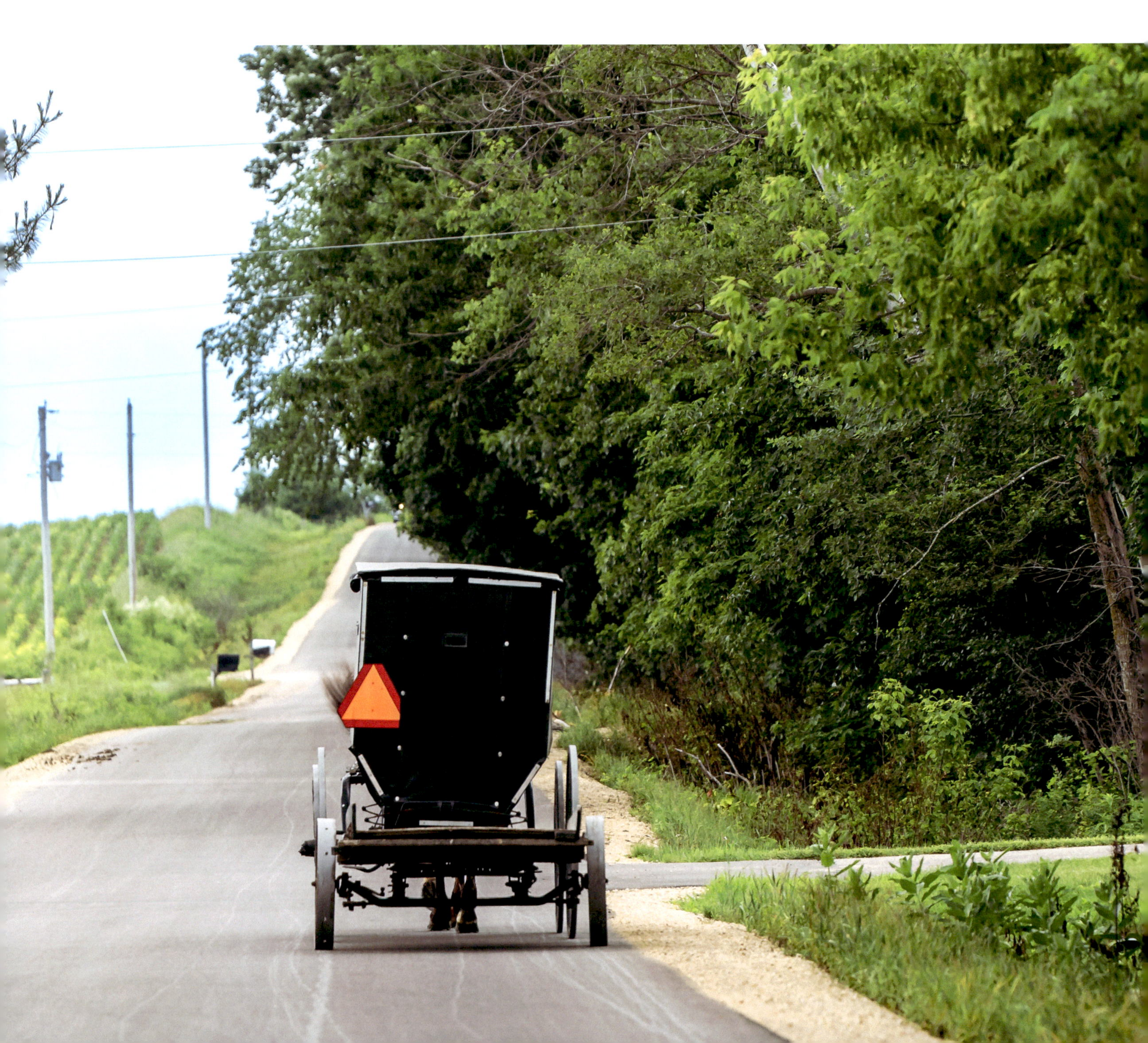

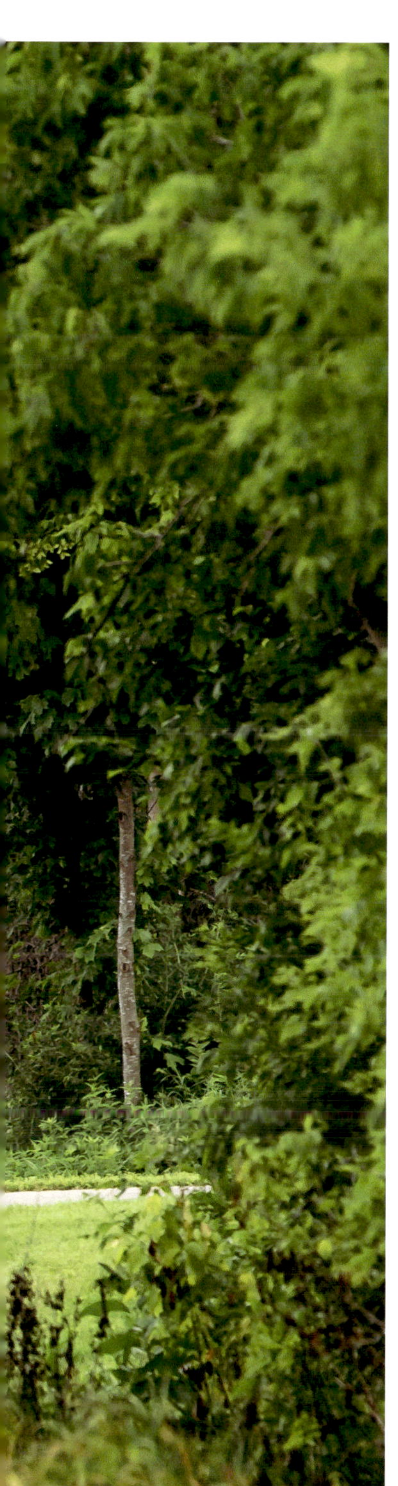

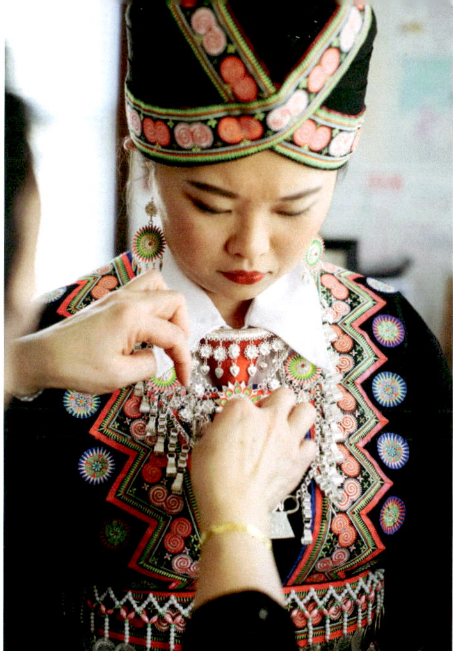

Left: The largest Hmong community in the United States thrives in the Twin Cities. Here, a Hmong bride prepares for her wedding. LEE VUE/UNSPLASH

Far left: A horse-drawn Amish buggy eases down a country road. More than 100 Old Order Amish families farm near Harmony in the state's southeast corner. DEBRA ANDERSON/SHUTTERSTOCK

Below: As its name suggests, the town of Scandia is a stronghold of Swedish and Norwegian cultures. This Dala horse statue at Gammelgården Museum is painted in a traditional style. MELISSAMN/SHUTTERSTOCK

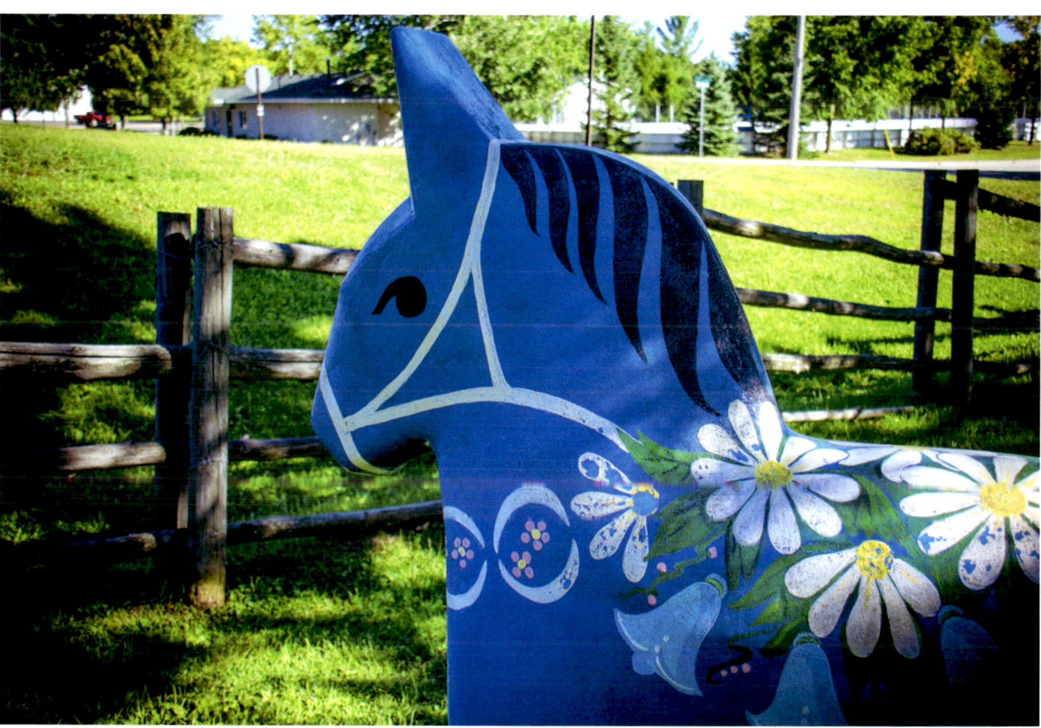

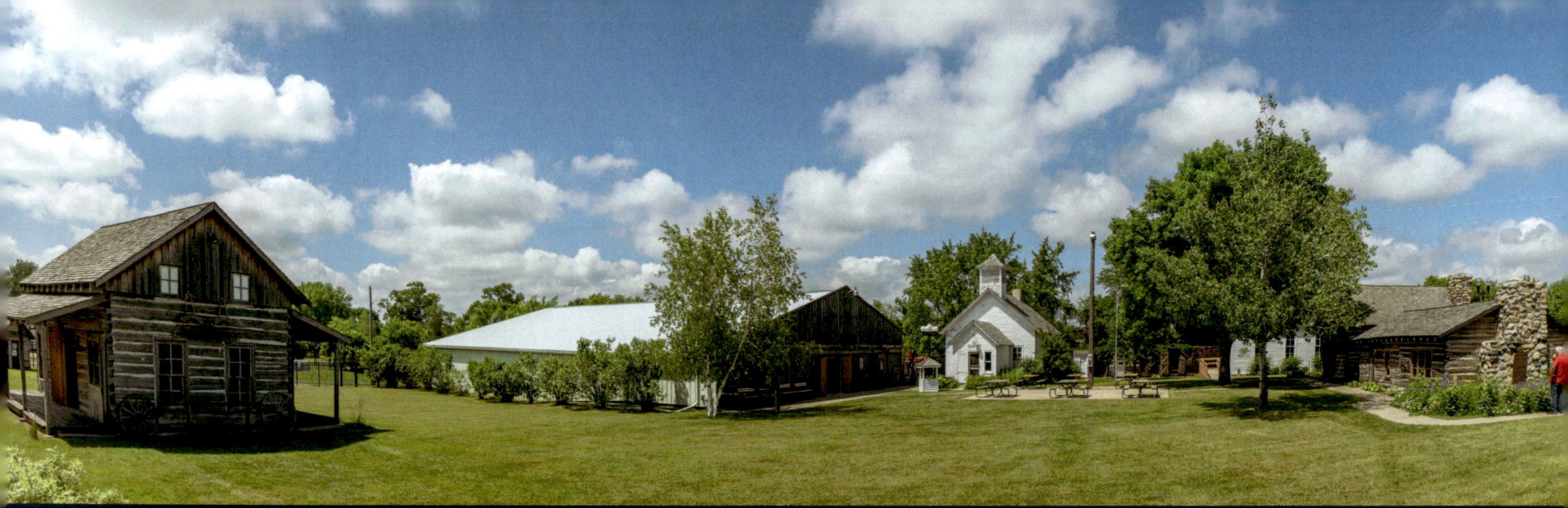

Above: The Runestone Museum in Alexandria is home to the Kensington runestone, a stone slab unearthed by a Minnesota farmer in 1898. The controversial stone's inscription claims the slab was left by Scandanavian explorers in 1362! The museum also features a Viking ship display and exhibits on local and Native cultures. BARBARAJO/SHUTTERSTOCK

Facing page: Strategically situated at the confluence of the Minnesota and Mississippi Rivers, historic Fort Snelling sits on Dakota homelands and today serves as a center for learning about the clash of cultures that once darkened the region. KEN LUND/WIKIMEDIA COMMONS

Below: Grand Portage National Monument preserves the history of the partnership between the Grand Portage Anishinaabe and the North West Company during the North American fur trade era. NATIONAL PARK SERVICE

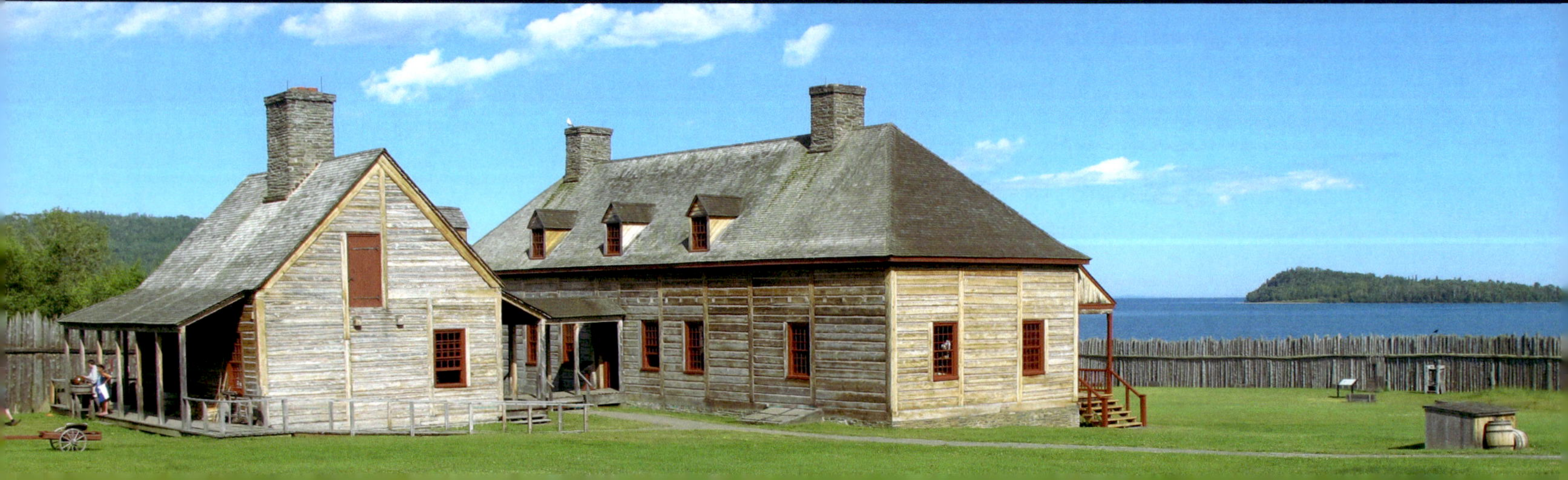

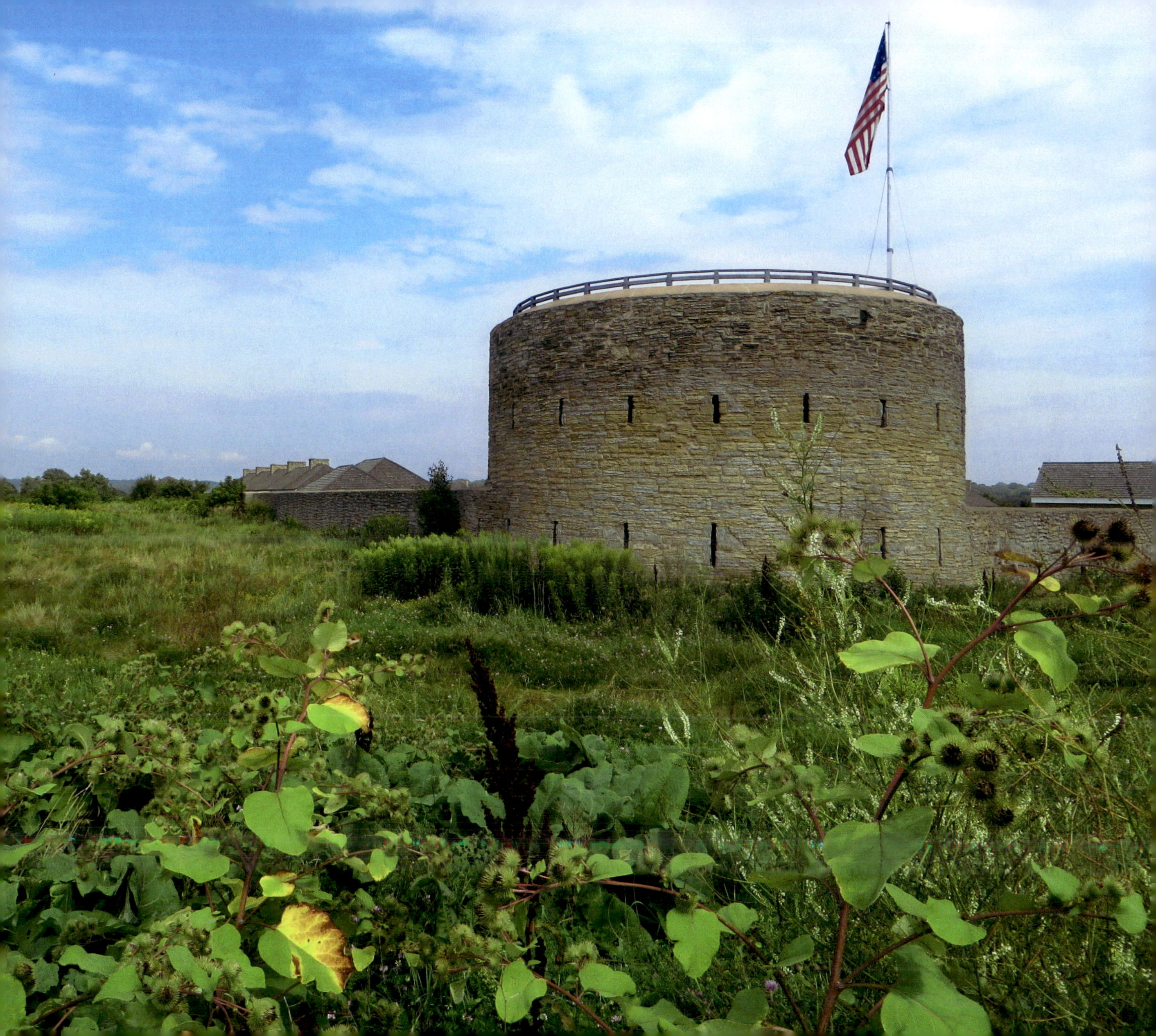

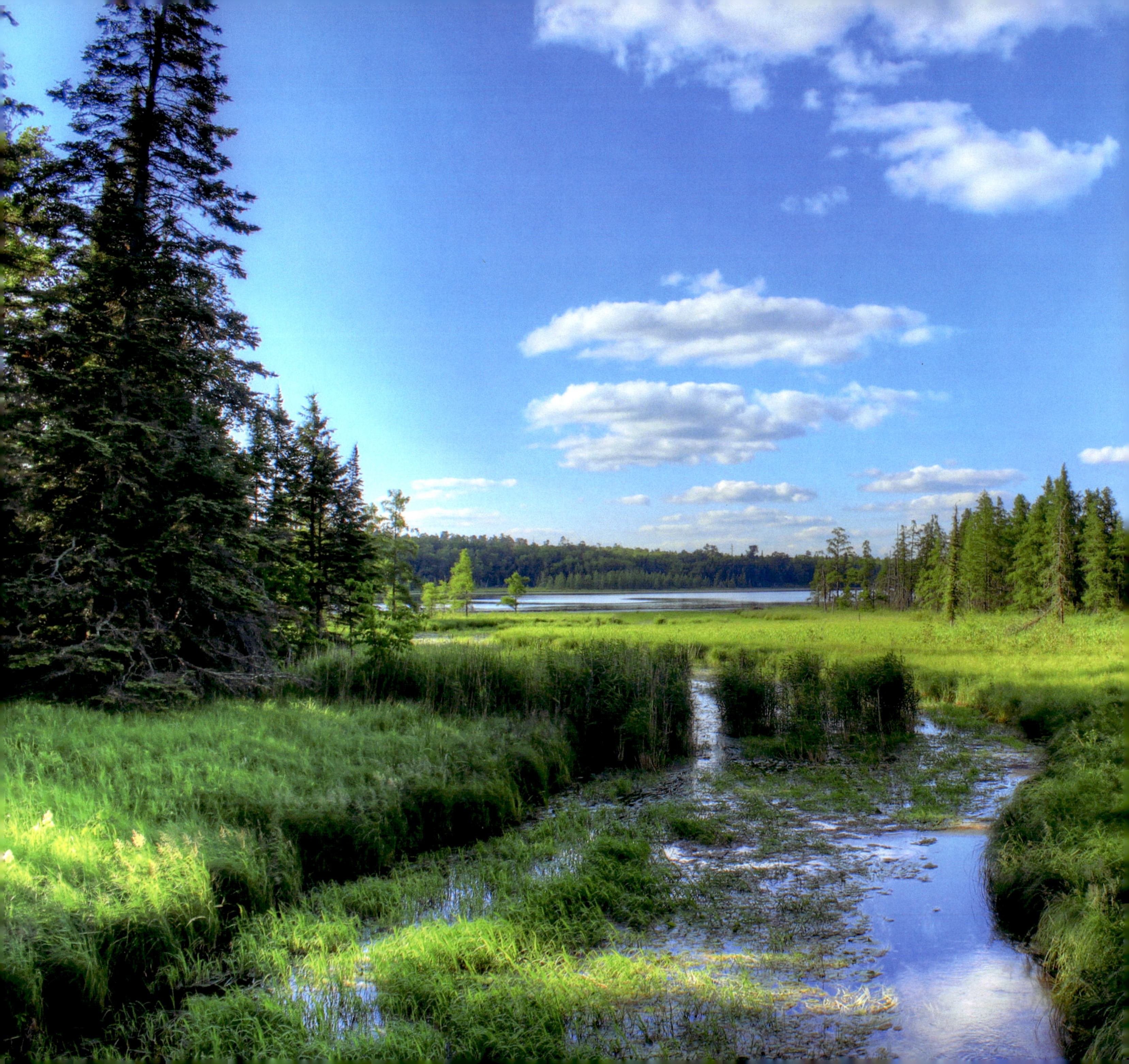

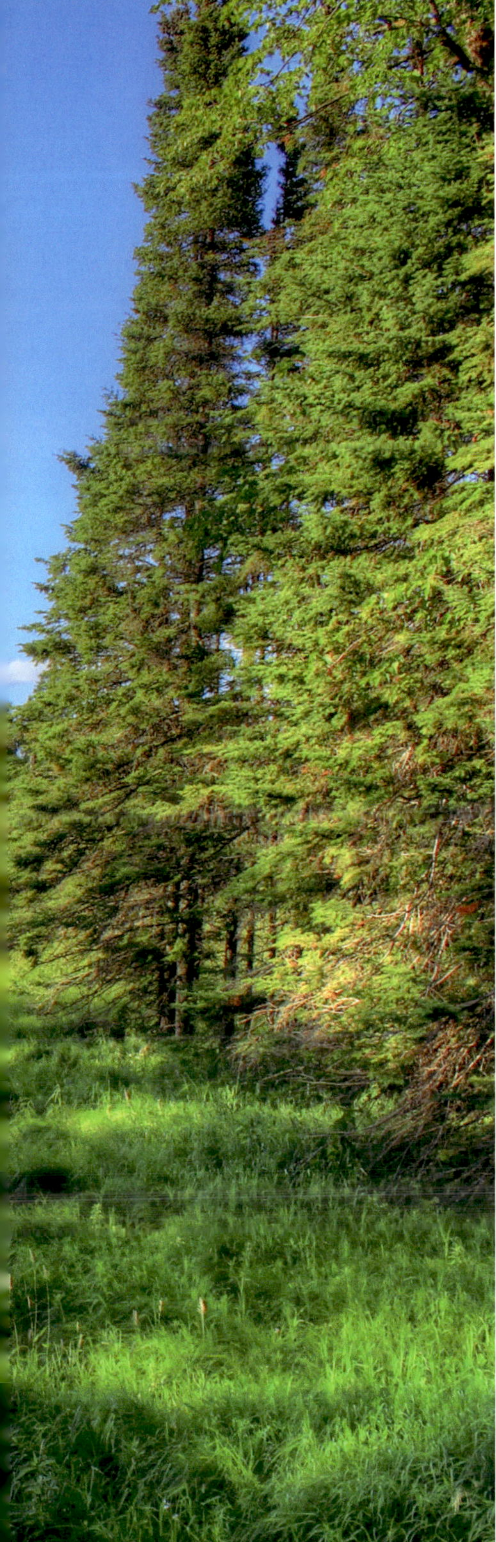

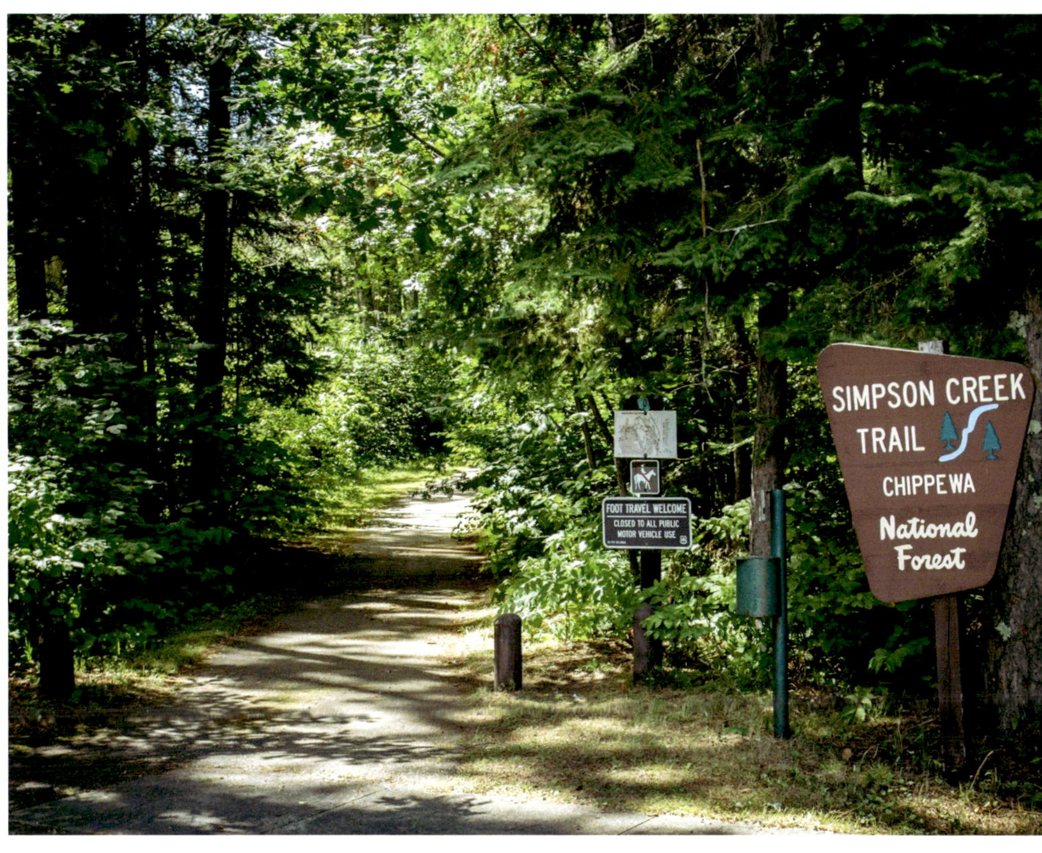

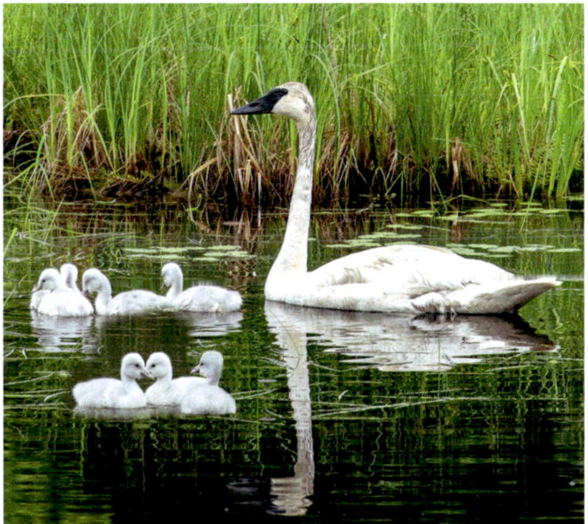

Above: On the Chippewa National Forest, the 13-mile Simpson Creek Trail, popular with cyclists, follows old tote roads and dirt paths through pine woods, swamps, and along glacial eskers. U.S. FOREST SERVICE

Left: A swan watches over seven cygnets. Four species of swans known to occur in North America—tundra, trumpeter, mute, and whooper—can be found in Minnesota. 21947960/PIXABAY

Far left: Home to the headwaters of the Mississippi River, Lake Itasca State Park was established in 1891, making it Minnesota's oldest state park, and second oldest in the country after Niagara Falls State Park in New York. GOOD FREE PHOTOS

Right: On the Normandale Community College campus in Bloomington, visitors can relax in a Japanese garden among more than 300 cold-hardy flowers and trees, and from May through October, may watch koi swim in a lagoon. RUNNER1928/WIKIPEDIA

Far right: The Beaux-Arts architecture of the Glensheen Mansion in Duluth is as beautiful as its summer garden. CRAIG HINTON/SHUTTERSTOCK

Below: Two tracts of land, long ago donated to the city of St. Cloud by thoughtful citizens, are today the Munsinger Clemens Gardens on the east bank of the Mississippi River across from St. Cloud State University. Visitors enjoy winding paths, a gift shop, musical concerts, and an annual art fair. RANDY RUNTSCH/SHUTTERSTOCK

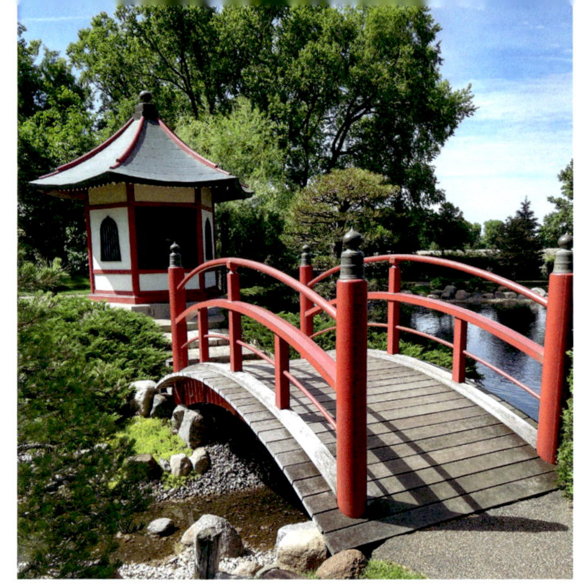

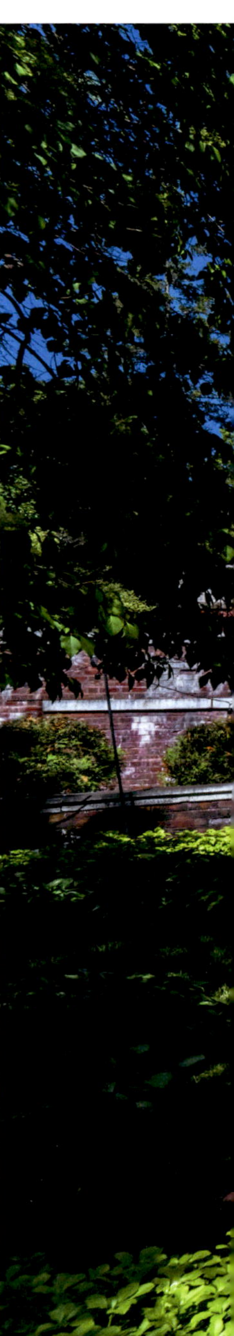

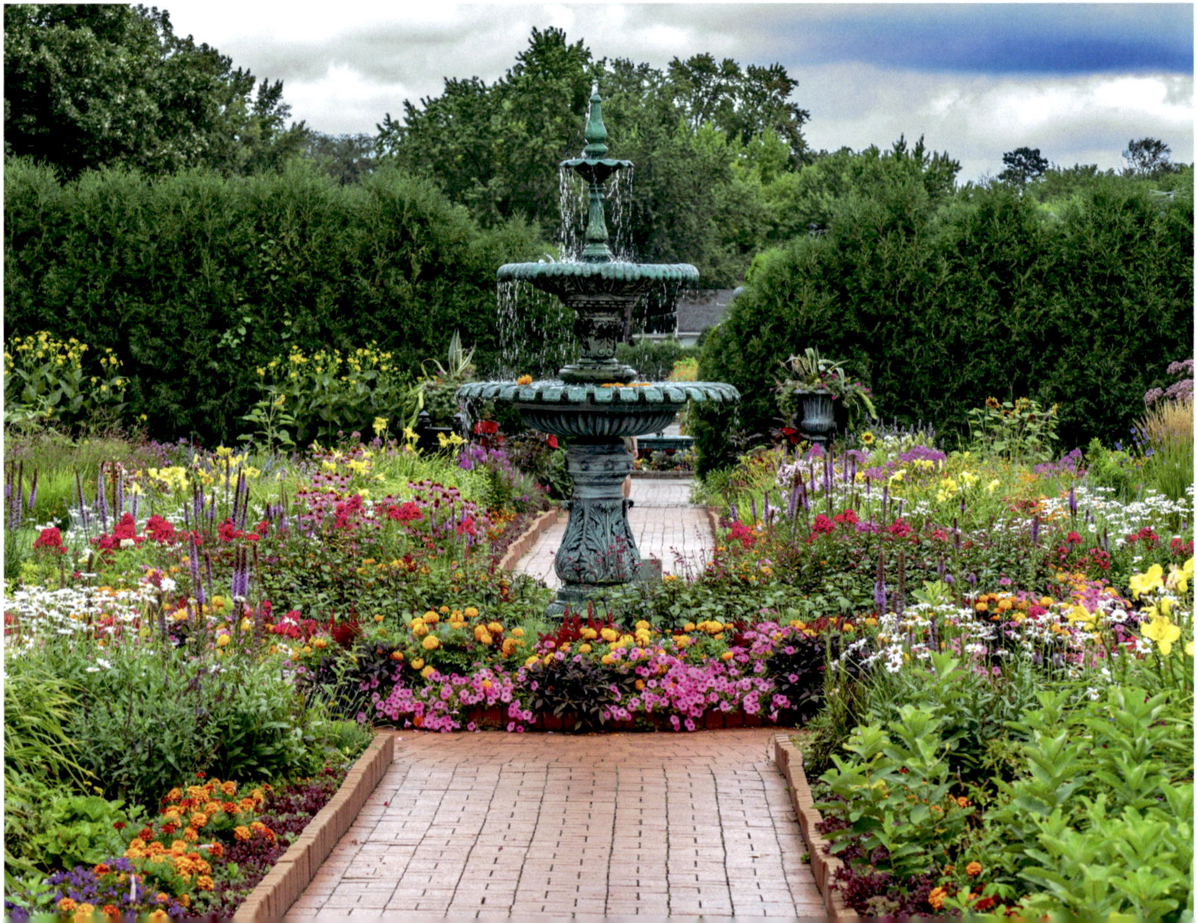

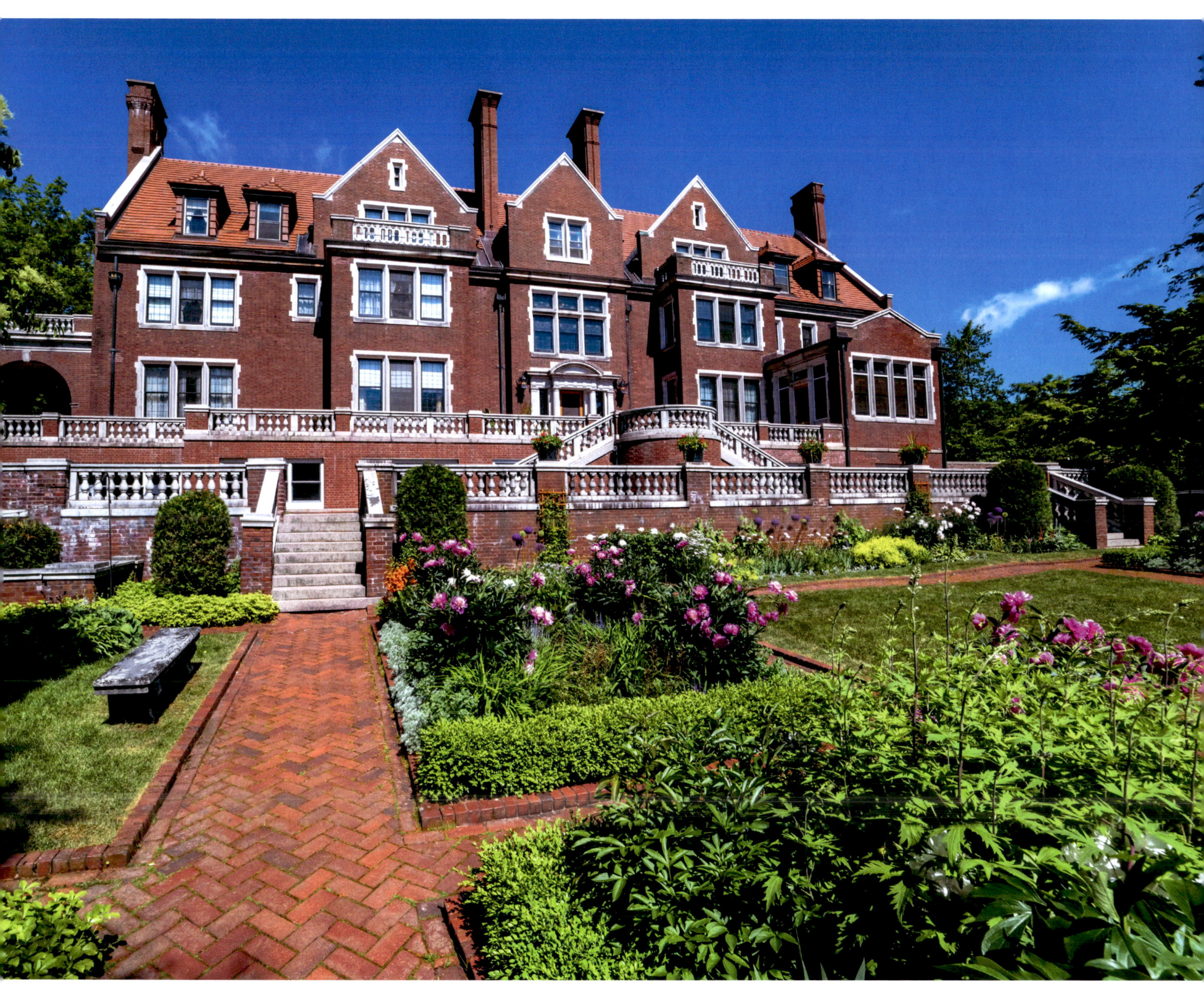

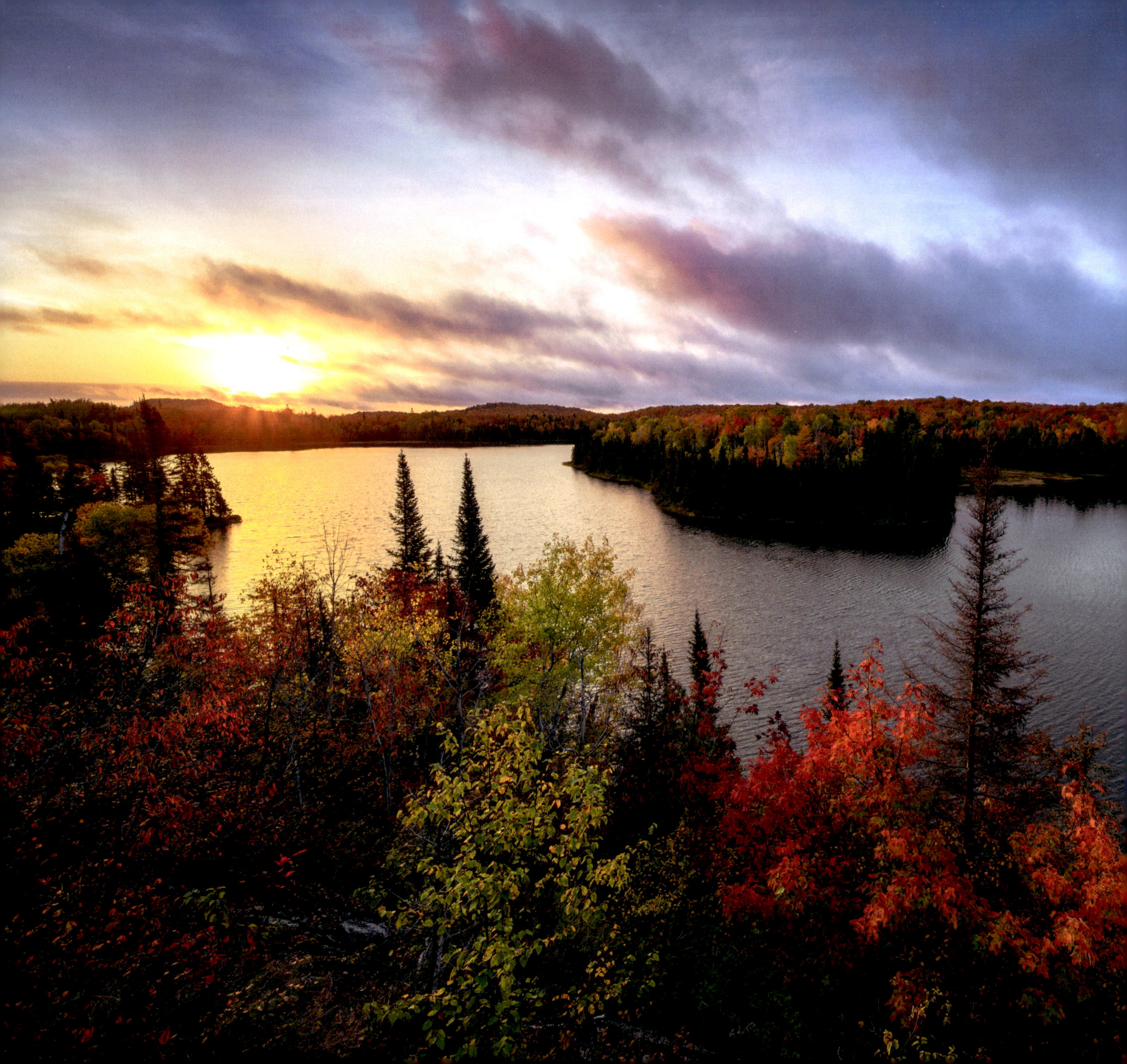

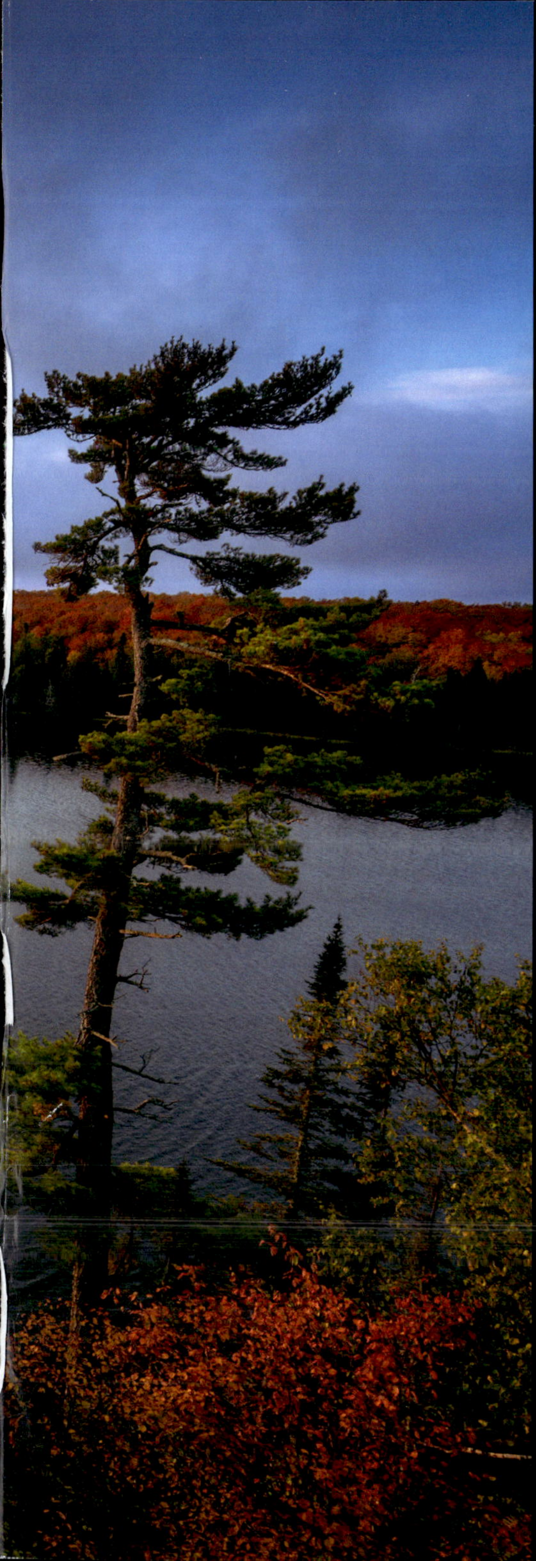

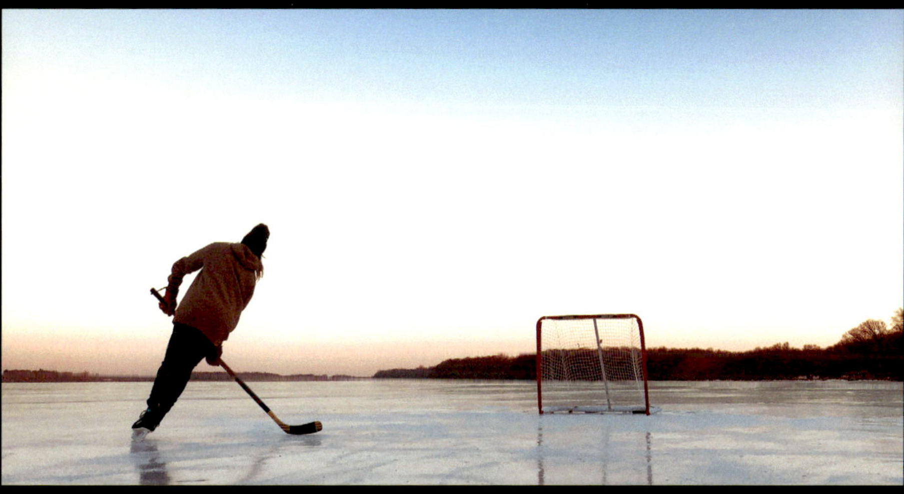

Above: Nearly everyone plays pond hockey in the "Land of 10,000 Lakes." Some Minnesotans prefer the unofficial nickname, "The State of Hockey." TAYLOR FRIEHL/UNSPLASH

Left: Not far from Lutsen, an easy hike to Lake Agnes on the Superior Hiking Trail leads to a scenic overlook of serene backcountry waters. Two campsites accommodate overnighters. MAX FOSTER

Below: One of the state's most popular fishing spots, 207-square-mile Mille Lacs Lake, holds walleye, northern pike, muskie, perch, bass, black crappie, and burbot. MIKE GOAD/PIXABAY

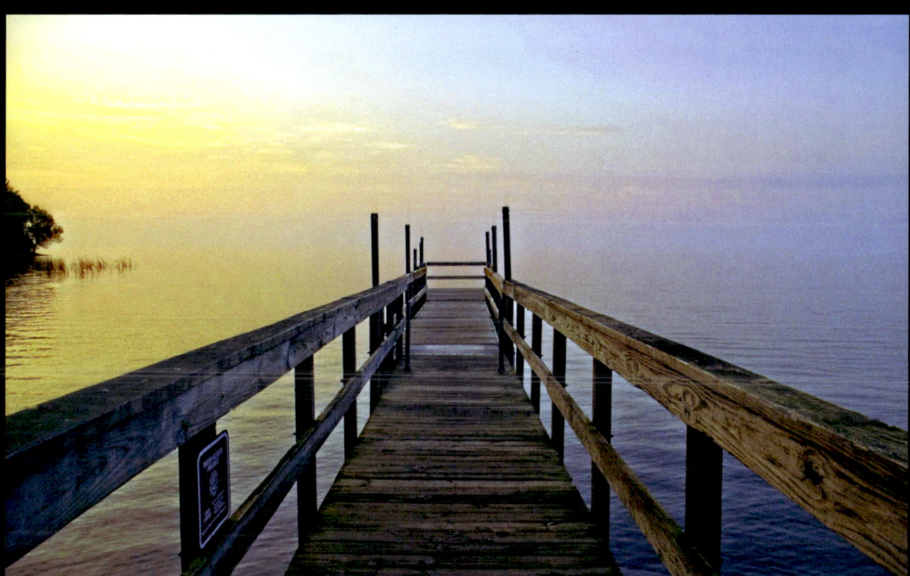

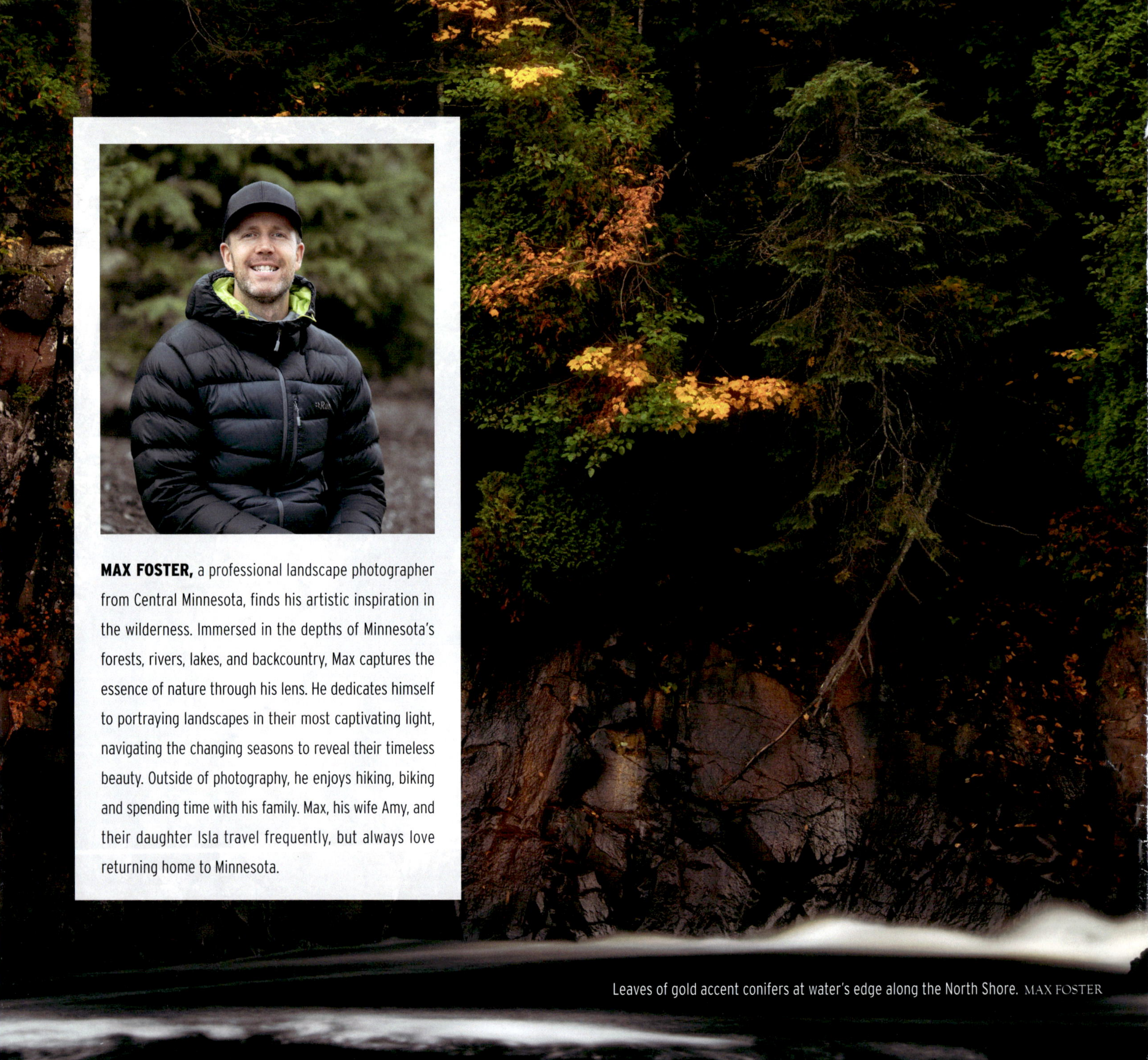

MAX FOSTER, a professional landscape photographer from Central Minnesota, finds his artistic inspiration in the wilderness. Immersed in the depths of Minnesota's forests, rivers, lakes, and backcountry, Max captures the essence of nature through his lens. He dedicates himself to portraying landscapes in their most captivating light, navigating the changing seasons to reveal their timeless beauty. Outside of photography, he enjoys hiking, biking and spending time with his family. Max, his wife Amy, and their daughter Isla travel frequently, but always love returning home to Minnesota.

Leaves of gold accent conifers at water's edge along the North Shore. MAX FOSTER